Creating Apps with React Native

Deliver Cross-Platform 0 Crash, 5 Star Apps

M. Holmes He

Apress®

Creating Apps with React Native: Deliver Cross-Platform 0 Crash,
5 Star Apps

M. Holmes He
Bucklands Beach, New Zealand

ISBN-13 (pbk): 978-1-4842-8041-6   ISBN-13 (electronic): 978-1-4842-8042-3
https://doi.org/10.1007/978-1-4842-8042-3

Copyright © 2022 by M. Holmes He

Managing Director, Apress Media LLC: Welmoed Spahr
Acquisitions Editor: Aaron Black
Development Editor: James Markham
Coordinating Editor: Jessica Vakili

Distributed to the book trade worldwide by Springer Science+Business Media New York, 233 Spring Street, 6th Floor, New York, NY 10013. Phone 1-800-SPRINGER, fax (201) 348-4505, e-mail orders-ny@springer-sbm.com, or visit www.springeronline.com. Apress Media, LLC is a California LLC and the sole member (owner) is Springer Science + Business Media Finance Inc (SSBM Finance Inc). SSBM Finance Inc is a **Delaware** corporation.

For information on translations, please e-mail booktranslations@springernature.com; for reprint, paperback, or audio rights, please e-mail bookpermissions@springernature.com.

Apress titles may be purchased in bulk for academic, corporate, or promotional use. eBook versions and licenses are also available for most titles. For more information, reference our Print and eBook Bulk Sales web page at http://www.apress.com/bulk-sales.

Any source code or other supplementary material referenced by the author in this book is available to readers on the Github repository: https://github.com/Apress/Creating-Apps-with-React-Native. For more detailed information, please visit http://www.apress.com/source-code.

Printed on acid-free paper

Table of Contents

About the Author

M. Holmes He Muyang (Holmes) He is a software engineer. He spent four years working with Tencent on hyperscale social network products. At the time when this book is written, he is a mobile engineer with Microsoft. He is also an active advocate and a practice leader of using React Native to create 0 crash, 5 star apps (05 apps).

About the Technical Reviewer

Akshat Paul is a technology leader and author of four books on React Native, Ruby, and RubyMotion. He has extensive experience in mobile and web development and has delivered many enterprise and consumer applications over the years. In other avatars, Akshat frequently speaks at conferences and meetups on various technologies. He has given talks at React Native EU, Cross-Platform Mobile Summit, Devops@Scale Amsterdam, TheDevTheory Conference India, RubyConfIndia, and #inspect-RubyMotion Conference Brussels and was a keynote speaker at technology leadership events at Bangkok and Kuala Lumpur. Besides writing code, Akshat likes to spend time with his family, is an avid reader, and is obsessive about healthy eating.

The Path to a *05 App*

User experience and developer experience (*U & D experiences*) are coiled double helix that spiral up a great product. **React Native** offers awesomeness of both. **React Native** is neither as luxurious and fabricated as other comparable frameworks, such as Xamarin and Flutter, nor as plain and simple as a WebView. Nonetheless, it successfully reconciles the *U & D experiences* on various mobile platforms by leveraging the timeworn front-end technologies, **JavaScript** and **React**, which marks a sweet spot on the frontier of mobile development.

No framework is perfect. **React Native** is no exception. The question is whether the shortcoming can be contained, and the answer is "yes." In the experience of the author, **React Native** is capable of delivering high-quality user experiences as the market has seen a lot of apps of such kind. Nevertheless, underoptimized apps and unsuccessful stories also shadow. The purpose of this book is to provide you with a solid information source to achieve the former, a *0* crash, *5* star app, a.k.a. a *05 app*.

CHAPTER 1

Start Thinking in React

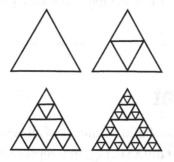

Figure 1-1. *A fractal topology*

React reflects the fractal topology (Figure 1-1) in which the whole system and each of its parts share the same geometrical form. This topology is found as a common phenomenon across scales spanning from a flake to a galaxy. In that sense, every ***React*** **component** shares the same programmatical form. This topology is the key factor, in the opinion of the author, that consistently drives the growth of ***React***-based systems and ecosystems in an organic fashion.

It is almost intuitive for a seasoned *React* developer to map between a tree of stylized **components** and the visual result. This ability can vastly enhance efficiency. To help you to become a React Native developer like this is the goal of this book. Let us start by looking at the basic building block of ***React***, a **component**.

© M. Holmes He 2022
M. H. He, *Creating Apps with React Native*, https://doi.org/10.1007/978-1-4842-8042-3_1

Note 🏛 The "drag and drop" UI builder, on the other hand, offers a tempting, painting-like development experience, ideally on a fix-sized canvas. However, the programmatic approach for the UI has been proven to be the putative winner when dealing with real-world complexity. More specifically, we need logic to control the adaptation of various dimensions and user interactions, which modern apps desire. We can naturally express logic in code. But things very soon become clumsy when the same logic is represented within a UI builder. I think this is for the discipline boundary between engineering and art.

1.1 Component

Components are the basic building blocks of all views. Technically, they are the underpinnings of the XML tags that represent various UI elements. For example, `<Text/>` represents a view that renders text, `<Image/>` is the one that renders graphic, and `<View/>` represents a plain rectangle area. Those tags are backed by their respective **components** encapsulating the presentation and business logic.

A **component** takes **props** (Section 1.2.3) as input. For instance, a `<Text/>` accepts attributes like `fontFamily`, `fontSize`, `fontWeight`, `color`, etc.; a `<View/>` takes `width`, `height`, and `borderRadius`; and an `<Image/>` takes `source` **prop** that indicates the image location. Most of the presentational **props** are categorized as **style**, a special type of **props** reserved by *React* (Section 1.2.3.1).

When a **component** works as a **flex container** (simplified as **container** in the following text), it takes certain **styles** that handle the layout of its **children** (Section 1.2.3.2). We use a technique called a **flexbox** to define adaptive layout. Since **flexbox** is presentational, the **flexbox**-related attributes are **styles** too. We are going to cover the basics as well as some handy techniques of **flexbox** in Section 2.1. As we will see very soon, the structural *component tree*, in conjunction with **flexbox**, results in a declarative, modernized semantic that makes UI layout a breeze. This semantic is called a **JSX** (Section 1.2.2).

Developers of the ***React Native*** core team and third parties have created more than enough stock **components** to address almost any difficulties and requirements for a mobile app. That said, it is essential to know how to create custom **components** to encapsulate the UI and logic units that suit our own business needs which could be very specific and specialized.

Let's start thinking of a social network with a billion expected users; we call it *Manyface*. One of the novel features of *Manyface* allows users to share with friends what is happening in their life by posting a short text along with a photo, and we call a post of this kind a *Feed*. On the other hand, the user can also get to know their friends' everyday lives by navigating a list with their recently posted *Feeds* mixed and sorted, and we decide to call this feature *Moment*. For the *Moment* list, it is nice to encapsulate one *Feed* as a **component**. Listings 1-1 and 1-2 show what a *Feed* **component** is like and how it is used by *Moment*.

Listing 1-1. A sample component

```
class Feed extends React.Component {
...
  render() {
    return (
      <View style={{
        flexDirection: 'row',
        justifyContent: flex-start
      }}> // ---------------------------------------------> 1)
        <Text>...</Text> // ---------------------------------> 3)
```

```
      <Image // ---------------------------------------> 2)
          source={{uri: 'https://xxx.xx'}} />
        <Image />
      </View>
    );
  }
...
};
```

Listing 1-2. How Feed component is used

```
class Moment extends React.Component {
...
  render() {
    return (
...
      <Feed/>
      <Feed/>
      <Feed/>
      <Feed/>
      <Feed/>
...
    );
  }
...
};
```

Note   Here, the example is given for simplicity. In practice, `map()` is normally used to render an array of similar **components**. This technique will be used in the case study in Section 2.2.

Starting from the top, every **component** is required to inherit from `React.Component` which is a template class that instructs *React* how to construct, render, and deallocate itself. With that information, *React* can then incorporate the **component** into the **component tree** and construct the whole app.

Next, let's take in some of the basics of a **component** by focusing on the `render()` method:

1) `<View>` is the most basic library **component** in *React* that simply represents a rectangle in the user interface. It defines the attributes of the rectangle such as background color, rounded corner, and shadows. Since `<View>` does not render anything special, a plain `<View>` **component** is normally used as a container that lays out its children **components**. As mentioned just now, the layout engine in *React* is **flexbox** (Section 2.1). For now, we can see the **flexbox**-related attributes are `flexDirection` and `justifyContent`.

2) As a more advanced **component**, `<Image>` renders graphic. Here, the graphic is fetched from `'https://xxx.xx'` that is indicated by the `source` **prop**.

3) As mentioned, `<Text>` renders text.

What is returned by the `render()` of a **component** is nothing but a tree of other **components**. In the preceding case, the root node of the tree is `<View>`. Those **components** inside `render()` are called **subcomponents**. Each **subcomponent** recursively calls their `render()` and renders their **subcomponents** to complete a subtree. Let's now take a higher perspective; the whole app is a cascading tree of **components** started from a **component** named `<App>`, and now we can see the whole picture of the fractal topology mentioned in the beginning.

Now let's magnify the tree by looking at its leaves. Those leaf **components** are backed directly by native UI entities. They are the concrete UIViews in **UIKit** and one kind of Views or ViewGroups in **Android UI**. The translation of the **components** to native UI objects is the cutting point between **React** and **Native**; we will examine this mechanism in Chapter 4.

One important property of a **component** is its life cycle (Figure 1-2). Predefined life cycle methods are constructor(), componentDidMount(), componentDidUpdate(), componentWillUnmount(), and shouldComponentUpdate(). They are invoked by the **React** runtime at the appropriate time during the life cycle of the **component**, which provides us chances to carry out additional work. For instance, we might need to fetch data from the network (Chapter 5) in componentDidMount() and to carry out clean up and free in componentWillUnmount().

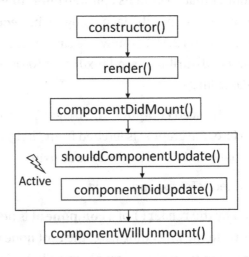

Figure 1-2. *Life cycle methods*

Note   shouldComponentUpdate() is a method used primarily for performance optimization. We will discuss its usage in Chapter 6.

1.1.1 Key Takeaways

In this section, we introduced some *React* basics by looking at what a **component** roughly looks like. We noted some of the key concepts of a **component**, such as (a) **props**, (b) **component tree**, and (c) **subcomponent**, which will be used repeatedly in the following learnings. We also introduced the unique layout system called **flexbox** and the declarative syntax **JSX**, but we didn't get into too much depth. Most importantly, we now have a purpose, the *Manyface* as an ongoing project. We are going to use it as a medium to learn all the mentioned concepts and techniques in detail throughout this book.

1.2 The "Hello World" App in Pieces

We've got a rough idea of what a **component** looks like and how an app is structured from a high-end perspective. But that level of understanding does not help a lot when it comes to a real-world project. We need more in-depth and extensive knowledge in order to accomplish *Manyface*. One of the good ways to establish such knowledge is by examining the autonomy of another real app. What we are going to examine is the "Hello world" app shipped with any *React Native* projects. It contains almost everything of a runnable app while being minimal. For now, we forget about *Manyface* and take a detour on this "Hello world" app shipped with every *React Native* project.

1.2.1 React Native Development Environment

The React Native development environment is a NodeJS project that enlists several subprojects targeting native platforms such as iOS, Android, and desktop. These subprojects represent the native facets of the main project. React Native supports most mainstream operating systems (e.g., Windows, Linux, and macOS) as the development host. Nonetheless, we need macOS if we want to target iOS.

For most of the time, we should work only on the main NodeJS project which contains the business and UI logic in JavaScript. The native projects, on the other hand, are app projects conforming to the structure of the platform IDE. Native projects also contain the React Native runtime that loads and executes the JavaScript code in the main project. Customized native modules and native components (Chapter 4) are included also in the native projects.

React Native adopts npm to manage the dependencies. So most of the awesomeness in the npm ecosystem, like TypeScript, Jest, and linting tools, are supported by nature. Moreover, this setting makes a React Native project work well with Visual Studio Code.

React Native apps should be executable seamlessly on various platforms, so should its dependencies. Just like in the main project, most dependencies contain native facades managed by iOS CocoaPods and Android Gradle. More specifically, npm loads all the required source code and binaries to local storage of the host, and dependency managers on the respective native projects load the native parts into the native IDEs for compiling and linking to the platform specific executables.

Note   There are also React Native libraries implemented in pure JavaScript. And sometimes we can also use libraries implemented for the Web. Those projects do not have native facades.

In production mode, the main project produces a JavaScript bundle which is embedded into the native projects as a plain resource file. When the app is loaded, the React Native runtime loads the bundle file to execute the business and UI logic.

In dev mode, the code is loaded from a metro server running on the development host and is reloaded whenever the code is changed locally (a.k.a. hot reload). 🏛 Hot reload is a killer feature equipped with React Native. It gives a nearly zero compiling turnaround, which not only enhances the development efficiency but also opens up developer experience that is extravagant in mobile development. For instance, we can have ten phones of various operating systems and screen sizes and hot reload the code to all of them simultaneously when programming adaptive layouts and compatible features; we can also sit side by side with designers and product managers and fine-tune parameters together in real time for features that require cross-disciplines such as UI and data validation and verification.

In dev mode, we can also access various debugging tools by shaking the device (or sending the shaking command to a simulator). For instance, we can set breakpoints or step into the code through Chrome; we can inspect the layout and metadata of the components in display; and we shall send commands to reload the entire app when the states are corrupted.

Lastly, the React Native version in use is 0.63.4.

Note   Reducing the compiling turnaround is one of the major demands on mobile development. On iOS, we need to resort to advanced lldb commands to change some of the behaviors of the app without recompiling the code base. In React Native, we can change everything we wrote and hot reload it. All these come by nature and free of cost.

Now let's create a ***React Native*** project from scratch by executing the following command:

```
npx react-native init Manyface
```

Then we can execute npm start to boot up the metro server.

Note   The original code of the "Hello world" project is modified for demonstration purposes.

Let's start the reading from the index.js which is the entry point (Listing 1-3).

Listing 1-3. The hello world app – index.js

```
import {AppRegistry} from 'react-native';
import App from './App';
import {name as appName} from './app.json';

AppRegistry.registerComponent(appName, () => App);
```

The only line of logic registers a **component** App as the root of the entire app. Here, App is just a naming convention; feel free to rename it as, for example, MyAwesomeAppCreatedByAwesomeMe.

Next, we look at the main body of the App (Listing 1-4).

Listing 1-4. The hello world app – skeleton

```
class Section extends Component { // --------------------> 8)
  render() {
  return (
    <View style={styles.sectionContainer}> // ----------> 1)
      <Text style={styles.sectionTitle}> // ------------> 1)
        {props.title} // -------------------------------> 1)
      </Text>
      <Text style={styles.sectionDescription}> // ------> 1)
        {props.children}
      </Text>
    </View>
  );
  }
}
```

```
export default class App extends Component {
  render() {
  return (
    <View>
    <StatusBar barStyle="dark-content" /> // -------> 3) 7)
    <SafeAreaView> // --------------------------------> 7)
      <ScrollView // --------------------------------> 7)
        contentInsetAdjustmentBehavior="automatic" // -> 3)
        style={styles.scrollView}> // ----------------> 1)
        <Header />
        {global.HermesInternal == null ? null : ( // --> 6)
          <View style={styles.engine}> // -------------> 1)
            <Text style={styles.footer}> // -----------> 1)
              Engine: Hermes // ----------------------> 4)
            </Text>
          </View>
        )}
        <View style={styles.body}>
          <Section title={'Step One'}> // ----------> 2) 8)
            Edit <Text style={ styles.highlight } > // > 1)
                 App.js // ----------------------> 4) 5)
            </Text> to change this // ---------> 4) 5)
          screen and then come back to see your edits.
          </Section>
          <Section title={'See Your Changes'}> // --> 2) 8)
            <ReloadInstructions />
          </Section>
          <Section title={'Debug'}> // -------------> 2) 8)
            <DebugInstructions />
          </Section>
```

```
        <Section title={'Learn More'}> // --------> 2) 8)
          Read the docs to discover what to do next:
        </Section>
        <LearnMoreLinks />
      </View>
    </ScrollView>
  </SafeAreaView>
  </View>
  );
  }
};

const styles = StyleSheet.create({
...
});
```

1.2.2 JSX

Now it's a good chance to examine **JSX**. As we have seen before, **components** are used in the form of XML tags called **JSX** in the render() method. This declarative way of defining a "page" is very similar to that using HTML. The major advantage of **JSX** over static HTML is that **JSX** supports inline *JavaScript* which offers runtime controls over visual outcome. Its name could also hint at this advantage, **JSX** = inline JS + XML tags. Embedding inline *JavaScript* to **JSX** is simple; just wrap the expression in curly braces {}. Next, we look at **JSX** in the "Hello world" app:

1) The most common embedded expression returns a single variable object. For instance, the expression {props.title} returns the value props.title and sets it as the body of the wrapping <Text> **component**. {styles.engine} returns the value of styles.engine and sets it as View's **style prop**.

We will cover **props** in Section 1.2.3; for now, we only need to know that **props** define the **component** input and a **style prop** defines its visual style.

2) You can also use a constant string in an expression, for example, `<Section title={'Learn More'}>`.

3) And in the above case (2) where the prop value is a string, curly braces can be omitted, for example:

```
<StatusBar barStyle="dark-content"/>
```

4) Moreover, if the static string is under a tag, double quotes can be omitted too. See this one:

```
<Section title={'Step One'}>
  Edit <Text style={ styles.highlight }
        App.js
      </Text>
  screen and then come back to see your edits.
</Section>
```

One interesting point here is that the complete amalgam of string and `<Text>` (Edit ... your edits) is passed down to `<Section>` as `props.children`. The real rendering point is actually the `<Text>` in `<Section>`:

```
...
<Text style={styles.sectionDescription}>
  {props.children}
</Text>
...
```

Here, **children** is another important concept, which we will cover very soon in the next section.

5) `<Text>` is a very versatile **component** as it can be
    nested, and each of the nested individuals can be
    applied with different **styles**. So a rich text box is
    supported by `<Text>`.

Note   In general principle, the UI layer shouldn't contain any complex
logic that normally belongs to the other software layers. In some large
scale industrial applications, business logic are carried out solely from
server-side to give the most flexibility. So it is reasonable that each
expression can only contain one line of code.

---

6) Since we have this one-line restriction, the ternary
    expression is used in place of an `if...else...`:

    ```
    {global.HermesInternal == null ?
                            null :
                            <View>...
    }
    ```

    This is called a *conditional rendering*. Here, if the
    condition is false (i.e., **Hermes** is not detected),
    the expression returns `null`, which will be simply
    ignored and render nothing. Otherwise, it returns a
    `<View>` with the **Hermes**-related information.

Note   `null` instead of `undefined` is the recommended value
to render nothing. Later, we will see expressions that are more
interesting than an `if...else` equivalence. For example, you shall
use `map()` to render a list of **components** based on an array or use
a **component** state to drive animation.

---

7)   Some handy stock **components**, their names are self-explained: `<StatusBar>` occupies the phone status bar and defines the attributes of the area; `<SafeAreaView>` places bottom and top insets that avoid overlapping between the app content and system items such as screen rounded corners, sensor housing and area for home indicator. All its **children** can be positioned away from those areas to avoid occlusion or clipping; `<ScrollView>` makes a `<View>` scrollable when its size is larger than that of the screen.

8)   Lastly, we defined a `<section/>` component and reuse it in various places. This is the first custom **component** we have seen. To better understand how it works, let's quickly move on to the next section.

1.2.3 props

props define the **components** inputs. Since *React* is data driven, there is a very limited need for public methods and properties. All interfaces and potential interactions of a **component** are exposed in the form of **props**. So whenever you are not sure about the usage of a **component**, look at its **props**.

Note   *React* has very good support of *TypeScript*. In fact, all code in *React* can be written in *TypeScript* to give an explicit type and type check in packaging time, which is way safer for large-scale projects. A side benefit of *TypeScript* is that it makes the interfaces of **components** crystal clear with the explicitly typed **props**.

For instance, an `<Image>` or a `<video>` could expose a `source` props to indicate where to fetch the content, and a `<Button>` could expose an `onPress()` method to define what happens when it is pressed.

There are also predefined **props** that are reserved for special cases. Next, we examine two most common predefined **props**, **style** and **children.**

1.2.3.1 Style

Style is well self-explained by its name; it defines the **components** visual style and layout. A **style prop** is no different than an ordinary **prop** by its usage. In Listing 1-5, we include the **style prop** of the "Hello world" app.

Listing 1-5. The hello world app – styles

```
const styles = StyleSheet.create({
  scrollView: {
    backgroundColor: Colors.lighter,
  },
  engine: {
    position: 'absolute', // -------------------------------> 1)
    right: 0,
  },
  body: {
    backgroundColor: Colors.white,
  },
  sectionContainer: {
    marginTop: 32, // ----------------------------------------> 2)
    paddingHorizontal: 24, // -------------------------------> 2)
  },
```

```
sectionTitle: {
  fontSize: 24,
  fontWeight: '600',
  color: Colors.black,
},
sectionDescription: {
  marginTop: 8, // ----------------------------------------> 2)
  fontSize: 18,
  fontWeight: '400',
  color: Colors.dark,
},
highlight: {
  fontWeight: '700',
},
footer: {
  color: Colors.dark,
  fontSize: 12,
  fontWeight: '600',
  padding: 4, // --------------------------------------------> 2)
  paddingRight: 12, // --------------------------------------> 2)
  textAlign: 'right',
},
});
```

Most of the **styles** are for individual attributes and are self-explained; Figure 1-3 gives the **components**' corresponding positions on the screen to demonstrate the visual outcome of the **styles**.

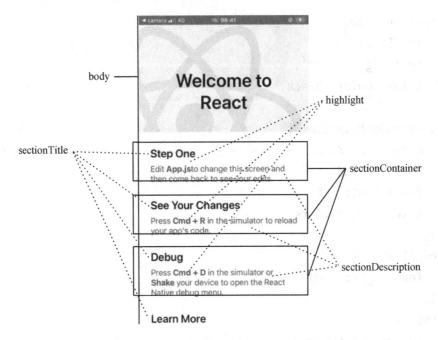

Figure 1-3. *Visual outcome when styles are applied*

Note   When defining your own **component**, nothing stops you from exposing all related **styles** as custom, first-level **props**. It is just nice to group all the visual- and layout-related **props** into **style**. One special case of using custom, first-level **props** for **styles** is when stylizing **children** (Section 1.2.3.2) of **subcomponents**. 🏛 It is preferred to define their **styles** as custom, first-level **props** in order to be distinguished from the **styles** associated with the **component** itself.

Apart from individual visuals, **styles** can be used to define the layout:

1) `position: 'absolute'` is used to opt out the default
   flexbox layout. Instead, you indicate the absolute
   position inside the **component**'s container. For example:

```
{
  position: 'absolute',
  top: 0,
  left: 0
}
```

lays out the **component** to the top-left corner:

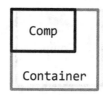

One use case of absolute position is an overlay:

```
{
  position: 'absolute',
  top: 0,
  left: 0,
+   width: '100%',
+   height: '100%',
}
```

2) margin adds space outside of the **component** border, so it is normally used to adjust the position of the **component** itself:

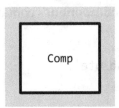

while padding adds space inside; hence, it is used to adjust the positions of its **children component**:

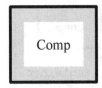

Another common style you might see in production source code is style={{xxx1: yy1, xxx2: yy2}}. Here, the outer pair of braces is for *JSX*, and the inner pair of braces is part of the *JavaScript* object. ✳ This way is called an *inline style*, which is slightly less performant as it creates new anonymous objects each time the render() is called. 🚀 So the static **styles** variable used earlier is the best practice.

Besides a single object, you can also assign an array of objects for **style**, for example, style={[{xxx1: yy1, xxx2: yy2}, {xxx3: yy3}]}. A style array is normally used when you want some style attributes to be dynamically defined by **states**. The change of those **styles** is driven by setState() invocations (Section 1.2.5).

Note   ✳ stands for performance issue; 🚀 is the hint for resolving it.

1.2.3.2 Children

Children are **components** that are wrapped inside another **component**. **Children** are passed to the **container** as a special **prop** for custom layout within. Listing 1-6 demonstrates their relationship.

Listing 1-6. Container and children

```
...
render() {// the render method of some component
...

    <Container> // The wrapper tag is a container
      <Child1/> // The lower ordered tags are children
      <Child2/>
    </Container>

...
}
...
```

Another similar notion to **children** is a **subcomponent** which is discussed in Section 1.1.1. As a reminder, if **children** are **components** under a **container** geologically, a **subcomponent** belongs to the **super-component** itself logically. In "Hello world," <View> and <Text> are Section's **subcomponents**.

Let us continue with the "Hello world" example and look at **children** of Section (Listing 1-7).

Listing 1-7. The hello world app – children of Section

```
...
            <Section title={'Step One'}>
              Edit <Text style={ styles.highlight } // ---> 1)
                  App.js
                </Text> to change this
```

```
        screen and then come back to see your edits.
      </Section>
      <Section title={'See Your Changes'}>
        <ReloadInstructions /> // ------------------> 2)
      </Section>
      <Section title={'Debug'}>
        <DebugInstructions /> // ------------------> 3)
      </Section>
      <Section title={'Learn More'}>
        Read the docs to discover what to do next: // 4)
      </Section>
```

. . .

They are as follows:

1) The nested <Text>

```
Edit <Text style={ styles.highlight }
      App.js
    </Text> to change this
screen and then come back to see your edits.
```

2) The <ReloadInstructions />

3) The <DebugInstructions />

4) The plain text "Read the docs to discover what to do next:"

We have explored what **children** are like. Now it's time to explain props.children and where it comes from. Like **styles**, props.children is another predefined **prop** that refers to the current **children** of the **component** instance. This **prop** gives the current **component** a chance to lay out its potential **children**.

Note   Figure 1-5 in the next section (Section 1.2.4) is a good place to refer to as it illustrates how `props.children` works in the big picture.

If a **component** omits the `props.children` passed through, it cannot be used as a **container** at all as all its children will not be rendered. Conversely, 🏛 when designing a **component** as a **container**, it's compulsory to handle `props.children` in `render()`.

Note   🏛 stands for architecture and design principles.

Back to the source code (Listing 1-8).

Listing 1-8. The hello world app – layout subcomponents of Section

```
class Section extends Component {
  render() {
  return (
    <View style={styles.sectionContainer}>
      <Text style={styles.sectionTitle}>
        {props.title}
      </Text>
      <Text style={styles.sectionDescription}>
        {props.children} // ----------------------------> 1)
      </Text>
    </View>
  );
  }
}
```

1) Section explicitly renders its **children** (under one
    of its <Text> **subcomponents**). So, whenever it is
    used as a container, its **children** will be displayed
    properly.

OK, we can say that Section is a container by design since render()
settles the positions of **children**. But what if it does not? Lastly, let us take a
quick counterexample where **children** are omitted:

```
<Text style={styles.sectionDescription}>
    {props.children} // <-------------------------- remove
</Text>
```

As expected, all its **children** (the section bodies) are dismissed as
Section does not know how to lay out them (Figure 1-4).

Figure 1-4. *Section without handling props.children*

1.2.4 JSX Internals

Note   Understanding how **JSX** works internally does not only satisfy our curiosity as a developer but also offers insight into how a UI update works, which is one critical point in *React Native*'s performance.

If **JSX** is on one side of a coin, the other side would be React.createElement(type, config, children) which is the internal implementation of **JSX**. The parameters are extracted directly from what you declared in **JSX**. type is the tag name, config is what you passed as **props**, and children are all the **children** components which, in turn, are represented as a group of createElement() invocations. We can look at the transformed version of the Section **component** in the "Hello world" app to get a practical view of how **JSX** is mapped into parameters of createElement() as shown in Listing 1-9.

Listing 1-9. The hello world app – the real form of Section

```
function Section(props) {
  return React.createElement(
    View, // --------------------------------> type
    { style: styles.sectionContainer }, // ---> config
    React.createElement( // ------------------> children 1

    Text,
    { style: styles.sectionTitle },
    props.title
  ),
```

```
  React.createElement(// -------------------> children 2
    Text,
    { style: styles.sectionDescription },
    props.children
  )
);
}
```

As shown in Listing 1-9, the cascading createElement() is actually one line of code where the **children components** (also created by createElement()) are passed as the container's last parameters. Likewise, deeper nested **components** are passed through in a similar way to their corresponding container.

This transformation is carried out by *babel*. We shall use the following command to uncover the thin veil of *JSX* and look at the App in its real form. Alternatively, we can use https://babeljs.io/repl to achieve the same.

```
./node_modules/.bin/babel --plugins transform-react-jsx App.js
```

Note   You might need to install *bable-cli* and *babel-plugin-transform-react-jsx* if you haven't.

Now let's look at the whole App **component** (Listing 1-10).

Listing 1-10. The hello world app – the real form of App

```
export default class App extends Component {
  render() {
    return React.createElement(
      View,
      null,
      React.createElement(StatusBar,
```

```
  { barStyle: 'dark-content' }),
React.createElement(
  SafeAreaView,
  null,
  React.createElement(
    ScrollView,
    {
      contentInsetAdjustmentBehavior: 'automatic',
      style: styles.scrollView },
    React.createElement(Header, null),
    global.HermesInternal == null ? null : React.
    createElement(
      View,
      { style: styles.engine },
      React.createElement(
        Text,
        { style: styles.footer },
        'Engine: Hermes'
      )
    ),
    React.createElement(
      View,
      { style: styles.body },
      React.createElement(
        Section,
        { title: 'Step One' },
        'Edit ',
        React.createElement(
          Text,
          {
            style: styles.highlight
          },
```

```
          'App.js'
        ),
        'to change this screen and then come back to see
        your edits.'
      ),
      React.createElement(
        Section,
        { title: 'See Your Changes' },
        React.createElement(ReloadInstructions, null)
      ),
      React.createElement(
        Section,
        { title: 'Debug' },
        React.createElement(DebugInstructions, null)
      ),
      React.createElement(
        Section,
        { title: 'Learn More' },
        'Read the docs to discover what to do next:'
      ),
      React.createElement(LearnMoreLinks, null)
      )
    )
   )
  );
 }
};
```

You might have heard about a **virtual DOM tree (VDOM tree)**. This is the core data structure *React* uses to render the UI and to drive its updates. However, createElement() does not create the **virtual DOMs**. Instead, it returns a blueprint that can be used by **React** to create the final **VDOMs**. The blueprint of createElement() is also what the render() method returns.

Note   So your render() method does not actually render anything. It kickstarts the whole render process.

Back to the "Hello world" app, what **React** generates based on our render() method is illustrated in Figure 1-5.

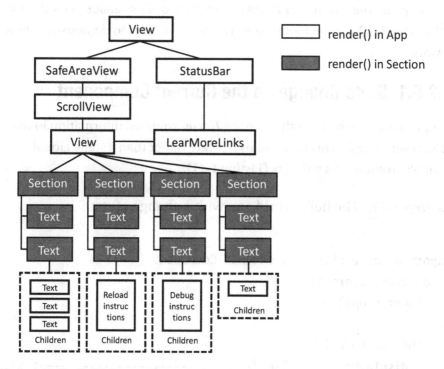

Figure 1-5. *DOM tree of app*

1.2.5 States

Like **props**, **states** are data that drive the behavior or, more specifically, the UI behavior of a **component**. Unlike **props** that are passed from outside, **states** are intrinsic. In other words, all moving parts of the UI are converged in the form of **states** combined. Thanks to the data-driven design of *React*, all the visual changes are driven by a single function, setState(). This is true for all sources or forms of the changes, text editing, button press, device rotation, and so forth. When you call setState() of one component, you basically tell *React* to do two things: (1) to update the **component**'s **state** and (2) to call its render() method to refresh the UI. Next, we modify the "Hello world" a bit to demonstrate how it works.

1.2.5.1 State Change on the Current Component

I hope you still remember the missing *Hermes*-related information in the "Hello world" app. This time, we use a **state** rather than a static global variable to control its visibility (Listing 1-11).

Listing 1-11. The hello world app with a change of state

```
...
export default class App extends Component {
+ constructor(props) {
+   super(props);
+
+   this.state = {
+     displayHermes: false // ----------------------------> 1)
+   };
+}
```

```
+ headerTouched() {
+   let display = !this.state. displayHermes;
+   this.setState({displayHermes}); // -------------------> 4)
+ }

  render() {
  return (
    <View>
    <StatusBar barStyle="dark-content" />
    <SafeAreaView>
      <ScrollView
        contentInsetAdjustmentBehavior="automatic"
        style={styles.scrollView}>
+       <TouchableOpacity
+         onPress={this.headerTouched.bind(this)} // -----> 3)
+       >
+         <Header />
+       </TouchableOpacity>
+-      {this.state.displayHermes === false ? null : ( // -> 2)
          <View style={styles.engine}>
            <Text style={styles.footer}>
              Engine: Hermes
            </Text>
          </View>
        )}
        <View style={styles.body}>
          <Section title={'Step One'}>
            Edit <Text style={ styles.highlight }
                   App.js
                 </Text> to change this
            screen and then come back to see your edits.
          </Section>
```

```
            <Section title={'See Your Changes'}>
              <ReloadInstructions />
            </Section>
            <Section title={'Debug'}>
              <DebugInstructions />
            </Section>
            <Section title={'Learn More'}>
              Read the docs to discover what to do next:
            </Section>
            <LearnMoreLinks />
          </View>
        </ScrollView>
      </SafeAreaView>
      </View>
    );
    }
};
```

...

1) state is nothing but an ordinary *JavaScript* object. All the **states** of a **component** are required to be declared in its constructor. 💣 Otherwise, setState() throws an exception and could potentially crash the app. ♡ Again, *TypeScript* is extremely helpful to avoid this kind of crash as it enforces the **state** structure at a very early stage of compiling.

Note   Here, 💣 means a crash point and ♡ is its countermeasure. The relentless vigilance to all categories of crashes is one key to **0 crash**.

---

2) We replace the global.HermesInternal with the added **state** to be used to control the visibility of the **Hermes** information.

3) We add a TouchableOpacity which can turn any **component** into a clickable button. The onPress **prop** accepts an instance method which will be called back when TouchableOpacity is pressed.

4) Call setState() to update the UI. 🚀 Note that if the name of the key and the value are the same, we can take the shortcut of setState({name}) instead of setState({name: name}).

Besides an instance method, we can also pass an arrow method to this **prop**, for example, onPress={() => {...}}. ❋ Like an inline style, an inline callback has a performance hit as a new method instance needs to be created for every render pass. 🚀 We'd better use the instance method as shown earlier.

1.2.5.2 Cascading State Changes

Changing the visual of the current **component** is of less interest. Very often, we need to simultaneously conduct the change to a nested **subcomponent**, or more than one **subcomponent**, in a cascading way.

A cascading change is carried out using setState() in conjunction with a **prop** which is the single point that connects a **component** to the outside, its caller **component**. More specifically, when a **prop** of a **component** is set with the reference of a **state**, the change of the **state** can be replayed into its **subcomponent**.

Back to the "Hello world." Now we want to change the title of the first section to blue when the TouchableOpacity is pressed (Listing 1-12).

Listing 1-12. The hello world app with a cascading change of state

```
class Section extends Component {
  render() {
  return (
    <View style={styles.sectionContainer}>
+-    <Text style={[
+-      styles.sectionTitle,
+      {color: this.props.redTitile ? 'red' : 'black'} // > 3)
+-    ]}>
        {props.title}
      </Text>
      <Text style={styles.sectionDescription}>
        {props.children}
      </Text>
    </View>
  );
  }
}

export default class App extends Component {
  constructor(props) {
    super(props);

    this.state = {
+-    redTitle: false // --------------------------------> 1)
    };
  }

  headerTouched() {
+-  let redTitle = !this.state.redTitle;
+-  this.setState({redTitle}); // ----------------------> 1)
+-}
```

```
render() {
return (
  <View>
  <StatusBar barStyle="dark-content" />
  <SafeAreaView>
    <ScrollView
      contentInsetAdjustmentBehavior="automatic"
      style={styles.scrollView}>
      <TouchableOpacity
        onPress={this.headerTouched.bind(this)}
      >
        <Header />
      </TouchableOpacity>
      {this.state.displayHermes === false ? null : (
        <View style={styles.engine}>
          <Text style={styles.footer}>
            Engine: Hermes
          </Text>
        </View>
      )}
      <View style={styles.body}>
        <Section
          title={'Step One'}
          redTitle={this.state.redTitle} // ---------> 2)
        >
          Edit <Text style={ styles.highlight }
                App.js
              </Text> to change this
          screen and then come back to see your edits.
        </Section>
```

```
          <Section title={'See Your Changes'}>
            <ReloadInstructions />
          </Section>
          <Section title={'Debug'}>
            <DebugInstructions />
          </Section>
          <Section title={'Learn More'}>
            Read the docs to discover what to do next:
          </Section>
          <LearnMoreLinks />
        </View>
      </ScrollView>
    </SafeAreaView>
    </View>
  );
  }
};

...
```

1) We adjust the name of the state in accordance with the purpose of this time.

2) We associate the **state** of App to the **prop** of Section and prepare for the cascading change.

3) We use the designated **prop**, that is, this.props. redTitle, to control the text color of the title.

1.2.6 setState() Internals

setState() invokes the **component**'s render() method with the **states** that are newly set to update the UI. But this doesn't answer the question of how cascading state changes are carried out. To understand that part, we need to look closer.

In fact, setState() does not only trigger the current component render() method but all the render() methods of the subtree rooted by the current **component**. Then, all the changes occurring along the subtree are collected, and a **VDOM tree** is derived based on the changes. Last, the new **VDOM tree** is compared with the existing one, and actual updates are carried out on components that are changed.

This operation is expensive. The time complexity is linearly correlated to the scale of the **component tree**. We have demonstrated one in Figure 1-5. In real-world applications, the tree is much bigger, and ❋ setState() becomes extremely heavy. In such a scenario, the user will experience unresponsive UX. This is because most of the user interactions take place on the same thread as setState() (Chapter 6). As such, setState() stands as one of the most critical performance bottlenecks of *React Native*.

What are the cures? 🚀 The simplest trick is to keep the **component tree** small by relentlessly trimming it down. Simple but not easy. In the next chapter (Section 2.1), we will give some techniques of doing away superfluous layers or nodes. 🚀 It's also very crucial to avoid calling setState() on a node with a large subtree, or, in other words, very close to the root. Here, *Redux* (Chapter 6) is our friend. Please refer to Chapter 6 for more information. *View flatting* introduced by Fabric is a "nice to have" optimization that trims down the **component tree**. As app developers, it is still recommended for us to be mindful about the tree size as the always caring of performance leads to a 5 star app.

Lastly, it is worth noting that multiple invocations of setState() are a typical antipattern. ❋ It exacerbates the rendering process as the *React* runtime needs to repeat the heavy lifting work each time a setState() is invoked. 🚀 In React 18, *automatic batching* can alleviate the preceding issues. Nevertheless, coalescing the state updates is still highly recommended for occasions that *automatic batching* cannot cover, for example, promises, callbacks from timeout, etc. So we should keep a close eye on it.

1.2.7 Key Takeaways

In this section, we examined the "Hello world" app shipped with the *React Native* project. All the terminology brought up in Section 1.1 were examined with concrete code. We learned how **components** are composed and aggregated using **JSX** syntax, how to define a **component**'s external input using **props**, how to define a **component**'s internal visual state using **state**, and how to define the visual and conduct basic layout using **styles** and **flexbox**. Then we modified the "Hello world" app to demonstrate how a **component** can change its visual outcome in runtime by leveraging setState() which is the key method that updates the UI and proceeds the UX. We also peeked into the **VDOM tree**, the mechanism underlying **JSX** and setState() that drives the UI in all *React*-based apps. Besides, we also learned the concepts of **children** and **subcomponents** which are sometimes confused with each other. We didn't stop at the concept level; we took a step further to illustrate the practical layout of **children** in **subcomponents**.

1.3 Summary

In this chapter, we grasped some general knowledge of *React*. We brought up those key concepts in the beginning and illustrated with the assistance of real code, the "Hello world" app shipped with *React Native*. Knowledge gained through "learning" and "reading" are neither sufficient nor fast enough to make a real app, but they are enough to assist us in going on with the rest of this book which will be emphasizing on "do."

We set *Manyface* as the main quest to consolidate our learning. As we proceed, *Manyface* will grow side by side with us. Each time we learn new skills, advance in knowledge, and gain matching confidence, *Manyface* iterates to its next version better.

We started using notion to highlight the key points, which are summarized as follows:

1) ❄ Stands for a performance issue.

2) 🚀 Stands for an efficiency boost trick.

3) 💣 Stands for a crash point, an antipattern, or simply a pitfall.

4) 🛡 Stands for the approach to defend a crash or to circumvent a pitfall.

5) 🏛 Stands for a hint at app architecture, principles, philosophy, or pattern.

CHAPTER 2

Foundations of React

React is built on top of very minimal theoretical concepts, and we have covered, well, pretty much all of them in the last chapter. However, to get things done, we need to get to know the meticulous technical details, the various framework particularities, and hands-on, factory techniques. Some of them are clean, well-abstracted principles that can be applied not only to *React*-based applications but anywhere else in the programming world, while others are just unspoken Konami codes.

Starting from this chapter, we are going to learn those techniques, well documented and unspoken alike. This chapter will continue focusing on the *React* part; hence, it emphasizes on the user interface in practice. At the end of this chapter, we will complete the basic interface for the moment screen of *Manyface*.

2.1 Flexbox, a Practical Guide

Basically, **flexbox** assists in arranging a group of **components** within a **container** representing a rectangle area, or a box. For each box, **style** `flexDirection` is the general guide that indicates whether the **children** should flow horizontally (`'row'`) or vertically (`'column'`). Then, we can use **styles** like `justifyContent` and `alignItems` to lay out the **children**. In a similar way, these boxes with various layout settings are in turn put together to fill bigger boxes, which ultimately fill the full screen.

© M. Holmes He 2022

M. H. He, *Creating Apps with React Native*, https://doi.org/10.1007/978-1-4842-8042-3_2

The two most used **styles** for layout are justifyContent and alignItems. Here, justifyContent determines in what order **children** should occupy the available space along the mentioned flow direction (main axis), while alignItems aligns **children** across the direction. For instance, the combination of flexDirection: 'column', justifyContent: 'flex-start', and alignItems: 'center' should lay out the **children**, as shown in Figure 2-1.

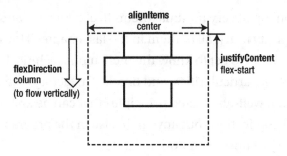

Figure 2-1. *justifyContent: 'flex-start'*

Figure 2-2 gives the visual outcome if we change the justifyContent to 'flex-end'.

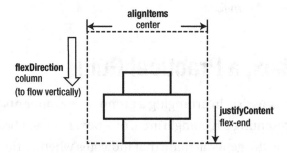

Figure 2-2. *justifyContent: 'flex-end'*

Figure 2-3 gives the result of 'space-between' for justifyContent.

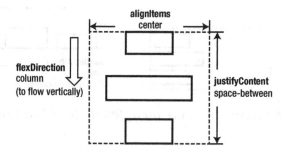

Figure 2-3. *justifyContent: 'space-between'*

alignItems works as a supplementary means of justifyContent. It applies alignments on the cross axis after the main flow direction is settled. Due to this variance, some of the values for justifyContent such as 'space-between' do not exist in alignItems. Figure 2-4 shows what alignItems: 'center' looks like for flexDirection: 'column' and flexDirection: 'row', respectively.

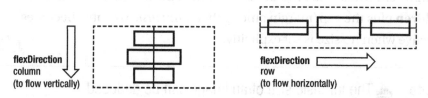

Figure 2-4. *alignItem: 'center' on different flow directions*

Besides 'center', another common value for alignItems is 'flex-start' as shown in Figure 2-5.

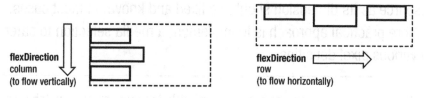

Figure 2-5. *alignItem: 'flex-start' on different flow directions*

Lastly, Figure 2-6 is the layout of 'flex-end'.

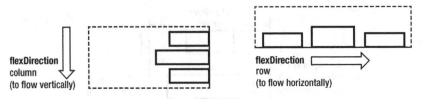

Figure 2-6. *alignItem: 'flex-end' on different flow directions*

2.1.1 Component Size

The **component** size is determined in three ways: *intrinsic size, given size,* and *flex size.*

Intrinsic size is decided by the content size of the **component**. For instance, the *intrinsic size* of a Text is determined by the font size and text length combined; and the *intrinsic size* of an Image is the dimension of the graphic resource in use. A more complex example is a **container component** whose *intrinsic size* is the sum of the *intrinsic sizes* of all its **children** plus the gap/margin among them. *Intrinsic size* only becomes effective when no size is set explicitly.

Note 🏛 The intrinsic size of an image can be deduced automatically only when it is a local resource and loaded in the packaging phase (source={require('local-directory-to-the-resource')}). When the graphic is loaded from the network, we must use the given *size* to represent the *intrinsic size* of the resource as its dimension should be fixed and known in most cases. A more practical approach is to implement a media selection to cater to various pixel densities.

We know that one way to set size explicitly is to use style.width and style.height (Section 1.2.3.1). We can call sizes of this kind *given size*. The value of these **props** can be an absolute value in **points** or percentage

compared to the container, for example, `width: '80%'`. The concept of
point might be unfamiliar to developers with non-front-end background.
Simply put, **points** describe the logical size regardless of the pixel density.
So, if sizes of two objects are the same in **points**, you see they are about the
same size in handhold.

Flex size is another kind of explicit size. *Flex size* is indicated with
`style.flex`, which dictates the relative size compared to sibling
components. In other words, it determines how the full space of a
container is distributed among **children**. Figure 2-7 shows what it looks
like if three **components** (a, b, c) `style.flex` is set to 1, 1, 2, respectively.

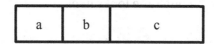

Figure 2-7. *Flex sizes*

Armed with the basics explained earlier, we are now capable of a very
complex layout. Let's get back to the *Manyface*. This time, we are going to
take it more seriously by composing its core component *Feed*.

2.1.2 Case Study: *Feed*

We look at the requirements first:

1) We want the thumbnail of the user's avatar to be
displayed on the left top of each *Feed*. And we want
the image to be rounded corners.

2) We want the user's nickname to be on the right
of her avatar, aligned to the top, and we need a
reasonable margin in between.

3) We want the time right beneath her nickname. It is
aligned with a nickname to the left and aligned with
a thumbnail to the bottom.

4) Then follows the text and image.

5) If the *Feed* is liked, we want to show the likes and number of comments and number of shares. We also give control to the users so they can like, comment, or share the *Feed*. In terms of the visual, we want to list the control buttons and numbers in the same row.

6) Lastly, the *Feed* should be adaptable to any length of the content.

Figure 2-8 is what the outcome looks like.

Figure 2-8. *Feed visual outcome*

Our first impression is that the main flow direction of this view is vertical. Following this direction, we can then take a top-down approach to divide the view into three major areas: (1) metadata area, (2) *Feed* body, and (3) control panel. Now we can conquer them separately (Figure 2-9).

At this stage, all the resources are hard coded for now. They will be aggregated in a model layer and eventually fetched from the network (Chapter 5) as we progress.

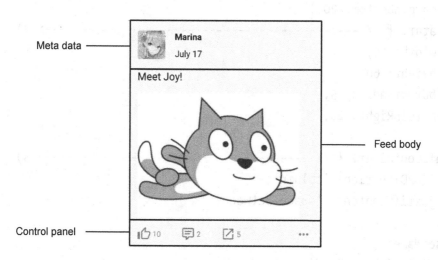

Figure 2-9. *The divided mock*

We look at the code for the area of metadata first (Listing 2-1).

Listing 2-1. Metadata area

```
...
<View style={styles.metaContainer}> // ------------------> 1)
  <Image style={styles.avatar} source={{uri: 'https://holmeshe.
me/05apps/avatar01.jpeg'}}/> // -------------------------> 2)
  <View style={styles.infoContainer}> // ----------------> 3)
    <Text style={styles.userName}>{'Marina'}</Text>
    <Text style={styles.date}>{'July 17'}</Text>
  </View>
</View>
...
```

```
metaContainer: { // -------------------------------------> 1)
  width: '100%',
  flexDirection: 'row',
  marginBottom: 20,},
avatar: { // ---------------------------------------------> 2)
  width: 60,
  height: 60,
  borderRadius: 5,
  marginRight: 20,
},
infoContainer: { // --------------------------------------> 3)
  flexDirection: 'column',
  justifyContent: 'space-between'
},
userName: {
  fontWeight: 'bold',
  fontSize: 18,
},
date: {
  fontSize: 18,
},
...
```

1) We notice that the height of the metadata area can be determined by the height of the image; hence, we refrain from giving explicit height to make this view more adaptable.

2) As said, Image can deduce its intrinsic size only when it is loaded locally using a require(...) expression. So we give an explicit size to the **component**.

3) A subcontainer is created to give a vertical layout for
the texts.

Note   *React Native* does not have margin collapsing. So we
need to apply `marginBottom` explicitly for all the containers when
appropriate.

Next, we look at the *Feed* body which is relatively simpler (Listing 2-2).

Listing 2-2. Feed body area

```
... // ----------------------------------------------------> 1)
<Text style={styles.textPost}> // ------------------------> 2)
  Meet Joy!
</Text>
<Image style={styles.imagePost} source={{uri:
'https://holmeshe.me/05apps/post01.png'}}/> // ----------> 3)
...
textPost: { // ------------------------------------------> 2)
  fontSize: 22,
  marginBottom: 20,
},
imagePost: { // -----------------------------------------> 3)
  width: '100%',
  aspectRatio: 4/3,
  marginRight: 20,
},
...
```

1) Since there is no change of **flex** direction as in metadata (`infoContainer`), we decide to try not to enlist a **container** for the *Feed* body. Rather, we let the *Feed* content flow along the main flex direction.

Note 🏛 Less **components** reduce memory and CPU overhead, and less code spares time and energy for the developer in the long run. Here is one approach: try introducing a new layer only when the flex direction changes. Though there are a few exceptional cases, this approach can make us more vigilant by using less layers consciously.

---

2) We need to apply the `marginBottom` to make the layout consistent.

3) 🏛 `width: '100%'` and `aspectRatio` are the golden combo styles applied for `Image`.

Let's continue along with the flow direction and examine the layout for the control panel (Listing 2-3).

Listing 2-3. Control panel area

```
...
<View style={styles.controlContainer}> // -----------------> 1)
  <NumberedWidget style={{flex: 1}} type={widgetTypes.LIKE}
number={10}/> // ------------------------------------------> 2)
  <NumberedWidget style={{flex: 1}} type={widgetTypes.COMMENT}
number={2}/> // ------------------------------------------> 2)
  <NumberedWidget style={{flex: 1.5}} type={widgetTypes.SHARE}
number={5}/> // ------------------------------------------> 2)
  <Widget type={widgetTypes.MORE} /> // -------------------> 2)
</View>
```

```
...
controlContainer: {
  flexDirection: 'row',
  justifyContent: 'space-between',
},
...
```

1) We encounter another flex direction change. So we added another container here.

2) By examining the visual requirement, it is very tempting to divide the control panel into two major portions using two containers like this:

```
<View style={{flex:3}}>
  <Like/>
  <Comment/>
  <Share/>
</View>
<View style={{flex:1}}>
  <More/>
</View>
```

But since there is no change of flex direction, we find a way to use flex applied for individual control buttons to reduce another layer of container.

Next, we look at how a widget is implemented (Listing 2-4).

Listing 2-4. Widget

```
...
const widgetTypes = {
  LIKE: 'like',
  COMMENT: 'commnet',
```

```
  SHARE: 'share',
  MORE: 'more',
}

function Widget(props) { // --------------------------------> 3)
  let iconName = 'thumb-up-outline';
  switch (props.type) {
    case widgetTypes.LIKE:
      iconName = 'thumb-up-outline';
      break;
    case widgetTypes.COMMENT:
      iconName = 'comment-text-outline';
      break;
    case widgetTypes.SHARE:
      iconName = 'launch';
      break;
    case widgetTypes.MORE:
      iconName = 'dots-horizontal';
      break;
  }

  return (
    <Icon name={iconName} color={'grey'} size={30} />
  );
}

function NumberedWidget(props) { // ----------------------> 1)
  return (
    <View style={[{...props.style}, styles.widget]}> // ----> 2)
      <Widget type={props.type}/>
      <Text style={styles.widgetText}>{props.number}</Text>
    </View>
```

```
  );
}
...
widget: { // ----------------------------------------------> 2)
  flexDirection: 'row',
  alignItems: 'center',
  justifyContent: 'flex-start',
},
widgetText: {
  marginLeft: 3,
  fontSize: 16,
  color: 'grey',
},
...
```

1) NumberedWidget is the composition of Widget and Text. We will see very soon that composition is favorable than inheritance for code encapsulation and reusing (Section 2.2).

2) The styles of NumberedWidget are divided into two portions. The **subcomponents** layout is inherent in the NumberedWidget; hence, it is defined as a constant style. On the other hand, the layout of NumberedWidget itself should be defined by its container. So the passed through styles are expanded as is.

3) Widget is a factory **component** that returns an Icon in an on-demand manner.

Lastly, we look at how **components** are put together to implement *Feed* (Listing 2-5).

Listing 2-5. Feed

```
class Feed extends React.Component {
  render() {
    return (
      <View
        style={[
          {...this.props.style}, styles.commonPadding
        ]}
      >
        <View style={styles.metaContainer}>
          <Image
            style={
              styles.avatar
            }
            source={
              {uri: 'https://holmeshe.me/05apps/avatar01.jpeg'}
            }
          />
          <View style={styles.infoContainer}>
            <Text style={styles.userName}>{'Marina'}</Text>
            <Text style={styles.date}>{'July 17'}</Text>
          </View>
        </View>
        <Text style={styles.textPost}>
          Meet Joy!
        </Text>
        <Image
```

```
          style={styles.imagePost}
          source={
            {uri: 'https://holmeshe.me/05apps/post01.png'}
          }
        />
        <View style={styles.controlContainer}>
          <NumberedWidget
            style={{flex: 1}}
            type={widgetTypes.LIKE}
            number={10}
          />
          <NumberedWidget
            style={{flex: 1}}
            type={widgetTypes.COMMENT}
            number={2}
          />
          <NumberedWidget
            style={{flex: 1.5}}
            type={widgetTypes.SHARE}
            number={5}
          />
          <Widget type={widgetTypes.MORE} />
        </View>
      </View>
    )
  }
}
```

2.1.3 Key Takeaways

In this section, we went through the usage of **flexbox**, namely, to lay out and to set size. Then we took it into action by composing the Feed, the building block of the core user experience of *Manyface*. This section could set up the foundation to handle most basic layout tasks. For more complex scenarios, we are going to learn some high-end principles and advanced techniques for layout in Chapter 6. What? You want to own a complete vertical feature? You will! Just read on.

2.2 Composition vs. Inheritance, HOC

I suppose it is tempting, if the only tool you have is a hammer, to treat everything as if it were a nail.

—Abraham Harold Maslow

Coming from a traditional OOP background, it could be tempting to use inheritance for code reusing and logic encapsulation. But it is inappropriate in **React** which adopts a declarative paradigm. To understand why, let us look at the tool and the object more closely.

In traditional OOP, classes are mechanical centric, and all the logic and properties can be accessed or overridden directly by a subclass. This makes inheritance an efficient tool for code reusing and logic encapsulation.

On the other hand, **components** are presentational centric, and the most valuable method that is worth being inherited could be the render() method. This is what makes inheritance clumsy. There are generally three options to use inheritance for **components**, to override completely, to inherit as is, and to call super.render() in the overridden render(). Let's look at them separately and understand why none of them are optimal.

First, completely overriding a render() makes no sense – if a **component** has its own version of render(), it is better off being a stand-alone rather than being a subclass of any **component** as a superclass. Moreover, completely overriding a render() could potentially invalidate all the supplementary methods and states built around the original one.

Second, directly inheriting the super.render() without overriding is less optimal as any specialization introduced in the subclass (that controls the render() behavior of the superclass) can be achieved in a simpler and more standard form, **props** in the superclass.

Third, we can also override the render() and call super.render() to reuse the superclass' render(). This causes an adversary called code fragmentation and makes the render() much harder to reason or, in other words, not scalable. 🏛 When it comes to complex layout and animations, it's important to ensure that all the involved elements are in one centralized place.

In a more fundamental sense, inheritance is not applicable for **components** because the *specialization order* of the inheritance chain (in OOP) is reversed from that of a **JSX** structure in a render() method. In inheritance, the downer a class is in the inheritance chain, the more specialized it is. On the other hand, in the **JSX** structure, the deeper a **component** is nested to the tag structure, it represents a more specialized or detailed feature and layout. They are not compatible when put together because it is not possible, or too tricky, to put a child class of a **component** to be in the **children** position of the super **component** in the render() method.

As such, a composition-based technique, higher-order component (**HOC**), is favored to achieve the same end result of inheritance. A **HOC** is like a superclass that conforms to the previously discussed specification order of **components**. Listing 2-6 gives a typical **HOC** example.

Listing 2-6. A HOC example

```
function HOC(Subcomponent) {
  return class extends React.Component {
    constructor(props) {
      super(props);
...
    }
    Render() {
      <ComponentThatProvidesBasicFunctionality>
          <Subcomponent/>
      </ComponentThatProvidesBasicFunctionality>
    }
  }
}
```

Next, we look at how **HOC** is used in real projects.

2.2.1 Case Study: Multiple Photo Feeds

This time, we are going to add more types of *Feed* (Figure 2-10). Let's look at the requirements first:

1) We give users the option to publish more than one photo in one of their *Feeds*.

2) If the user posts more than one and less than four photos, we want the photos to be displayed in a 2 x 2 grid.

3) If the user posts more than four and less than nine photos, we want the photos to be displayed in a 3 x 3 grid.

Figure 2-10. *Multiple photo Feeds*

We could implement three variances of *Feed* using a factory **component** (as we did for Widget in 1.3.2.) that returns the right version in accordance with the number of photos. And we soon find out that the code for the control panel and metadata area has to be duplicated for each *Feed*. Moreover, similar duplication could occur for other feed-related features such as comment. So instead of applying a short-term, ad hoc solution, let's take one step further to solve the problem the right way.

Firstly, we need a factory **component** to meet the new requirement (Listing 2-7).

Listing 2-7. Feed factory

```
export default function FeedFactory(props) { // -----------> 1)
  let numOfImages = props.item.feed.images.length;

  if (numOfImages > 4 && numOfImages <= 9) {
    return <Feed3x3 {...props}/>; // ----------------------> 2)
  } else if (numOfImages > 1 && numOfImages <= 4) {
    return <Feed2x2 {...props}/>; // ----------------------> 2)
```

```
  } else if (numOfImages === 1) {
    return <Feed {...props}/>; // -------------------------> 2)
  }

  return <Feed3x3 {...props}/>; // -------------------------> 2)
}
```

1) This factory **component** simply returns another **component** based on the condition derived from the **props**.

2) It also sincerely passed through all the props it received. This is achieved with a spread operator.

Note 🏛 As we mentioned in the beginning of this section, for the purpose of easy layout (and animation as we will see very soon in Chapter 3), it is preferred for a `render()` method to return a monolithic JSX layout free of logic as much as possible. However, there is one exception, that is, when a component works as a factory and sincerely returns a set of homogeneous components as is, logic such as `if else` or `switch case` is acceptable and will not cause trouble to further layout and animation effort.

Next, we implement the **HOC** that adds metadata and control panels to plain *Feeds* (Listing 2-8).

Listing 2-8. HOC that adds the metadata to the feed

```
export default function withMetaAndControls(Feed) {
  return class extends React.Component { // ---------------> 1)
    render() {
      return (
```

```
<View style={[
      {...this.props.style},
      styles.commonPadding
    ]}
>
  <View style={styles.metaContainer}>
    <Image style={styles.avatar}
         source={{
           uri:this.props.item.meta.avatarUri // --> 2)
         }}
    />
    <View style={styles.infoContainer}>
      <Text style={styles.userName}>
        {this.props.item.meta.name} // ------------> 2)
      </Text>
      <Text style={styles.date}>
        {this.props.item.meta.date} // ------------> 2)
      </Text>
    </View>
  </View>
  <Feed {...this.props}/> // --------------------> 3)
  <View style={styles.controlContainer}>
    <NumberedWidget
      style={{flex: 1}}
      type={widgetTypes.LIKE}
      number={ this.props.item.meta.numOfLikes } // -> 2)
    />
    <NumberedWidget
      style={{flex: 1}}
      type={widgetTypes.COMMENT}
      number={ this.props.item.meta.numOfComments }//> 2)
```

```
        />
        <NumberedWidget
          style={{flex: 1.5}}
          type={widgetTypes.SHARE}
          number={ this.props.item.meta.numOfShares } //-> 2)
        />
        <Widget type={widgetTypes.MORE} />
      </View>
    </View>
  )
 }
 }
}
```

1) **HOC** returns an enhanced class of the **component** passed through.

2) We start replacing all the hard-coded values with proper **props** which can be dynamically customized by the caller.

3) **HOC** is responsible to pass through the **props** to the target **component** being wrapped. This is achieved with the spread operator.

Next, we implement the three types of *Feed*. Listing 2-9 is how the original one-photo *Feed* looks after some of the functionalities are pulled out to the **HOC**.

Listing 2-9. The original Feed

```
class Feed extends React.Component {
  render() {
    return (
      <>
```

```
    <Text style={styles.textPost}>
      { this.props.item.feed.text }
    </Text>
    <Image
      style={styles.imagePost}
      source={{uri: this.props.item.feed.images[0]}} // -> 2)
    />
  </>
  )
 }
}

export default withMetaAndControls(Feed); // --------------> 1)
```

1) This is how **HOC** is used. Here, we export the enhanced class returned by the **HOC** instead of the *Feed* itself.

2) Unprotected access to array elements is error-prone. Safer approaches and ways to handle potential exceptions will be introduced in Section 2.4.

The two new types of *Feed* are implemented as in Listings 2-10 and 2-11.

Listing 2-10. Feed2x2

```
class Feed2x2 extends React.Component {
  render() {
   return (
     <>
       <Text style={styles.textPost}>
         { this.props.item.feed.text }
```

```
        </Text>
        <View style={styles.gridContainer}> // ------------> 1)
          {this.props.item.feed.images.slice(0, 4).map(e =>//> 2)
          <View style={styles.cell}> // -------------------> 1)
            <Image // -------------------------------------> 3)
              style={styles.imagePost}
              source={{uri: e}}
            />
          </View>
          )}
        </View>
      </>
    )
  }
}
const styles = StyleSheet.create({
  textPost: {
    fontSize: 22,
    marginBottom: 20,
  },
  gridContainer: {
    flexDirection: 'row',
    flexWrap: 'wrap', // ------------------------------------> 1)
  },
  cell: {
    width: '50%', // -----------------------------------------> 1)
    paddingRight: 12, // ------------------------------------> 3)
    marginBottom: 12, // ------------------------------------> 3)
    justifyContent: 'center',
    alignItems: 'flex-start'
  },
```

```
  imagePost: {
    width: '100%', // ----------------------------------> 3)
    aspectRatio: 4/3, // --------------------------------> 4)
  },
});
```

```
export default withMetaAndControls(Feed2x2); // -----------> 5)
```

1) We use `flexWrap: 'wrap'` on the container to enable the grid layout. Each row of the grid will contain two cells as the width of the **children** is set to `'50%'` of the container.

2) We use `map()` as the **JSX** expression to transform the image URLs from the **props** to the list of cells in the grid. We also use `slice(0, 4)` to ensure the number of cells in the grid is less than four; hence, the number of rows will always be less than two.

3) We use a combination of styles to maintain a consistent horizontal and vertical margin among the cells. Firstly, we set the width of the graphic to be `'100%'` which will be offset by the padding (12) given to the cell. Then the same amount of margin is also given to the cell correspondingly.

4) We set the `aspectRatio` of the cells the same as before.

5) The **HOC** is applied to the Feed2x2 the same way as to the *Feed*.

Listing 2-11. Feed3x3

```
class Feed3x3 extends React.Component {
  render() {
    return (
```

```
      <>
        <Text style={styles.textPost}>
          { this.props.item.feed.text }
        </Text>
        <View style={styles.gridContainer}>
          {this.props.item.feed.images.slice(0, 9).map(e =>//> 2)
          <View style={styles.cell}>
            <Image style={styles.imagePost} source={{uri: e}}/>
          </View>
          )}
        </View>
      </>
    )
  }
}
const styles = StyleSheet.create({
  textPost: {
    fontSize: 22,
    marginBottom: 20,
  },
  gridContainer: {
    flexDirection: 'row',
    flexWrap: 'wrap',
  },
  cell: {
    width: '33%', // ----------------------------------------> 1)
paddingRight: 3, // ----------------------------------------> 3)
marginBottom: 3,
    justifyContent: 'center',
    alignItems: 'flex-start'
  },
```

```
imagePost: {
  width: '100%', // ------------------------------------> 3)
  aspectRatio: 4/3,
},
});
```

```
export default withMetaAndControls(Feed3x3);
```

1) We use '33%' to set the grid to be 3 x N.

2) `slice(0, 9)` makes the grid 3 x 3.

3) We reduce the gap value to be three in accordance with a grid of more density.

2.2.2 Key Takeaways

In this section, we learned the fundamental difference between a **React component** and an ordinary class in the traditional OOP paradigm.

2.3 ScrollView and FlatList

One of the key mobile experiences distinguished from desktop is swipe. Whether the swiping is smooth or not by and large determines the success of the user experience of an app. Here is where `ScrollView` comes into play. `ScrollView` is backed by the native scroll view and inherits all the smoothness and fluency optimized for the mobile platform. Moreover, the fine-tuned snapping and momentum mimicking real world physics are sincerely relayed in **React Native**. So `ScrollView` is one key ingredient to unlock a highly user-interactive animation experience (Chapter 3).

FlatList extends ScrollView catering for the need of a long list. In addition to the excessive length, a long list is required to grow dynamically. When triggered by certain user interactions, for example, scrolling to the end, additional rows could be added. FlatList is more appropriate as rendering everything in one shot is not optimal or not feasible for most long list use cases. FlatList implements a concept *virtual list* which renders only a necessary portion of it at any point of time. The user will be under the impression that they are navigating a list fully populated at all times because the **component** ensures that the visible area of the list is always being covered within the portion that has been rendered. As noted, FlatList or, more specifically, the scrolling mechanism of FlatList is based on ScrollView; hence, FlatList also inherits all the native-level performance and user experience merits by nature.

As you might already be figuring out, FlatList is more suitable for Moment in *Manyface*. And this is what we are going to do.

Note   In the terminology of the virtual list, the visible area is called *viewport*, and a rendered area is called a *window*. By default, FlatList can cope with most scenarios of a long list. In extreme cases, nevertheless, it is desirable to deeply squeeze the performance of the component by adjusting the sizes of windows and anticipated viewport. Such heuristics are examined in detail in Chapter 6.

2.3.1 Case Study: Moment

This time, we are going to complete the layout for *Moment*. The requirement of *Moment* is simple: a scrollable list of *Feeds* (Figure 2-11).

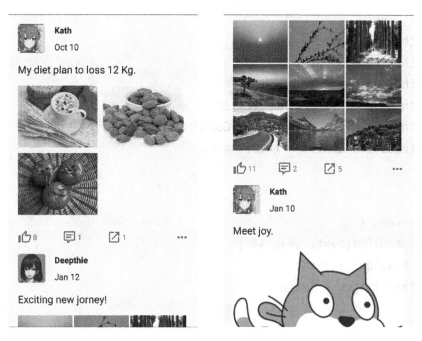

Figure 2-11. *Moment*

Firstly, let's move the hard-coded *Feeds* content to a model layer which could be read by the FlatList (Listing 2-12). As we progress, we are going to gradually remove the hard-coded content and fetch everything from a web API.

Listing 2-12. FeedModel

```
class Meta {
  constructor(
    avatarUri,
    name,
    date,
    numOfLikes,
    numOfComments,
    numOfShares
```

```
  ) {
    this.avatarUri = avatarUri;
    this.name = name;
    this.date = date;
    this.numOfLikes = numOfLikes;
    this.numOfComments = numOfComments;
    this.numOfShares = numOfShares;
  }
}

class Feed {
  constructor(text, images) {
    this.text = text;
    this.images = images;
  }
}

class FeedModel { // -----------------------------------------> 1)
  constructor(obj) {
    this.meta = new Meta(
                  obj.avatarUri,
                  obj.name,
                  obj.date,
                  obj.numOfLikes,
                  obj.numOfComments,
                  obj.numOfShares
                );

    this.feed = new Feed(obj.text, obj.images);
  }
}
```

1) It is common to create a model layer to capture the underlying data structure that the app is running on. In practice, *TypeScript* is more favorable than vanilla *JavaScript* used here.

Next, we fill the model with some mock data (Listing 2-13).

Listing 2-13. Mock data

```
const mockData = [{
  avatarUri: 'https://holmeshe.me/05apps/avatar08.jpeg',
  name: 'Kath',
  date: 'Oct 10',
  numOfLikes: 8,
  numOfComments: 1,
  numOfShares: 1,
  text: 'My diet plan to loss 12 Kg.',
  images: [
    'https://holmeshe.me/05apps/hoc-2x2-1.jpg',
    'https://holmeshe.me/05apps/hoc-2x2-2.jpg',
    'https://holmeshe.me/05apps/hoc-2x2-3.jpg',
  ]
}, {
  avatarUri: 'https://holmeshe.me/05apps/avatar02.jpeg',
  name: 'Deepthie',
  date: 'Jan 12',
  numOfLikes: 11,
  numOfComments: 2,
  numOfShares: 5,
  text: 'Exciting new jorney!',
  images: [
    'https://holmeshe.me/05apps/hoc-3x3-1.jpg',
    'https://holmeshe.me/05apps/hoc-3x3-2.jpg',
```

```
    'https://holmeshe.me/05apps/hoc-3x3-3.jpg',
    'https://holmeshe.me/05apps/hoc-3x3-4.jpg',
    'https://holmeshe.me/05apps/hoc-3x3-5.jpg',
    'https://holmeshe.me/05apps/hoc-3x3-6.jpg',
    'https://holmeshe.me/05apps/hoc-3x3-7.jpg',
    'https://holmeshe.me/05apps/hoc-3x3-8.jpg',
    'https://holmeshe.me/05apps/hoc-3x3-9.jpg',
  ]
}, {
  avatarUri: 'https://holmeshe.me/05apps/avatar08.jpeg',
  name: 'Kath',
  date: 'Jan 10',
  numOfLikes: 3,
  numOfComments: 1,
  numOfShares: 0,
  text: 'Meet joy.',
  images: [
    'https://holmeshe.me/05apps/post01.png',
  ]
}];

let mockModel = mockData.map((obj) => { return new
FeedModel(obj); });

export default mockModel;
```

Lastly, we encapsulate the Moment **component** (Listing 2-14).

Listing 2-14. Moment

```
import React from 'react';
import { FlatList } from 'react-native';

import FeedFactory from './feeds/FeedFactory';
```

```
import data from '../models/FeedModel';

const Moment = () => {
  const renderItem = (entry) => // -------------------------> 1)
    <FeedFactory meta={entry.item.meta} // ------------------> 2)
                 feed={entry.item.feed}
    />

  return (
    <FlatList // ------------------------------------------> 3)
      data={data} // -------------------------------------> 1)
      renderItem={renderItem} // -------------------------> 1)
    />
  );
};

export default Moment;
```

1) The two essential props that FlatList requires
   are (a) data which defines its data source and (b)
   renderItem() which defines how to render data in
   the granularity of entry. FlatList can work out of
   the box with these two props set properly.

2) FeedFactory is the same one we use in our last case
   study (Section 2.2.1).

3) We use FlatList to render the whole list.

2.3.2 Key Takeaways

This section introduced the basic ScrollView and its enhanced version,
FlatList, which empower the long list experience. As the scrolling
is backed directly by the corresponding native **component**, it has no

difference than the native experience performance wise. Then we used a minimal setup of `FlatList` to complete the core user experience of *Manyface*. As mentioned, `FlatList` deserves some derivative optimization when it comes to extreme scenarios. We are going to review some of the critical performance aspects of `FlatList` and common optimization approaches in Chapter 6. Moreover, as we will see in Chapter 3, ScrollView is also the key to implement user-interactive animation.

2.4 Error Handling

When designing systems of any kinds, it is important to understand that every component could potentially fail. A robust system is not one that does not have any failure, but the one that is always tolerant to setbacks and is able to degrade gradually to the next acceptable state when a failure occurs. Bottom line, the system in design should never quit the game with a crash or any other kinds of undefined behaviors (e.g., blank screen), in exception, by design. To build a system that never crashes, the very first step is to define the boundaries for exceptions so as to confine the exceptions inside one logic unit that causes them. As you will see very soon in this section, a clear boundary does not only make the exceptional behavior easier to be defined but also makes the potential issue easier to be debugged. This technique is called exactly as an **error boundary**.

An **error boundary** is very similar to a *try-catch* semantic that defines the exception flow along with the normal logic flow. Unlike the traditional imperative programming paradigm where the logic flow is grouped into functions, ***React*** is declarative and logic units are made up with presentation-oriented **components**. An **error boundary** is an error handling mechanism catering for this paradigm and is itself a **component**. More specifically, an **error boundary** is a container **component** designed with presentation and behavior for types of exception that **children** could potentially throw. 🏛 In practice, an **error boundary** is strategically placed on cutting points of the domain logic unit so as to, again, confine the exceptions inside one logic unit that causes them.

As you might be thinking of right now, **HOC** is the fitting technique to apply **error boundaries**. To be more concrete, a **HOC** is an ideal place to encapsulate some of the common logic for error handling (e.g., log, exception filtering) and to execute the custom exception presentation or behavior of a specific **component** in design. Those **components** with **error boundaries** enabled, in turn, are determined as the noted strategic points that are embedded with the exception flow for itself and all its **children** and **subcomponents**.

Note   A stand-alone **error boundary** is also a common practice that is suggested by the community. We take the approach of using **HOC** to implement **error boundaries** as we see more merits in this practice.

How to identify those strategic points mentioned earlier? Luckily, we are in the middle of implementing *Manyface*. Let's find out together with real-world examples.

2.4.1 Case Study: Moment (Reinforced)

Before we move forward, let's slow down here and think about one question: Is Moment production ready? No. Because it lacks an exception flow despite the complete and seemingly bug-free functionalities. As a result, any hidden flaws within the **component** logic or the data from the model layer could cause a crash of the app. Figure 2-12 shows how *Manyface* is represented in debugging mode when one metadata is undefined. In production, it will be an instant crash.

Figure 2-12. A crash

In practice, the flaw could come from a malfunctioning endpoint, a bug from one of us programmers, or a premature configuration flag turned on remotely. Nonetheless, a crash in any of the preceding cases is not acceptable. We know that an **error boundary** is our friend. But how to use it effectively? To answer this question, we firstly look at the nature of exception flows.

Unlike the normal logic flow where each branch pinpoints a certain expected logic case, an exception flow targets each time an undetermined range of cases that are exceptional and could not be anticipated beforehand. A common narrative of an exception flow is "when one category of unexpected happened, whatever it is, what would you do?". Sometimes, even the error category itself is not known. In order to deal with this uncertainty, exception flows are deployed strategically as layers of defending lines.

We shall take a top-down approach to identify the strategic points to place **error boundaries**, starting from the Moment. If anything unexpected happens inside Moment, what should we render? Correct, an error page like a 404. Take a step down; what if the unexpected exception happens inside a Feed, should we block the user experience of Moment with the 404 error page? No, right? We can simply make the Feed in problem invisible. So the problem will not surprise the user. On the other hand, we should log the incident with all the contexts within the exception flow predefined. We call this technique a *silent log*. We now have two defending lines to make our **component** robust in a way that in any case of unexpected exceptions, it can degrade gradually to the next acceptable state. And voila, we just defined the requirements for this case study:

1) When an exception happens inside a Feed,
   the Feed should be invisible.

2) When an exception happens inside a Moment,
   it should be replaced with an error page.

Firstly, let's implement the utility **component** that makes our lives better. As discussed, we are going to count on our old friend, **HOC**, this time again (Listing 2-15).

Listing 2-15. withErrorBoundary

```
export default function withErrorBoundary(Comp, ErrorPage,
ErrorHandler) { // ----------------------------------------> 1)
  class Error extends React.Component { // ----------------> 2)
```

```
  constructor () {
    super()

    this.state = {
      error: undefined,
      info: undefined
    }
  }

  componentDidCatch (error, info) { // -----------------> 2)
    this.setState({ error, info })

    // Common exception related logic comes here // -----> 3)
    // e.g., log, report, etc.,

    if (ErrorHandler) { ErrorHandler(error, info); } // --> 1b)
  }

  render() {
    if (undefined !== this.state.error) {
      const { error, info } = this.state
      if (!ErrorPage) { // -----------------------------> 1a)
        return <View/>;
      }

      return (
        <ErrorPage // --------------------------------------> 1a)
          error={error}
          info={info}
        />
      )
    }
    return this.props.children; // ----------------------> 2)
  }
}
```

```
class WithError extends React.Component { // ------------> 4)
  constructor () {
    super()
  }

  render () {
    return <Error><Comp {...this.props} /></Error> // ----> 2)
  }
}

return WithError; // -------------------------------------> 5)
}
```

1) (a) To achieve the two requirements defined earlier,
   we give the protected **component** a chance to
   define its error page in exception. If this page is
   passed as a nil value, nothing will be rendered.
   (b) The protected **component** could also define its
   behavior when an exception happens. Normally,
   the behavior could drive changes outside of the
   component (e.g., navigation back and forward,
   make a global banner (no network) visible, etc.).

Note 🏛 In order to avoid double fault (fault within the exception handler), a rule of thumb when designing an exception flow is to be a minimalism.

---

2) Error is the **error boundary** that can catch
    exceptions thrown within its **children**. In normal
    execution, it simply returns its **children**. When
    such an exception occurs, on the other hand,
    componentDidCatch is invoked by the *React*
    runtime, and the ErrorPage defined in step 1 is
    rendered.

3) Being in the funnel position of all exception flow,
    the componentDidCatch is also an ideal place for
    other common actions such as log, report, and
    debugging dialog boxes.

4) WithError is the actual **HOC** that wraps the
    protected **component** inside the Error defined
    in step 2.

5) Lastly, the **HOC** is returned in place of the original
    component.

Now we can enhance *Feeds* using the **HOC** defined earlier
(Listing 2-16).

Listing 2-16. Feeds reinforced

```
class Feed extends React.Component {
  render() {
    return (
      <>
        <Text style={styles.textPost}>
          { this.props.item.feed.text }
        </Text>
        <Image
          style={styles.imagePost}
          source={{uri: this.props.item.feed.images[0]}}
```

```
        />
      </>
    )
  }
}

const styles = StyleSheet.create({
  textPost: {
    fontSize: 22,
    marginBottom: 20,
  },
  imagePost: {
    width: '100%',
    aspectRatio: 4/3,
    marginBottom: 20,
  },
});
export default withErrorBoundary(withMetaAndControls(Feed),
undefined, undefined); // --------------------------------> 1)

...// Feed2x2 definition

export default withErrorBoundary(withMetaAndControls(Feed2x2) ,
undefined, undefined); // --------------------------------> 1)

...// Feed3x3 definition

export default withErrorBoundary(withMetaAndControls(Feed3x3) ,
undefined, undefined); // --------------------------------> 1)
```

1) As per the requirement, when anything happens
   inside the Feed, we simply return an empty view and
   omit the **component** completely.

Next, we enhance the Moment which is a bit more complex than Feed as it requires a default error page (Listing 2-17).

Listing 2-17. Moment reinforced

```
const ErrorPage = () => { // ----------------------------> 1)
  return (
    <View style={{
            flex: 1,
            justifyContent: 'flex-start',
            alignItems: 'center',
            paddingTop: 180,
            paddingHorizontal: 60
        }}
    >
      <Icon name={'alert-circle-outline'}
            size={88}
            color={'#6c8ca5'}
      />
      <Text style={{fontSize: 28, color: '#6c8ca5'}}>
        Oops but no worries!
      </Text>
      <Text style={{
              fontSize: 20,
              color: 'darkGray',
              paddingTop: 15
          }}
      >
        Our engineers are working hard at the moment. So please
        give another try soon later!
      </Text>
    </View>
```

```
  );
}

const Moment = () => {
  const renderItem = (entry) =>
  <FeedFactory item={entry.item}/>

  return (
    <FlatList
      data={data}
      renderItem={renderItem}
    />
  );
};

export default withErrorBoundary(Moment, ErrorPage,
undefined);// ------------------------------------------> 2)
```

1) This is the error page we now define specifically for Moment. Later, we shall move it to a global position we see fit. 🏛 This page is programmed in the most rudimentary way so as to avoid double fault as mentioned earlier.

2) Again, we protect the Moment using the withErrorBoundary **HOC**. And this time, we pass it with the error page.

Lastly, let's see if the whole **error boundary** facility works. In common sense, the foremost presumption for a safety test is to assume it's unsafe. So let's inject some random errors to those protected **components**, starting from Feed3x3 (Listing 2-18).

Listing 2-18. Feed in problem

```
class Feed3x3 extends React.Component {
  render() {
    const errorObj = undefined;
    errorObj.error(); // ------------------------------------> 1)
    return (
      <>
        <Text style={styles.textPost}>
          { this.props.item.feed.text }
        </Text>
        <View style={styles.gridContainer}>
          {this.props.item.feed.images.slice(0, 9).map(e =>
          <View style={styles.cell}>
            <Image style={styles.imagePost} source={{uri: e}}/>
          </View>
          )}
        </View>
      </>
    )
  }
}

...// styles

export default withErrorBoundary(withMetaAndControls(Feed3x3),
undefined, undefined);
```

1) This line throws. As per the discussion, an exception
    thrown in a Feed will only affect the Feed itself.
    Hence, the user will not sense it. The development
    team, on the other hand, will know it through an
    exception report (Figure 2-13).

Note 🏛️ We call the technique a *silent log* that (1) makes the exception transparent from the user's perspective, while (2) it makes it obvious to developers with meticulous logging.

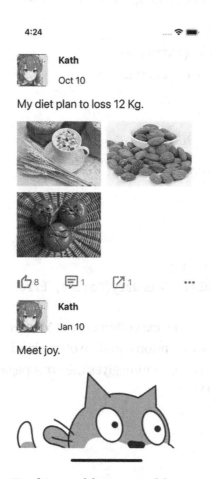

Figure 2-13. *Make Feed in problem invisible*

Next, we give some problems to the Moment (Listing 2-19).

Listing 2-19. Moment in problem

```
// ErrorPage is defined here

const Moment = () => {
  const errorObj = undefined; // -------------------------> 1)
  errorObj.error();

  const renderItem = (entry) =>
  <FeedFactory item={entry.item}/>

  return (
    <FlatList
      data={data}
      renderItem={renderItem}
    />
  );
};

//export default Moment;
export default withErrorBoundary(Moment, ErrorPage, undefined);
```

1) We throw the same exception here at Moment.
   In reality, the exception could be of any kind.
   The Moment in exception gives the error page
   (Figure 2-14).

5:03   ...⋆ ■

Oops but no worries!

Our engineers are working
hard at the moment. So please
give another try soon later!

Figure 2-14. *Give error page when Moment is in problem*

2.4.2 Key Takeaways

In this section, we completed the **components** for *Feed* and *Moment*
which make up the core user experience of *Manyface*. We firstly reviewed
the nature of an exception flow in general. Then we introduced **error
boundaries** and the way of handling exceptions in *React*. We took a step
further to use **HOC** as the means to implement an error boundary and
apply it on *Moment* and *Feed* **components**.

The most valuable part of this section is the methodology to define the
critical points in a project. Through the practice, we know that the general
principle here is "least surprise to the user," even in the case of exceptions.

To be more specific, we hide the problematic **component** and conduct a *silent log* if possible; or we show an error page letting users know what is going on when we have no choice. In the real scenario, navigation, alert box, toast, and status banner are all in your utility suit. When applying the methodology in your particular cases, you could take the practical approach of reasoning carried out in this section as well.

The scope of an exception flow in a ***React Native*** app is more extensive than what we see in this section. In particular, two more scenarios are not covered in this section: (1) exceptions thrown within services that enlist asynchronous operations and (2) exceptions thrown in **native modules and native components**. The error handling of the two scenarios will be covered in their respective chapters (i.e., Chapters 4 and 5). And we are going to escalate our point of view by abstracting a more generalized methodology for exception handling in Chapter 6.

2.5 Summary

In this chapter, we established a rock-solid foundation of ***React*** development. We started the development journey from the Feed **component** with the basic understanding and skill in **flexbox**. We diversify the Feed using a technique called **higher-order component** (**HOC**). Then we put the diversified *Feeds* into a scrollable list using FlatList. Lastly, we set up an exception flow for all **components** including categories of Feed and Moment so the core user experience can survive the errors and exceptions in the coming iterations.

The knowledge and skill discussed in this chapter are sufficient for you to take charge of one user interface module of reasonable complexity. To expand the scope to other aspects of a ***React Native*** app, read on.

CHAPTER 3

Animation in React Native

FPS delayed is UX denied.

—Holmes

Animation does not seem to belong to the core user experience of any apps. Not true. Conversely, it is vital to do the animation correctly. Why? Read on.

The first key usage of animation is to avoid abrupt user interface change. For example, when an image is just loaded from the network, a looming animation is more optimal than a sudden popping up. This principle applies to some other user interface changes, as we will see very soon that the text expanding transition in Feeds is made smooth using a ***React Native*** animation technique called *layout animation*.

The second one is to maintain the impression that the app is being responsive while loading. Instances are a spinning indicator that an individual item is being loaded, a glimmering skeleton view in app initialization, and an animated bubble when an AI is thinking. In these cases, the animation assures the user that the app is still active though it is not actually responsive to any user interactions. The absence of the animation could lead to inappropriate or incomplete experiences in the preceding scenarios.

© M. Holmes He 2022
M. H. He, *Creating Apps with React Native*, https://doi.org/10.1007/978-1-4842-8042-3_3

The last but most valuable use of animation is the instinctive touch screen experience, which is especially critical to mobile user experience. This type of animation should mimic real-world objects by reflecting its velocity and inertia and by following the user's gesture frame by frame. We call this type gesture-driven animation to distinguish it from other simpler playback animations discussed earlier. Gesture-driven animation is in demand when multitouch is introduced by iPhone, and fingers become the major means for the users to interact with apps. In today's mobile ecosystem, the users have already been used to smooth touch screen experiences. Hence, doing it right, although not easy, is just the minimal baseline.

Note   If you are looking at the home page of an iPhone, please pay attention to (1) the smooth sliding that follows your finger when you drag and swipe and (2) the natural momentum when you release.

3.1 Introduction to React Native Animation

React Native contains three types of animation targeting different scenarios. The first one is *layout animation. Layout animation* is bound to a setState(). After a successful invocation, **React Native** will "guess" the most reasonable animation by comparing the layout change incurred by the setState(). This is normally used for playback animation such as view fly-in or area expanding.

Layout animation cannot handle complicated and compounded layout changes. When we need finer control, we shall use *value animation*. Technically, those values are associated to transform or opacity of a **component**'s props.style and are changed during runtime to facilitate playback animation.

Gesture-driven animation is different fundamentally from the first two ways to facilitate playback animations. This is the most sophisticated animation in that each frame needs to reflect the current position of the user's finger so as to give a smooth and instinctive user experience.

Animation can be powered by either native or *JavaScript*. *JavaScript* is not slow. But the asynchronous operation and interthread communication are. We will cover native-powered animation only in that *JavaScript*-powered animations cannot meet the quality bar of production-level apps more often than not. The good news is we don't need a single line of native code to facilitate a native-powered animation. All the functionalities are well encapsulated within the *React Native* core and surface out elegantly to be in pure *JavaScript*.

Next, we examine each type of animation. And you know the drill; each learning section is followed by a practical hands-on section(s). And *Manyface* will be enhanced in each iteration. Let's go!

3.2 Layout Animation

For each relayout triggered by setState(), we can opt in an animation effect that smooths out the transition. As said, *layout animation* is normally used to kick off a one-off playback animation. In some situations, it also can facilitate looping animation such as pulsating. *Layout animation* works only when the layout change introduced by setState() is simple enough to be guessed by the runtime. That means the layout changes should not involve correlated **states** nor nested **components**.

3.2.1 Presets

The easiest way to invoke *layout animation* is to use shortcut methods which fire a linear or bouncing animation using predefined configurations (Listing 3-1). Since the properties in regard to the animation, for example, `velocity`, `springDamping`, `duration`, **create/update/delete** configs, etc., are all hard coded within the shortcuts, these methods are the least flexible among other approaches to issue a *layout animation*.

Listing 3-1. Shortcut methods

```
LayoutAnimation.linear()
LayoutAnimation.easeInEaseOut()
LayoutAnimation.spring()
```

Note   Here, the **create/update/delete** configs are not straightforward by their names, but don't worry, we are going to cover their meanings very soon when we go through more advanced APIs.

🔴 The *layout animation* is configured for the **next** `setState()` in code execution order. Hence, a wrongly abstracted layer of methods could incur unwelcomed animation with *layout animation* configured by accident. This kind of bug is contextual and hence is very time-consuming to pinpoint. So 🤍 constantly revising the layer of responsibilities is vital. 🏛 Alternatively, we shall make the architecture flatten. Anyway, no abstraction could be better and less expensive than overabstraction.

3.2.2 LayoutAnimation.create( )

Normally, the preset parameters are not set with the most optimal values. If we have higher demand on the animation elegance, we shall leverage the finer control offered by the combination of two other layout animation methods, LayoutAnimation.configureNext() and LayoutAnimation. create(). Listing 3-2 gives an example.

Listing 3-2. Customize layout animation using .configureNext() + .create()

```
LayoutAnimation.configureNext(
  LayoutAnimation.create(
    300,
    LayoutAnimation.Types.linear,
    LayoutAnimation.Properties.opacity
  )
);
```

LayoutAnimation.create() is a handy utility method that helps create the primary parameter config for LayoutAnimation.configureNext(). Usually, we don't need to understand what is the actual format of the raw animation config taken by LayoutAnimation.configureNext(). So the specialization level offered by LayoutAnimation.create() is sufficient for most use cases.

3.2.3 Raw Animation Config

If we need finer adjustment to the animation outcome, we can create the animation config object manually and pass it through directly to LayoutAnimation.configureNext(). Listing 3-3 gives LayoutAnimation. create() as a helper to assist us in understanding the exact format of the animation config object.

Listing 3-3. Implementation of .create()

```
function create(
  duration: number,
  type: Type,
  property: Property,
): LayoutAnimationConfig {
  return {
    duration,
    create: {type, property},
    update: {type},
    delete: {type, property},
  };
}
```

For the example in Section 3.2.2, the actual config object created is given in Listing 3-4.

Listing 3-4. The result config object got created by .create()

```
{
  duration: 300, // ----------------------------------------> 2)
  create: { // --------------------------------------------> 1)
    type: LayoutAnimation.Types.linear, // ----------------> 2)
    property: LayoutAnimation.Properties.opacity // -------> 3)
  },
  update: {
    type: LayoutAnimation.Types.linear // -----------------> 2)
  },
  delete: {
    type: LayoutAnimation.Types.linear, // ----------------> 2)
    property: LayoutAnimation.Properties.opacity // -------> 3)
  }
}
```

1) The **create** subconfig defines the presenting
   animation when a new component is created after a
   setState(). Conversely, **delete** defines the dismiss
   animation for the **component** when it got removed.
   Similarly, **update** defines the animation when the
   same **component** is changed in size or position.

2) The duration and type parameters passed to
   LayoutAnimation.create() are applied to all
   subconfig entries.

3) The property parameters, on the other hand, are
   applied to **create** and **delete** subconfig only. This
   is to define a symmetric behavior for these two
   opposite actions of the respective **component**.
   In particular, we want to fade in a newly created
   component and to fade out the deleted one.

Note   Despite its simplicity, *layout animation* is also very
performant. This is because after the declaration of the animation, the
actual animation is calculated and is carried out all in the native layer.
So here only the standard performance overhead of setState()
applies.

3.2.4 Android

Lastly before we jump into hands-on, we need to add one extra line to
enable *layout animation* on **Android** (Listing 3-5).

Listing 3-5. Extra one line to enable layout animation on Android

```
UIManager.setLayoutAnimationEnabledExperimental?.(true);
```

3.2.5 Case Study, Read More

In *Moment*, we don't want an excessive long feed to occupy the screen. Instead, if the texts of a feed exceed a certain length, we fold the text portion up so as to make the experience more fluent. The exact requirements are as follows:

1) When the number of characters is less than 180, we display the full message without any truncation.

2) If the number of characters is equal or greater than 180, we truncate the text to three lines and add a three-dot symbol below. This symbol gives a visual effect like a synopsis and also works as a button that expands the message when clicked.

3) After a long message is expanded, we switch the button to an up arrow that folds up the message once again (Figure 3-1).

4) We want the user experience to be smooth; hence, animation is desired for all the moving parts.

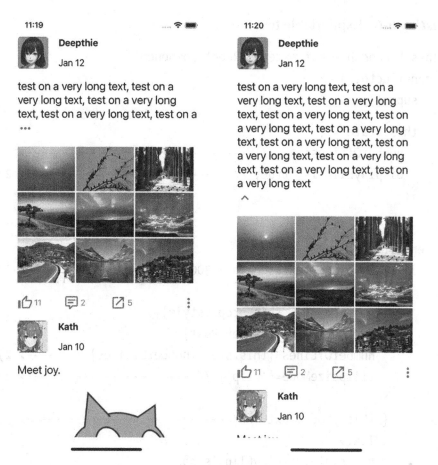

Figure 3-1. Expandable message

Firstly, let's implement the core **component** that enables the expandable text (Listing 3-6).

Listing 3-6. Expandable text

```
class ExpandableText extends React.Component {
  constructor() {
    super();

    this.state = {
      numberOfLines: 3, // ----------------------------------> 2)
      displayElipsis: true, // ----------------------------> 2)
    };
  }

  render() {
    if (this.props.text.length > 300) { // ----------------> 1)
      return (
      <View style={{...this.props.style}}>
        <Text style={styles.textPost}
          numberOfLines={this.state.numberOfLines} // -----> 2)
          ellipsizeMode={'clip'} // ----------------------> 2)
        >
        { this.props.text } // ----------------------------> 5)
        </Text>
        {this.state.displayElipsis &&
        <TouchableOpacity onPress={this.expand.
        bind(this)}> // 3)
          <Icon name={'dots-horizontal'} // ---------------> 2)
                color={'grey'}
                size={30}
          />
        </TouchableOpacity>
        }
        {!this.state.displayElipsis &&
        <TouchableOpacity onPress={this.fold.bind(this)}>
```

```
        <Icon name={'chevron-up'} // --------------------> 4)
               color={'grey'}
               size={30}
         />
       </TouchableOpacity>
       }
     </View>
     );
   } else { // ---------------------------------------------> 1)
     return (
     <Text style={[{...this.props.style}, styles.textPost]}>
     { this.props.text } // -------------------------------> 5)
     </Text>
     );
   }
 }

 expand() { // -------------------------------------------------> 3)
    this.setState({numberOfLines: null, displayElipsis:
false});
 }
 fold() { // ---------------------------------------------------> 4)
    this.setState({numberOfLines: 3, displayElipsis: true});
 }
}

const styles = StyleSheet.create({ // --------------------> 5)
  textPost: {
    fontSize: 22,
  },
});
```

```
export default ExpandableText;
```

1) This is where we return different layouts according to text length. We have seen conditional rendering in Section 2.2.1. Although 🏛 the render() method should avoid fragmented **JSX** in that monolithic **JSX** is easier to be laid out and be reasoned, this pattern works fine only when a render() needs to return different, complete **components** according to certain conditions.

2) These props are set for the expandable text logic. Firstly, numberOfLines is set to three initially to truncate the text. Then we set the ellipsisMode to 'clip' to hide the ellipsis for the button. Next, we use 'dots-horizontal' to render the button.

3) Bind the expand() method to the TouchableOpacity to enable the pressing. In this method, we (a) remove the restriction of three lines to fully display the message and (b) flip the state of displayEllipsis to hide the button.

4) The folding button is displayed only when the state of numberOfLines is set to zero and displayEllipsis is set to false. This button is linked to fold() that reverses the preceding two **states** and hence folds back the message.

5) The actual text set with the style is embedded in the preceding logic.

Next, we apply the ExpandableText to the existing Feed **components** (Listings 3-7 to 3-9).

Listing 3-7. ExpandableText applied to Feed

```
class Feed extends React.Component {
  render() {
    return (
        <>
        <ExpandableText
          style={styles.textPost}
          text={this.props.item.feed.text} />
        <Image
          style={styles.imagePost}
          source={{uri: this.props.item.feed.images[0]}}
          />
        </>
    )
  }
}
```

Listing 3-8. ExpandableText applied to Feed2x2

```
class Feed2x2 extends React.Component {
  render() {
    return (
        <>
        <ExpandableText
          style={styles.textPost}
          text={this.props.item.feed.text}
        />
        <View style={styles.gridContainer}>
          {this.props.item.feed.images.slice(0, 4).map(e =>
          <View style={styles.cell}>
            <Image style={styles.imagePost} source={{uri: e}}/>
          </View>
```

```
            )}
        </View>
    </>
    )
  }
}
```

Listing 3-9. ExpandableText applied to Feed3x3

```
class Feed3x3 extends React.Component {
  render() {
    return (
        <>
        <ExpandableText
          style={styles.textPost}
          text={this.props.item.feed.text}
        />
        <View style={styles.gridContainer}>
          {this.props.item.feed.images.slice(0, 9).map(e =>
          <View style={styles.cell}>
            <Image style={styles.imagePost} source={{uri: e}}/>
          </View>
          )}
        </View>
    </>
    )
  }
```

There is still one missing piece in the puzzle, that is, to make a smooth transition when the text is expanded or folded. Listing 3-10 gives its implementation.

Listing 3-10. Add animation

```
...
expand() {
  LayoutAnimation.configureNext( // ----------------------> 1)
    LayoutAnimation.create(
      300,
      LayoutAnimation.Types.linear,
      LayoutAnimation.Properties.opacity
    )
  );

  this.setState({numberOfLines: null, displayElipsis: false});
}
fold() {
  LayoutAnimation.configureNext( // ----------------------> 1)
    LayoutAnimation.create(
      300,
      LayoutAnimation.Types.linear,
      LayoutAnimation.Properties.opacity
    )
  );

  this.setState({numberOfLines: 3, displayElipsis: true});
}
```

1) Yes, here we simply use the animation code from
   Section 3.2.3, which effectively turns the setState()
   invocations to layout animation.

Note   The animation outcome is exactly what we defined. Take expand() as an example; after the setState(), the expanding button is faded out by the **delete** action, while the folding button is faded in for **create**. The rest of the **components** move linearly to their destined position because of the **update** action.

3.2.6 Key Takeaways

In this section, we learned the *layout animation*. It is simple and performant, but it cannot deal with compounded change. As the name suggests, *layout animation* can automatically animate the next layout change that is issued by setState(). We also went through ways of invoking *layout animation*, from its simplest form with a single method call to the more complex one where you can manually fine-tune the parameters. It is worth noting again that *layout animation* cannot handle complex animation tasks, which should be tackled with more advanced techniques discussed in the following sections.

3.3 Value Animation

Unlike *layout animation* that impacts on the layout of the overall user interface, *value animation* targets individual **components**. To enable *value animation*, **components** need to be attached with an *animation value* (Animated.Value). More specifically, after the *animation value* is bound to the designated **component props**, animation can be driven by changing its value with APIs such as Animated.timing() or Animated.spring(). In contrast to the coarse-grained control offered by *layout animation, value animation* is capable of driving highly sophisticated and complicated animation behavior.

Value animation can be powered by either a native or a *JavaScript* thread. Technically, animation powered by *JavaScript* is slow as it requires constant involvement of the *JavaScript* thread and asynchronous interthread calls. Native-powered animations are free of those overheads as the computing is completely offloaded to a native thread and hence is no different from pure native animation performance wise. 💣 Due to the questionable quality of the *JavaScript* thread, ♡ we are going to focus only on native-powered animation. It is also a common practice to only rely on native-powered animation in production.

Note   Despite its low performance, *JavaScript-powered animation* provides a wider range of options of props to which the *animation value* can attach. For instance, 💣 one restriction of *value animation* at the native level is that the width and height cannot be attached with an *animation value*.

Next, let's go through the APIs. As said, a variable that can be used as an *animation value* should be initialized as Animated.Value(). Listing 3-11 declares an *animation value* that controls a **component**'s opacity.

Listing 3-11. Animated.Value, an example

```
let opacity = Animated.Value(0);
```

A **component** should be animation enabled before it can be attached with an *animation value*. This is achieved using Animated.createAnimatedComponent(). As you might expect, this method creates a **HOC** based on the **component** passed in. The *React Native* animation has already encapsulated common stock components with Animated.createAnimatedComponent() to make them directly usable, like the View's animation counterpart, Animated.View. Listing 3-12 gives an example.

Listing 3-12. Animated.Value and Animated.View

```
class SomeComponent extends React.Component {
  constructor() {
    this.opacity = Animated.Value(0); // ------------------> 1)
    ...
  }
  render() {
    return (
      <Animated.View style={{opacity: this.opacity}} />
    );
  }
}
```

1) It is suggested to put the *animation value* directly as an instance variable instead of **states**. The reason will be explained very soon in Section 3.3.1.4.

After this, the value could be changed in various ways to facilitate an animation.

3.3.1 Animate the Animation

3.3.1.1 Animated.timing( )

Animated.timing() is the most straightforward way to start a *value animation*. The first argument taken is the *animation value,* and the second is a configuration object that controls the animation speed and style.

What Animated.timing() creates is an actionable object which in turn calls start() to invoke the animation defined. The start() accepts a callback argument which will be called after animation completes. 🏛

Normally, this callback is used to call setState() to forward the layout to the next stable state post the animation. 🏛 In general principle, please refrain from locking/unlocking touch within this callback as fluent user interaction should be free of lock all the time. Listing 3-13 gives a typical invocation of an Animated.timing().

Listing 3-13. Animated.timing()

```
Animated.timing(this.opacity, {
  toValue: 1,
  duration: 300, -----------------------------------------> 1)
  useNativeDrive: true, ----------------------------------> 2)
}).start(() => {
  this.setState({
    done: true
  })
});
```

1) The **component** fades in (opacity: 1) for 300 milliseconds.

2) useNativeDrive indicates that this is a native-powered animation calculation. As said, we will always set it to true in this book.

Animated.timing() provides other configurations such as easing and delay for the animation. easings.net is a good place to refer to when we want to adjust those parameters to achieve the desired outcome.

3.3.1.2 Animated.spring( )

Animated.spring() kicks off bouncing animations. With Animated. spring(), we do not need to provide duration in the animation configuration (Listing 3-14).

Listing 3-14. Animated.spring()

```
Animated.spring(this.opacity, {
  toValue: 1,
  useNativeDrive: true
}).start();
```

The configurations provided by Animated.spring() include damping, friction, overshootClamping, etc. Likewise, we enable native-powered animation with useNativeDrive: true.

3.3.1.3 Animation Cohort

Besides the methods discussed earlier, we can also combine multiple animations together. The APIs are listed as follows:

1) Animated.parallel() combines multiple animation objects created using Animated.timing() or Animated.spring() and fires them all at once using start().

2) Likewise, Animated.sequence() takes multiple animation objects but fires them one by one in order. This method starts the next animation only after the previous one completes.

3) Animated.stagger() also starts multiple animations in order. However, this method does not wait for the completion of the previous animation to start the next animation. Rather, it waits for an interval to fire them one by one in order.

4) loop() takes an animation object created using Animated.timing() or Animated.spring() and repeats it.

5) All the animation objects can be cancelled using
    stop(). We can save the animation objects
    returned by the preceding methods including
    Animated.timing() and Animated.spring() as
    instance variables and call stop() on it at the
    appropriate time.

3.3.1.4 setValue( )

Animation values can be updated using a direct call of setValue(), for
example, this.opacity.setValue(100). The value given to setValue()
will be updated on the user interface, but this gives an abrupt change
instead of an animation. Hence, similar to setState(), this method is
used to forward a **component** to the next stable state, normally after an
animation transition completes. 💣 However, you can also call this method
very fast (e.g., in a gesture callback) to mimic an animation. As explained,
this is not recommended by all means due to the inevitable low animation
quality (i.e., frame loss, shaking) at the *JavaScript* level.

Furthermore, setValue() uses the direct *JavaScript-to-native*
communication channel separated from the normal *React* rendering
and layout pass. Hence, it is faster than the normal update issued by
setState(). In order to reflect this distinction, 🏛 using instance variables
is slightly preferred for *animation values* than **states** as mentioned. That
said, feel free to store the *animation values* anywhere that makes sense
to you. 🚀 For better performance, please always rely on setValue() to
update animation value when we want to opt out the associated animation.

3.3.2 Bind the Animation Value

3.3.2.1 The transform props.style

transform is another well-used props.style. We can use transform to animate a **component**'s shape, size, or location. 💣 It is worth noting that the changes taking place using transform do not respect the **flex** layout. ♡ Hence, in some cases, we might need additional *layout animation* in parallel to cater to a **component** size or position to make the general layout in order.

transform takes an array of objects. Each element of the array takes a predefined string as the key and expresses a *transform attribute*. Normally, an *animation value* is set as the corresponding value to make the attributes animatable. Nonetheless, we can use ordinary **states** or even const variables for the values as well.

🏛 **Anchor** is an important while undocumented attribute for transform animations. As illustrated in Figure 3-2, an **anchor** is the pivot point that the animation should be carried out. For instance, scaleX and scaleY indicate that a **component** should expand along the X and Y axes, respectively. From which original point the **component** should expand is defined by the **anchor**.

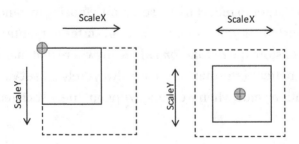

Figure 3-2. *Anchor of transform animation*

💣 In *React Native*, the position of the anchor is undocumented and obscured, albeit predictable. Instead of an explicit parameter, the position of the anchor is determined implicitly by how the **component** in animation is attached to its **container**. For example, the justifyContent: 'center', alignItems: 'center' in the **container** puts an anchor in the center of the animation, while the justifyContent: 'flex-start', alignItems: 'flex-start' puts the **anchor** on the top-left corner.

Commonly used attributes of transform are listed as follows:

1) scaleX and scaleY: As mentioned, width and height are not available in native-level animation. Hence, scaleX and scaleY are normally used instead to achieve a similar effect.

2) translateX and translateY: These two attributes define a change in position of the **component**.

3) rotateX, rotateY, and rotateZ: These attributes define the angle on which **component** flips.

We will see very soon in the case study section (Section 3.3.8) how transform is used to facilitate a spinning animation in action. Next, we start the first hands-on.

3.3.2.2 Value Interpolation

Sometimes, an *animation value* cannot be mapped directly to a transform. This is where *value interpolation* comes into play. For instance, the rotateZ attribute takes a string which cannot be directly represented by an *animation value*. Hence, a common practice is to use an integer as the *animation value* and then interpolate it to the destined string value. Listing 3-15 shows the interpolation from an integer animation value to the rotate angle.

Listing 3-15. Value interpolation

```
this.rotate = new Animated.Value(0);
...
this.rotate.interpolate({
  inputRange: [0, 1],
  outputRange: ['0deg', '360deg']
})
```

We are going to use this technique very soon when implementing a loading indicator that requires the rotateZ attribute in Section 3.3.8.

3.3.2.3 Value Calculation

Sometimes, one *animation value* alone cannot represent the destined transform. Rather, the attribute could be calculated from two or more *animation values* combined. As we will see in Section 3.4.2, the transparency of the loading indicator depends on two *animation values*: the first one is used to represent whether the user is dragging, and the second one indicates the current position of the scroll view.

Here is where *value calculation* comes into play. ***React Native*** provides numerous functions to calculate *animation values*, for example, Animated. add(). The return value of those methods is *animation value* as well; hence, those methods can be invoked in a cascaded manner. See the example in Listing 3-16.

Listing 3-16. Cascading invocation of animation value calculation

```
Animated.add(new Animated.Value(6 / 7),
  Animated.multiply(
    new Animated.Value(1 / 7),
    Animated.add(
```

```
Animated.subtract(
  this.pivotValue,
  new Animated.Value((someVal - 1) * someVal2)
).interpolate({
  inputRange: [-bound, -threshold, 0, threshold, bound],
    outputRange: [1, -threshold, 0, threshold, 1]
  }),
  new Animated.Value(threshold)
 )
 )
)
```

Note   The preceding code is to give the form of cascading invocation of *animation value* calculation. It does not have any practical means.

In Listing 3-17, we list the value calculation methods.

Listing 3-17. Methods for animation value calculation

```
Animated.add()
Animated.subtract()
Animated.divide()
Animated.multiply()
Animated.modulo()
Animated.diffClamp()
```

Note   It is reasonable to question the design of those calculation methods. Since *animation value*s are essentially ordinary numbers, why do we need methods to calculate their result? To answer this question, it is important to understand that those methods are not used to calculate *animation value*s; instead, they are for expressing a relationship between a pivot *animation value*(s) and the destined *transform attributes* in a declarative fashion. We will see how this technique is used in action in Section 3.4.1.

Declarative is not a silver bullet. It has the issue of debuggability. The more profound reason why we need declarative animation in the first place and the underlying mechanism of value calculation will be discussed in Chapter 6.

3.3.3 Case Study 1, Looming Animation for Image Loading

The feed images in *Manyface* are loaded from online, but the popping in the image loaded is abrupt (Figure 3-3). The exact requirements are as follows:

1) Add loading animation for feed images.

2) Before the image is loaded, show a light gray background as placeholders to make the loading process smoother.

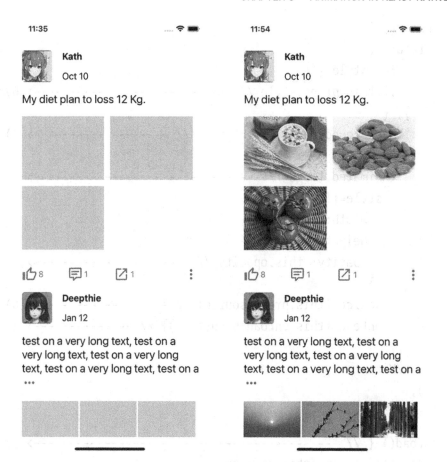

Figure 3-3. *Before and after the images are loaded*

Firstly, we implement the LoomingImage **component** (Listing 3-18).

Listing 3-18. LoomingImage

```
class LoomingImage extends React.Component {
  constructor() {
    super();

    this.opacity = new Animated.Value(0); // -------------> 1)
  }
```

115

```
render() {
  return (
    <View style={[{
      ...this.props.style // ----------------------------> 6)
    }, {
      backgroundColor: 'lightgrey' // -------------------> 5)
    }]}>
      <Animated.Image // ------------------------------> 2)
        style={{
          width: '100%',
          height: '100%',
          opacity: this.opacity // ---------------------> 2)
        }}
        source={this.props.source} // -------------------> 6)
        onLoad={this.onLoad.bind(this)} // --------------> 3)
      />
    </View>
  );
}

onLoad() { // ---------------------------------------------> 3)
  Animated.timing(this.opacity, {
    toValue: 1,
    duration: 300,
    useNativeDriver: true // --------------------------> 4)
  }).start();
}
}

export default LoomingImage;
```

1) As described, this.opacity is initialized as an
   Animated.Value.

2) We need to use the `Animated` version of the `Image`;
    otherwise, the animation we apply will not be
    effective. The *animation value* created in the
    preceding step is attached to the `opacity` **prop** of
    the `Animated.Image`.

3) `onLoad` is a callback **prop** provided by `Image` that
    signals a load complete of the `Image`. We leverage
    this prop to animate the `this.opacity` to 1 and
    hence make the `Image` visible.

4) We emphasize on performance throughout the
    text; hence, `useNativeDriver: true` is here for this
    purpose.

5) Use `Animated.Image` attached with opacity to
    implement the loading animation (requirement 2).

6) 🏛 Lastly but most importantly, we design the
    `LoomingImage` compatible with `Image` as possible;
    the **props.styles** that could potentially be the layout
    information are passed through to the **container**,
    while the `source` **prop** is passed through to the
    `Image`. Soon we will see the benefit of this design.

Then we replace the ordinary `Image` **components** used in various
positions with the `LoomingImage`. First is the `Image` in Feed (Listings 3-19
to 3-21).

Listing 3-19. LoomingImage applied to Feed

```
class Feed extends React.Component {
  render() {
    return (
      <>
        <ExpandableText
```

117

```
          style={styles.textPost}
          text={this.props.item.feed.text} />
        <LoomingImage // ---------------------------------> 1)
          style={styles.imagePost}
          source={{uri: this.props.item.feed.images[0]}}
      />
    </>
  )
  }
}
```

Listing 3-20. LoomingImage applied to Feed2x2

```
class Feed2x2 extends React.Component {
  render() {
    return (
      <>
        <ExpandableText
          style={styles.textPost}
          text={this.props.item.feed.text}
        />
        <View style={styles.gridContainer}>
          {this.props.item.feed.images.slice(0, 4).map(e =>
          <View style={styles.cell}>
            <LoomingImage // -------------------------------> 1)
              style={styles.imagePost}
              source={{uri: e}}
          />
          </View>
          )}
        </View>
      </>
```

```
    )
  }
}
```

Listing 3-21. LoomingImage applied to Feed3x3

```
class Feed3x3 extends React.Component {
  render() {
    return (
      <>
        <ExpandableText
          style={styles.textPost}
          text={this.props.item.feed.text}
        />
        <View style={styles.gridContainer}>
          {this.props.item.feed.images.slice(0, 9).map(e =>
          <View style={styles.cell}>
            <LoomingImage // -----------------------------> 1)
              style={styles.imagePost}
              source={{uri: e}}
            />
          </View>
          )}
        </View>
      </>
    )
  }
}
```

Avatars in withMetaAndControls use Image as well. We simply need to replace the Image with LoomingImage. Here, we omit supplementary **components** and some of the code for simplicity (Listing 3-22).

119

Listing 3-22. LoomingImage applied to avatars

```
export default function withMetaAndControls(Feed) {
  return class extends React.Component {
    render() {
      return (
        <View style={[
          {...this.props.style},
          styles.commonPadding]}
        >
          <View style={styles.metaContainer}>
            <LoomingImage // ------------------------------> 1)
              style={styles.avatar}
              source={{
                uri: this.props.item.meta.avatarUri
              }}
            />
            <View style={styles.infoContainer}>
              <Text style={styles.userName}>
                {this.props.item.meta.name}
              </Text>
              <Text style={styles.date}>
                {this.props.item.meta.date}
              </Text>
            </View>
          </View>
          <Feed {...this.props}/>
          <View style={styles.controlContainer}>
...
          </View>
        </View>
      )
```

```
      }
   }
}
```

1) 🏛 We design the `LoomingImage` with the
    compatibility in mind; hence, in the refactor we
    only need to replace the **component**'s name and
    keep the rest of the **props** untouched. This makes
    the similar refactor tasks much less error-prone. In
    Chapter 6, we are going to discuss the more general
    and actionable principles of designing a custom
    component.

3.3.4 Case Study 2, Loading Indicators

A loading indicator can be used in various places when the app is being
bootstrapped or loading additional resources. Although *React Native*
provides a default loading indicator, we need a custom one that fits the
style of *Manyface* better. More specifically, we need three kinds of loading
indicator:

1) A quarter circle that rotates: This could be used as
    part of a placeholder view when an individual UI
    element loading is prolonged (e.g., a video). In this
    section, we are going to apply the loading indicator
    to images. This is the variant that is the most similar
    to the default loading indicator.

2) A spinning envelope: This special loading indicator
    will be used by the pull down loading animation.

3)   A skeleton view of any size: This loading indicator is
used as a placeholder itself when a view (e.g., Image)
is being loaded. Unlike a loading indicator, this
loading style is applied to the whole page, so as to
make the whole loading experience integrated. We
also need a glimmering animation to assure the user
that the app is not frozen.

Note   Some of the **components** implemented in this hands-on will
not be used straightaway. For example, a rotating circle is mostly
useful only when the loading of a resource requires excessive time,
for example, a video; a skeleton view is normally needed during
bootstrap when the critical logical path is being blocked by network
fetching or other bootstrap steps. The practical use of the loading
indicators implemented in this section will be discussed in Chapter 5.

First, let's implement the simplest variant, the rotating quarter circle
(Listing 3-23).

Listing 3-23. Loading indicator – RotatingCircle

```
import Icon from 'react-native-vector-icons/
MaterialCommunityIcons';

const AnimatedIcon = Animated.createAnimatedComponent(Icon);// 2)

class RotatingCircle extends React.Component {
  constructor() {
    super();

    this.rotate = new Animated.Value(0); // ---------------> 1)
  }
```

```
componentDidMount() {
  Animated.loop( // -------------------------------------> 1)
    Animated.timing(this.rotate, {
      toValue: 1,
      duration: 1000,
      easing: Easing.linear, // ------------------------> 1)
      useNativeDriver: true // -------------------------> 1)
    })
  ).start();
}

render() {
  const size = this.props.size ?? 58;
  const color = this.props.color ?? 'white';

  return (
    <View style={[
      {...this.props.style}, styles.stablizer // --------> 5)
    ]}>
      <AnimatedIcon // ----------------------------------> 2)
        style={{
          transform: [{rotateZ: this.rotate.interpolate({ // 3)
            inputRange: [0, 1],
            outputRange: ['0deg', '360deg']
          })}]
        }}
        name={'loading'}
        color={color} // --------------------------------> 4)
        size={size} // ----------------------------------> 4)
      />
    </View>
```

```
      )
    }
}

const styles = StyleSheet.create({
    stablizer: { // ----------------------------------------> 5)
        justifyContent: 'center',
        alignItems: 'center'
    },
});

export default RotatingCircle;
```

1) We initialize an *animation value* this.rotate which is set to loop from zero to one in a one-second interval. Note that we set easing to Easing.linear (the default value Easing.inOut is jumpy when used in a loop) in order to give an even animation transition. Again, we set useNativeDriver to true to gain the performance point.

2) Instead of directly using the Icon from *react-native-vector-icon*, we create a **HOC** that enables the animation using Animated. createAnimatedComponent. So the following transform set in the props.style can be effective.

3) Here come our protagonists of this section, transform + interpolate(). interpolate() takes an *animation value* range as the input and output range of values that is acceptable by the transform attribute.

4) We expose two **props** as the interface of this **component** so it can be further customized by the user, size and color.

5) Lastly, we apply another layer of **components** as a stabilizer. This **component** becomes the **container**; hence, it also accepts the layout information the user might want to let it know using {...this. props.style}.

Now we can apply the RotatingCircle as part of the LoomingImage (Listing 3-24).

Listing 3-24. LoomingImage with a loading indicator

```
import RotatingCircle from './loadingIndicators/RotatingCircle'

class LoomingImage extends React.Component {
  constructor() {
    super();
    this.opacity = new Animated.Value(0);

    this.state = {loaded: false}; // ---------------------> 3)
  }

  render() {
    return (
      <View style={[{
        ...this.props.style
      }, {
        backgroundColor
      }]}>
        {this.state.loaded === false && // ---------------> 3)
        <View style={styles.overlay}>
```

```
            <RotatingCircle size={28}/>
          </View>
          }
          <Animated.Image // -------------------------------> 2)
            style={{
              width: '100%',
              height: '100%',
              opacity: this.opacity
            }}
            source={this.props.source}
            onLoad={this.onLoad.bind(this)}
          />
        </View>
    );
  }

  onLoad() {
this.setState({loaded: true}); // ----------------------> 3)
    Animated.timing(this.opacity, {
      toValue: 1,
      duration: 300,
      useNativeDriver: true
    }).start();
  }
}

const backgroundColor = 'lightgrey';

const styles = StyleSheet.create({
  overlay: { // -------------------------------------------> 1)
    backgroundColor,
    justifyContent: 'center',
```

```
    alignItems: 'center',
    position: 'absolute',
    left: 0,
    right: 0,
    top: 0,
    bottom: 0,
  },
});
```

1) We use position: 'absolute' to put an overlay that populates the loading indicator.

2) The Image is put after the loading indicator to make sure that it is on top of it when being rendered.

3) When the graphic has been loaded, we do away with the loading indicator completely by forwarding the **state** to the next phase (i.e., loaded) along with the animation.

Next, let's implement the spinning envelope using a similar technique of RotatingCircle (Listing 3-25).

Listing 3-25. Loading indicator – SpinningEnvelope

```
import Icon from 'react-native-vector-icons/
MaterialCommunityIcons';

const AnimatedIcon = Animated.createAnimatedComponent(Icon);

class SpinningEnvelope extends React.Component {
  constructor() {
    super();

    this.rotate = new Animated.Value(0);
  }
```

```
componentDidMount() {
  Animated.loop(
    Animated.timing(this.rotate, {
      toValue: 1,
      duration: 2000,
      easing: Easing.linear,
      useNativeDriver: true
    })
  ).start();
}

render() {
  const size = this.props.size ?? 58;
  const color = this.props.color ?? 'white';
  return (
    <View style={[{...this.props.style}, styles.stablizer]}>
      <AnimatedIcon
        style={{
          transform: [{rotateY: this.rotate.
          interpolate({ //1a)
            inputRange: [0, 1],
            outputRange: ['0deg', '360deg']
          })}]
        }}
        name={'email-outline'} // ----------------------> 1b)
        color={color}
        size={size}
      />
    </View>
  )
}
}
```

```
const styles = StyleSheet.create({
  stablizer: {
    justifyContent: 'center',
    alignItems: 'center'
  },
});
```

```
export default SpinningEnvelope;
```

1) This implementation is similar to that of
   RotatingCircle, except for (a) the rotation
   that is pivoting on Y axis instead of Z and (b) an
   envelope symbol.

Note 🏛 Why don't we converging the rotating logic into a single, generalized component if the two components are so similar? This is to avoid overabstraction. Overabstraction could lead to a rigid code base in that a change in one place could potentially have an effect on the other. Moreover, you are obligated to test feature(s) completely irrelevant to the current change. So a healthy level of duplication could make software projects more flexible and hence more extensible.

Lastly, let's start implementing the skeleton view (Figure 3-4). When doing so, it is tempting to implement a generalized **component** that can magically transform any layouts into a designated animated skeleton view. However, this idea only sounds good but is not practical. 🏛 More specifically, it's neither feasible to derive the complete layout of a **component** nor to orchestrate animation across placeholder **components** that could be scattered within the view hierarchy. So this time again, let's refrain from designing a brilliant high-end abstraction, but opt in an ad hoc, down-to-the-ground way (Listing 3-26).

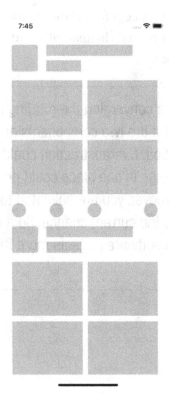

Figure 3-4. *A skeleton view*

Note 🏛 The general idea of a skeleton view is to give an expectation to the user how the view looks like when fully loaded. The blocks in a skeleton view are not the one-to-one placeholders, so their positions do not need to be exact. In contrast, making exact placeholders of the real UI elements sometimes gives weird visual outcomes. This is another reason why deriving a skeleton view from a normal **component** layout is not practically feasible.

Listing 3-26. A skeleton view

```
class Skeleton extends React.Component {
  constructor() {
    super();

    this.lightPos = new Animated.Value(0); // -------------> 1)
  }

  constructor() {
    super();

    this.lightPos = new Animated.Value(200); // -----------> 1)
  }

  componentDidMount() {
    Animated.loop( // -------------------------------------> 1)
      Animated.timing(
        this.lightPos, {
          toValue: -Dimensions.get('window').width,
          duration: 1200,
          delay: 500,
          easing: Easing.linear,
```

```
            useNativeDriver: true
        }
      )
    ).start();
  }

  render() {
    return (
      <View style={{...this.props.style}}>
        <FakeFeed/> // -------------------------------------> 2)
        <FakeFeed/>
        <Animated.View style={[styles.light, {
          transform: [
            {translateX: this.lightPos},
          ],
        }]}/>
        <Animated.View style={[styles.light, { // ---------> 3)
          right: -50,
          width: 30,
          transform: [
            {translateX: this.lightPos},
          ],
        }]}/>
      </View>
    );
  }
}

const styles = StyleSheet.create({
  light: {
    position: 'absolute',
    top: 0,
```

```
    right: 0,
    width: 60,
    opacity: 0.3,
    height: 1500,
    backgroundColor: 'white',
    transform: [
      {translateX: this.lightPos},
    ],
  },
});
```

```
export default Skeleton;
```

1) We use `Animated.loop()` to repeatedly move `this.lightPos` that determines the position of the reflection of light.

2) We omit the code for `FakeFeed` here as it is a pure flex layout similar to that of a `Feed`.

3) Again, we attach `this.lightPos` to an `Animated.View` to make the position animatable.

3.3.5 Key Takeaways

We have examined how to create various types of animation using an animation value. We firstly covered `timing()` and `spring()` to facilitate animations targeting particular **components**. Then we learned how to combine those animations in serial or in parallel using animation cohort techniques. 🖋 We also explained why `setValue()` is more efficient than `setState()` when it comes to the *animation value* and offered a general practical guide for using it. Lastly, we covered the basics of *value transform*, which, combined with value *interpolation and calculation*, can be used to express a very complex relationship between user gesture and the visual outcome. This technique will be especially useful when we use *native events* to implement *gesture-driven animation*.

We dedicated two hands-on subsections and implemented four **components** for *Manyface* for a better coverage of aspects of *animation value* usage. Some were applied straightaway to enhance the user experience of *Manyface*. The rest will be integrated eventually when the time comes.

🏛 Throughout the section, we always use native-powered animation in order to maintain the quality bar for all animations applied. It is a suggested practice in real projects as well.

3.4 Gesture-Driven Animation

This is the hardest type of animation which makes mobile experience special. Basically, we need to mimic real-world objects that do not only give real-time response to the user touch but also display attributes such as resistance, quality, and inertia. The goal is to conform to the user's expectation to the physics in their subconscious to avoid attention we don't want.

> *I thought that the dream space would be all about visual but, it's more about the feel of it.*
>
> —Inception

Generally speaking, *gesture-driven animation* enlists two parts corresponding to the two phases of a gesture, (1) gesture animation and (2) release animation. The gesture animation reflects the current position of the user's gesture frame by frame. For instance, a pan gesture animation should be able to move the UI element along with the user's finger, and to perform a finish off animation when the user releases the gesture. We normally call the user interface in a transitional stage during gesture animation and call the user interface in a stable stage after release animation completes. The release animation should account for the current velocity of the swiping gesture. Moreover, it should be redirectable whenever the user changes their mind. So release animation, as a vital link between those two stages, is critical and hard to implement. Luckily, *React Native* has provided us with the right tool, the ScrollView, to make the whole transition natural.

Note   We don't categorize all animations triggered by user gestures as *gesture-driven animation*. When being triggered by simple gestures, such as a tap, what gets involved is simply a playback animation and can be implemented using the *value animations* or *layout animations*. This kind of animation does not enlist a transitional state, nor should it be redirectable.

As said, a release animation leads to the next stable stage. Hence, we also need a threshold to determine what the next state is, a moving forward or a folding back. This threshold is the key to make the gesture transition redirectable.

Technically, *React Native* provides two means to carry out *gesture-driven animation*, the *gesture responder system* and the ScrollView. The *gesture responder system* relies on the *JavaScript* thread and is only good for playback animation once a gesture is determined. Another common option is provided by a third-party library, *react-native-gesture-handler* which supports *native event* (Section 3.4.1) for gesture animation. However, it imposes a subtle performance penalty to be used to implement the release animation, which can be noticeable by the users with very sharp eyes.

Note   *react-navigation* is one of the mainstream third-party libraries that relies on *react-native-gesture-handler*. Since *react-native-gesture-handler* only accounts for the gesture animation, the release animation is required to be implemented separately in ***JavaScript*** (using value animation). Though both animations are implemented using a native driver and are performant, we need to pass the current velocity from the native to the ***JavaScript*** thread. And this communication gives a very subtle halt in the middle of the gesture experience.

A ScrollView, though sounds animation irrelevant, is one of the key **components** in mobile ecosystems to achieve smooth gesture-based experiences in various occasions. To better understand the reason, read on.

3.4.1 Native Event

Native events are designed for high-performance *gesture-driven animation*. To enable the pure native-powered animation, the events are firstly bound, in the form of an *animation value*, to a certain **component** (*event source*) like a ScrollView. Then, a *value calculation* (Section 3.3.2.3) is derived from the *animation value*, to define the animation behavior which can be in turn executed in the native layer. *Value calculation* effectively forms a native-to-native communication channel which we will discuss in Chapter 6. Lastly, on the other side(s) of the communication channel reside the *event receivers*, which are **components** that take the calculation results as **props**.

Ideally, gesture animation must be completely offloaded to the native level in order to give an acceptable FPS. The principle is similar to that in *value animation*. Due to the high performance bar of *gesture-driven animation,* ***JavaScript****-powered animation* is not capable of this kind of task. As mentioned before, the bottleneck is the interthread, asynchronous communication mechanism.

Since the ***JavaScript*** thread should be excluded completely throughout the animation procedure, the output of the *native event* is made a single *animation value* and will not be attached with any logic (or callback). As mentioned, *value calculation* and *interpolation* are required as this value cannot be used directly. More specially, *value interpolation and calculation* define the animation behavior by declaring the relationship between an *animation value* and the destined transform. After the animation behavior is defined completely in one go, the ***React Native*** runtime will be able to carry out the animation purely in the native layer.

3.4.2 Case Study, a Pull Down Load Experience

This time, we are going to implement another feature involving *gesture-driven animation* – a pull down load effect. For now, we simply implement the animation effect only for the pull down, which will be used for the actual content network loading in Chapter 5. Let's look at the requirements first:

1) When the user pulls down the list, a loading indicator (the SpinningEnvelope we implemented in Section 3.3.8) appears on the top blank area.

2) The opacity of the loading indicator is determined by the position of the pull down gesture, meaning the more the user pulls down the list, the more opaque the loading indicator becomes.

3) When the user releases the gesture and the current position doesn't exceed a threshold, the list folds back to where it starts from.

4) When the user releases and the gesture position exceeds the threshold, the list starts folding back and is locked to a position for one second. Then the list folds back to the start position.

5) When the user is pulling, we want the maximum opacity to be 50%.

6) When the user releases the gesture, we want the value to be 100% when it's in phase 4 and to fade out during the list folding back.

Figure 3-5 shows how it looks.

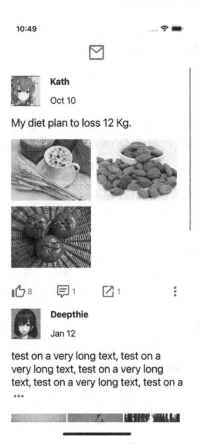

Figure 3-5. Pull down load

Listing 3-27 is the code snippet to tune up Moment. Though the structure is the same as the old Moment, the bulk of code is added to implement the pull down load experience. This can also give a hint on how much effort it takes to implement proper *gesture-driven animation.*

Listing 3-27. Moment

```
...
const LoomingSpinningEnvelope = Animated.createAnimatedComponent
(SpinningEnvelope); // ------> 3)
```

```
...
class Moment extends React.Component {
  constructor() {
    super();

    this.pullDownPos = new Animated.Value(0);
    this.autoScrolling= new Animated.Value(0);
    this.userPulling = new Animated.Value(0);

    this.scrollViewRef = undefined;

    this.state = {
      loading: false,
    }
  }

  renderItem(entry) {
    return (
      <FeedFactory item={entry.item}/>
    );
  }

  beginDrag() { // ----------------------------------------> 4)
    this.userPulling.setValue(1);
    this.autoScrolling.setValue(0);
  }

  endDrag(evt) { // ---------------------------------------> 4)
    this.userPulling.setValue(0);
this.autoScrolling.setValue(1);

const y = evt.nativeEvent.contentOffset.y;

if (y < -loadingIndicatorOffset) { // -----------------> 5)
    this.setState({loading: true});
```

```
    setTimeout(() => {
      this.scrollViewRef.scrollToIndex({ // ------------> 5b)
        index: 0,
        animated: true
      });
    }, 1000); // --------------------------------------> 5a)
  }
}

onReset(evt) { // ------------------------------------> 4)
  if (evt.nativeEvent.contentOffset.y === 0) {
    this.userPulling.setValue(0);
    this.autoScrolling.setValue(0);

    if (this.state.loading) {
      this.setState({loading: false}); // --------------> 5c)
    }
  }
}

getScrollViewRef(ref) {
  this.scrollViewRef = ref;
}

render() {
  return (
    <View style={{flex: 1}}>
      <Animated.FlatList // ----------------------------> 1)
        data={data}
        renderItem={this.renderItem.bind(this)}
        contentInset={{ // ----------------------------> 3)
          top: this.state.loading ? 5: 0
        }}
```

```
      onScroll={ // ------------------------------------> 1)
        Animated.event([{
          nativeEvent: {
            contentOffset: { y: this.pullDownPos } }
        }], { useNativeDriver: true })
      }
      onScrollBeginDrag={this.beginDrag.bind(this)}
      onScrollEndDrag={this.endDrag.bind(this)}
      ref={this.getScrollViewRef.bind(this)}
      onMomentumScrollEnd={this.onReset.bind(this)}
    />
    <View style={styles.overlay}> // ------------------> 6)
      <LoomingSpinningEnvelope // --------------------> 3)
        color={'#6291f0'}
        size={45}
        style={{
          opacity:
            Animated.add( // -------------------------> 2)
              Animated.multiply( // ------------------> 2a)
                this.userPulling,
                this.pullDownPos.interpolate({
                  inputRange: [-loadingIndicatorOffset, 0],
                  outputRange: [0.5, 0]
                })
              ),
              Animated.multiply( // ------------------> 2b)
                this.autoScrolling,
                this.pullDownPos.interpolate({
                  inputRange: [-loadingIndicatorOffset, 0],
                  outputRange: [1, 0]
                })
```

```
                ),
              )
          }}
        />
      </View>
    </View>
  );
  }
};

const loadingIndicatorOffset = 50;

const styles = StyleSheet.create({ // --------------------> 6)
  overlay: {
    position: 'absolute',
    top: 0,
    left: 0,
    width: '100%',
    height: loadingIndicatorOffset,
    justifyContent: 'center',
    alignItems: 'center',
  },
});

//export default Moment;
export default withErrorBoundary(Moment, ErrorPage, undefined);
```

1) First things first, we bind the *animation value* to the
    scrolling position of the FlatList. In order to enable
    the binding in the native level (useNativeDriver:
    true), we need to use Animated.FlatList instead of
    plain FlatList.

2) This is the core logic that translates the pivot
    animation value to the destined transform **props.**
    style. We use two flags to indicate the list's current
    state, being dragged or scrolled automatically.
    (a) We use Animated.multiply() to simulate an
    "AND" operator, so when the user is dragging (this.
    userPulling), we use 0 to 0.5 as the opacity range.
    (b) Likewise, after the user releases the gesture
    (this.autoScrolling), we use 0 to 1 as the opacity
    range. Here again, Animated.multiply() is used to
    simulate an "AND" operator. Lastly, Animated.add()
    is used to simulate the "OR" operator as only one of
    the flags will be true at a given time.

3) The opacity value calculated earlier is attached to
    LoomingSpinningEnvelope. It is worth noting that
    though SpinningEnvelope contains an animation
    effect, the **component** itself is not animatable as is.
    Hence, we need to use createAnimatedComponent to
    enable animation.

4) We update the preceding flags in the corresponding
    events, that is, when the user starts pulling
    (beginDrag), the user ends pulling (endDrag), and
    after the FlatList folds back (onReset).

5) After the user ends pulling, we also want to (a) stay
    to a position for one second, (b) fold back to the
    beginning position, and (c) after the list folds back,
    we reset the state indicating the loading is taking
    place (loading).

6) Lastly, we make some space sticking on top for the
    loading indicator.

3.4.3 Key Takeaways

In this section, we took a step deeper in *native-powered animation* by applying *value animation* combined with *native events*. This gives the *gesture-driven animation* as a result. To implement the task in this section, *native-powered animation* becomes more essential because *gesture-driven animations* have excessive demand in performance. We also examined why *animation interpolation and calculation* are used in practice and how to use those techniques in action.

In terms of *Manyface*, we implemented the pull down load effect for `Moment` and made use of the `SpinningEnvelope` developed in previous sections. In this case study, we applied in action the techniques of *gesture-driven animation*.

3.5 Summary

In this chapter, we went through the animation facilities provided by **React Native**. In particular, only *native-powered animations* were used to maintain a healthy level of quality bar. Nonetheless, if compromise of quality is acceptable, for example, in a prototype phase, **JavaScript-powered animation** can be used in a very similar way – we only need to set `useNativeDriver` to `false` in some cases.

In the sense of choosing hands-on practices, we used practical animation effects rather than fancy ones, and we emphasized on performance all the time. We also dove into detailed requirements which could be set by real-world product managers, and we excelled the **React Native** animation techniques learned to fulfill them. As a result, we enhanced the experience of *Manyface* to the next level.

Not all animation options in the **React Native** ecosystem are covered in this chapter. For instance, *lottie-react-native* brings to **React Native** the existing **iOS** and **Android** *Lottie* facility that offers controllable, predefined animations. *react-native-reanimated* and *react-native-gesture-handler* improve the existing ***React Native*** animation and *gesture response system* by leveraging *native events* extensively. Please refer to their respective GitHub pages for more information.

Again and again, performance is a big deal in animation. Though we covered some of the techniques to utilize the ***React Native*** animation, it will be helpful to understand the underlying mechanisms of `useNativeDriver` and *native events*, especially when you want to create a customized, high-performance animatable **component**. For that matter, we will analyze the mechanism and the performance implication of native-level animation in Chapter 6.

CHAPTER 4

Native Modules and Components

React Native is to app developers as ship is to sailors. Sailors still need to master swimming for critical tasks though they don't have to swim all the way through with a ship.

—Holmes

In this chapter, we are going to program majorly in the native layer using the languages of native platforms. Wait, isn't **React Native** a cross-platform that eliminates all needs of native development? True and false. Indeed, the **React Native** core bridges the native rendering system so the UI layout can be carried out on the **JavaScript** layer, like what we have accomplished in the previous chapters. Native layer programming comes into play when our app needs to access advanced functionalities (e.g., geolocation) or requires specialized rendering systems (e.g., SVG). For that purpose, **React Native** provides two ways – **native modules** and **native components**. A plethora of third-party projects have created **native modules** and **native components** catering for most of the commonly used functionalities. So in most cases, we just need to import them as dependencies to fit our needs. And this is for free. However, it is ideal for **React Native** developers to master a certain level of native programming, preparing for very specialized requirements and challenges that haven't

M. H. He, *Creating Apps with React Native*, https://doi.org/10.1007/978-1-4842-8042-3_4

been resolved yet. In this chapter, we are going to equip you with the technique by fully examining and discussing this native programming on both *iOS* and *Android*.

As mentioned, *React Native* provides us with two means to access the underlying native system, **native modules** and **native components**. **Native modules** expose functions to the *JavaScript* layer, so it fits in functionalities that are UI irrelevant. Examples are geolocation, file downloading, and Bluetooth. After proper initialization, functions exposed by **native modules** can be used as ordinary *JavaScript* functions. On the other hand, **native components** expose UI elements to *JavaScript* in the form of **components** which are integrated in the *React* life cycle and rendering routines. Hence, they are more suitable for UI features. Examples are video player, cached images, and specialized renderers like SVG and Lottie. **Native modules** can also actively push events to the *JavaScript* layer with external events for example, a new Bluetooth connection or a push notification.

Note   In practice, the boundary of **native modules** and **native components** is not so clear in some cases. Let's take haptic as an example. On *iOS*, haptic is exposed as an API method; on *Android*, however, haptic is attached to a certain view to determine the haptic position. So it could be reasonable to expose the functionality as both a **native module** and a **native component** in order to cater to the platform variance.

Native modules and **native components** are, as their names suggest, programmed in native languages. And inevitably, they need to be developed twice on *iOS* and *Android*. As such, 🏛 it is crucial to keep a consistent interface for both platforms so the **native module** or **native component** can be used in the *JavaScript* layer in a unanimous way. That means the signature of native methods and **props** of **native components**

are supposed to be implemented exactly the same on both platforms. In most cases, this is absolutely achievable. But when it is not possible due to the disparate implementation of the two underpinning platforms, we will need platform-specific logic in the *JavaScript* layer. We call this kind of logic a "hard fork," and it should always be our last resort and be avoided whenever possible.

Next, we look at how to program **native modules** and **native components**. We are going to use *Swift* and *Kotlin* for **iOS** and **Android**, respectively, as the major programming languages in this chapter.

4.1 Native Modules

Native modules are used to bridge native APIs to the *JavaScript* layer. This is very similar to cross-language communication technologies like JNI. A more comparable technology is *WebView* which supports native APIs and objects to be registered as *JavaScript* functions and variables.

Note   Cordova and Ionic are implemented based on the *JavaScript*-to-native communication abilities of *WebView*.

Like other cross-language communications, native types of function arguments are required to be mapped to *JavaScript* types. 💣 Failing to pass the correct type across the bridge incurs an exception which leads to a crash. An ordinary native function call in the *JavaScript* layer is technically a cross-thread communication. Hence, it is asynchronous. More specifically, all the *JavaScript* code is running on a *JavaScript* thread, while **native modules** are running on another dedicated thread. And the function calling is eventually translated to messages sent through an interthread communication queue. 💣 So it is unsafe for direct UI manipulation or to send notifications to UI controllers in **native module** functions.

Note   Turbo module makes the native method invocation
more performance by calling it synchronously directly on the
JavaScript thread.

One of the drawbacks of **native modules** is singleton. As you will
see very soon, all of the **native modules** are singleton in both *iOS* and
Android, which is far from ideal in terms of the design pattern. In more
concrete words, singleton classes have intrinsic concurrent and life cycle
issues, especially when asynchronous operations are involved and when
designed as stateful. More specifically, the state of a singleton could be
messed up easily with unwanted reentrant calls and overlapped responses
from asynchronous actions. Hence, we should avoid using **native modules**
beyond the purpose of bridging. 🏛 When you are designing your own
native modules, it is recommended to avoid handling asynchronous
operations directly inside the **native module** and to make **native modules**
stateless as possible. If asynchronous operations and native layer states are
inevitable, it is better to delegate those out to other modules or frameworks
that can handle more sophisticated logic and states.

Now let's see some code. We need to create a **native module** class
and register it along with all the methods that are required to be exported
using the *React Native* runtime. This **native module** will be available
to the *JavaScript* side and can be imported in a platform-agnostic way
(Listing 4-1).

Listing 4-1. Native module on the JavaScript side

```
import { NativeModules } from 'react-native';
const { OurAwsomeNativeModule } = NativeModules;
```

🏛 Again, it is highly recommended to keep the consistent function signatures exported by the **native module**. This is the magic that turns the *JavaScript* logic that consumes **native modules** into fully cross-platform. However, 💣 this could be tricky due to platform discrepancies and particularities. And we are going to cover some of the down-to-the-ground techniques to fulfill this principle in the hands-on.

4.1.1 iOS Native Module

4.1.1.1 Setup

To create the **native module**, we firstly open in *Xcode* the ***React Native*** project (Figure 4-1). The project file (`*.xcworkspace`) is located at the `ios/` subdirectory.

Figure 4-1. *Open the .xcworkspace in Xcode*

Right-click the *iOS* project root group and click *new file* (Figure 4-2).

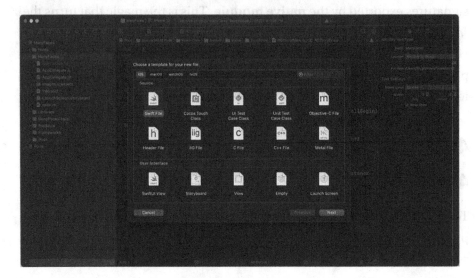

Figure 4-2. *Add a new Swift file to the project*

Select *Swift* which is the major programming language on *iOS* as mentioned (Figure 4-3).

Figure 4-3. *Add the HelloWorldManager*

Then we change the name to HelloWorldManager. Here, xxxManager is a naming convention of **native modules** both on *iOS* and *Android*.

Xcode will then prompt a message box asking to create a bridging header file; select *Create Bridging Header* (Figure 4-4).

Figure 4-4. *Automatically create a bridging header file*

Xcode then will automatically create a file named "ProjectName-Bridging-Header" along with a configuration *building-settings* ➤ *Objective-C Bridging Header*. This configuration entry activates the header file that bridges *Objective-C* to *Swift*. With this file, *Swift* can make use of classes in the *React Native* core which is written in *Objective-C*.

The last file we need to create is an *Objective-C* file that creates the *JavaScript* bridge with the **native module** written in *Swift* (Figure 4-5).

Figure 4-5. *Add a new Objective-C file to the project*

This time, we name it `HelloWorldManagerBridge` (Figure 4-6).

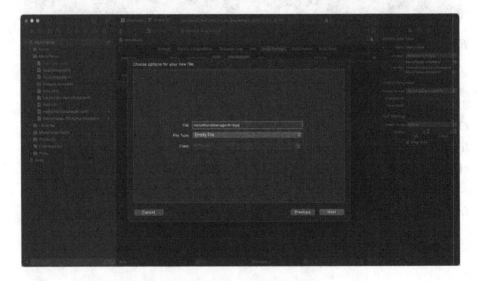

Figure 4-6. *Add the HelloWorldManagerBridge*

In short, we need to create three files for the **native module**: one *Swift* file which is the main implementation, one *JavaScript* bridge written in *Objective-C* that registers the *Swift* implementation to the *JavaScript* layer with the *React Native* runtime, and an *Objective-C* to *Swift* bridging header which is created automatically by *Xcode* to export *Objective-C* written classes to *Swift*. Figure 4-7 illustrates this relationship. The architecture applies to both **native modules** and **native components**.

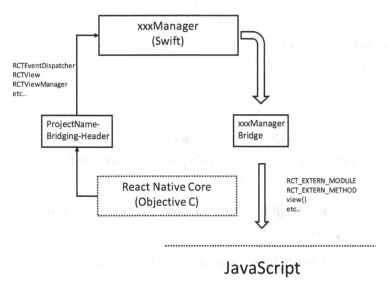

Figure 4-7. *JavaScript and native communication*

Note   The *React Native* core is written in pure *Objective-C*. The dynamic nature of this language is essential for framework code that emphasizes on performance and flexibility. However, *Swift* suits better for application logic by providing better code quality and readability. Additional bridge headers are required as a necessary trade-off so we can use *Swift* for the better good.

4.1.1.2 Implement the Native Module

Firstly, let's see the main logic of the **native module** in *Swift* (Listing 4-1a).

Listing 4-1a. HelloWorldManager.swift

```
@objc(HelloWorldManager) // --------------------------------> 1)
class HelloWorldManager: NSObject { // --------------------> 1)

  @objc(hello) // -------------------------------------------> 2)
  func hello() -> Void {
    print("Hello World!")
  }
}
```

1) To export *Swift* classes to *Objective-C*, we need
   to extend the class from NSObject and decorate it
   with @objc.

2) To export *Swift* functions to *Objective-C*, we need to
   use @objc.

Then we look at the *JavaScript* bridge (Listing 4-2).

Listing 4-2. HelloWorldManagerBridge.m

```
#import <React/RCTBridgeModule.h>

@interface RCT_EXTERN_MODULE(HelloWorldManager,
NSObject) // > 1)

RCT_EXTERN_METHOD(hello) // -------------------------------> 2)

@end
```

1) Use the macro RCT_EXTERN_MODULE to export the class to *JavaScript*.

2) Use the macro RCT_EXTERN_METHOD to export the function to *JavaScript*.

Next, let's see how a **native module** looks on *Android*.

4.1.1.3 Async Calls

Native method invocations discussed in this section are all asynchronous. Hence, we need a way to communicate back (with results) when the invocation completes. One way is **callback**. By passing in a parameter of type RCTResponseSenderBlock, we can invoke the **callback** within the native layer when the operation completes. RCTResponseSenderBlock takes an array of strings as its parameter. This array will be transformed in order to the parameters of the **callback** in the *JavaScript* layer. As a rule of thumb, the first parameter of the **callback** populates the error of this invocation, where an empty string indicates a success. See Listing 4-3.

Listing 4-3. Use a callback to complete a native method invocation

```
RCT_EXTERN_METHOD(someWork:(RCTResponseSenderBlock *) cb)
...

@objc(someWork:)
func someWork(_ cb: RCTResponseSenderBlock) -> Void {
  print("Done some work")
  cb(["", "result data"])
}
```

A **callback** is hard to manage especially when deeply nested. This scenario is commonly referred to as a **callback** hell. A **promise** is considered a more elegant way. To make a native method compatible with a **promise** chain (or its **await** parity), we need to pass

RCTPromiseResolveBlock and RCTPromiseRejectBlock as the last two parameters. Listing 4-4 gives an implementation of such translation. We are going to discuss in detail the **promise** and **await** in Chapter 5.

Listing 4-4. Make native method promise compatible

```
RCT_EXTERN_METHOD(someWork:(RCTPromiseResolveBlock *) resolve
                  rejecter:(RCTPromiseRejectBlock *) reject)

...

@objc(someWorkWithPromise:rejecter:)
func someWorkWithPromise(_ resolve: RCTPromiseResolveBlock,
rejecter reject: RCTPromiseRejectBlock) -> Void {
  print("Done some work")
  resolve (["result data"])
}
```

And make sure both methods are registered within the bridge (Listing 4-5).

Listing 4-5. Make native methods available through the bridge

```
RCT_EXTERN_METHOD(someWork:(RCTResponseSenderBlock *) cb)

RCT_EXTERN_METHOD(
  someWorkWithPromise:(RCTPromiseResolveBlock *) resolve
           rejecter:(RCTPromiseRejectBlock *) reject)
```

Note   Please try to make the method names explicit to the bridge. 💣 Please refrain from overloading methods, which confuses the bridge and gives undefined error when the method got invoked.

4.1.2 Android Native Module

Now let's implement the ***Android*** version of HelloWorldManager.

4.1.2.1 Setup

Firstly, we open the ***Android*** project in *Android Studio*. The subdirectory is android (Figure 4-8).

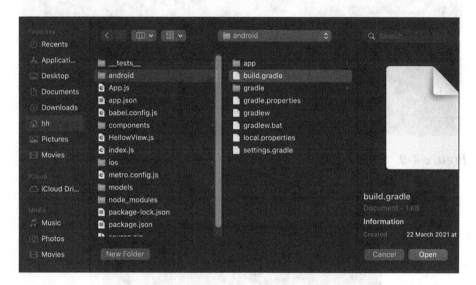

Figure 4-8. *Open the Android project in Android Studio*

Next, right-click the source code directory under the project; choose new Kotlin Class/File (Figure 4-9).

Figure 4-9. *Create a new Kotlin class*

Again, we type `HelloWorldManager` for the class name (Figure 4-10).

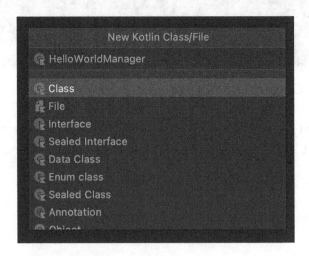

Figure 4-10. *Add HelloWorldManager*

Next, we create a package class where all **native modules** are registered. This package class is specific to *Android*. We name the package MomendCardPackage (Figure 4-11).

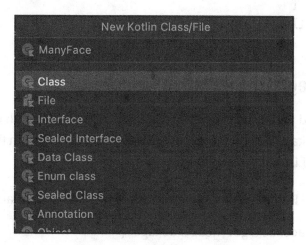

Figure 4-11. Add ManyfacePackage

4.1.2.2 Implement the Native Module

Firstly, we need to export the module to the *JavaScript* layer. This is the same step as the RCT_EXTERN_MODULE macro in *iOS* (Listing 4-6).

Listing 4-6. Export the module to the JavaScript layer

```
override fun getName(): String {
  return "HelloWorldManager"
}
```

Next, we can go ahead and implement the hello method as in *iOS* (Listing 4-7).

Listing 4-7. Implement hello()

```
@ReactMethod
fun hello() {
  Log.d("HelloWorldManager", "Hello World!");
}
```

4.1.2.3 Register the Native Module

Next, we need to register the newly created native module with the ManyfacePackage and then register the ManyfacePackage with the application (Listings 4-8 and 4-9).

Listing 4-8. Register the native module with ManyfacePackage

```
class ManyfacePackage: ReactPackage {
  override fun createViewManagers( // ---------------------> 1)
reactContext: ReactApplicationContext):
MutableList<ViewManager<out View, out ReactShadowNode<*>>>
  {
    return mutableListOf<ViewManager<View,
    ReactShadowNode<*>>>()
  }

  override fun createNativeModules( // -------------------> 2)
reactContext: ReactApplicationContext):
MutableList<NativeModule>
  {
    return mutableListOf(HelloWorldManager(reactContext))
    // > 3)
  }
}
```

1) We return an empty list for `createViewManagers`.
   The list will be populated very soon in Section 4.2.2.

2) `createNativeModules` is the method to register
   native modules.

3) We instantiate the **native module**
   `HelloWorldManager` and populate the list with it.

Listing 4-9. Register the ManyfacePackage with the application

```
...
  override fun getPackages(): List<ReactPackage> {
    val packages = PackageList(this).packages
    packages.add(ManyfacePackage())
    return packages
  }
...
```

4.1.2.4 Async Calls

The same as in *iOS* (Section 4.1.1.3), we can use either callbacks or
promises to resolve asynchronous native calls. Firstly, let's see how a
callback is used by implementing the *Android* counterpart of `someWork()`
(Listing 4-10).

Listing 4-10. Use a callback to complete a native method invocation
(Android version)

```
@ReactMethod
fun someWork(cb: Callback) {
  Log.d("HelloWorldManager", "Done some work");
  cb.invoke("", "success")
}
```

Next is the approach using Promise (Listing 4-11).

Listing 4-11. Make native method promise compatible (Android version)

```
@ReactMethod
fun someWorkWithPromise(promise: Promise) {
  Log.d("HelloWorldManager", "Done some work");
  promise.resolve("result data")
}
```

4.1.3 Use the Native Module in JavaScript

As we deliberately make method signatures exported from *iOS* and *Android* the same, we can call these methods in a unanimous way as given in Listing 4-12.

Listing 4-12. Use the native module in JavaScript

```
import { ..., NativeModules } from 'react-native';

const HelloWorld = NativeModules.HelloWorldManager; // ----> 1)

HelloWorld.hello(); // -------------------------------------> 2)

NativeModules.HelloWorldManager.someWork((err, res) => {
// -> 3)
  console.log('Result of the callback:' + res);
});

NativeModules.HelloWorldManager.someWorkWithPromise() // --> 4)
.then((res) => {
  console.log('Result of the promise:' + res);
});
```

1)   The name of the native module will be the same as the class name in Swift. This is guaranteed by the RCT_EXTERN_MODULE macro.

2)   This invokes the *Swift* implementation of the same method.

3)   The callback param could be either in the form of an arrow method or a normal *JavaScript* function.

4)   As discussed, the native method can be designed as part of an ordinary promise chain.

4.1.4 Key Takeaways

In this section, we looked at how to implement native modules that export native methods to the *JavaScript* layer. We firstly listed the files required by both *iOS* and *Android* to enable a full-fledged native module. Then we made a dummy native module to demonstrate how exactly a method is exposed from both platforms. Lastly, we discussed the asynchronous nature of native method calls. Although we adopted both callback and promise ways to implement asynchronous method calls, the promise is always the go-to approach in practice.

We also make a checklist of files required to create **native modules** as follows:

iOS

```
HelloWorldManager.swift
ProjectName-Bridging-Header.h
HelloWorldManagerBridge.m
```

Android

```
HelloWorldManager.kt
MomendCardPackage.kt
```

4.2 Native Components

Involved with the UI, **native components** are more complex than **native modules**. **Native components** turn existing native UI elements into ordinary **components**. For example, you may want to expose the system AirPlay button to the *JavaScript* layer. For teams who want to integrate *React Native* to their existing app, it is also a good practice to expose existing battle-ironed native UI elements out in the form of **native components** so as to reuse the wheel.

The **native component** is also the technique applied by the *React Native* community to create various third-party libraries. Some of them are the go-to component for their designated task. *react-native-fast-image* is by far the best image cache library based on *SDWebImage* and *Glide*; *react-native-video* is the most commonly used video library; and *react-native-vector-icons* allows for using vector icons on mobile apps, which largely enhance the development speed especially in the phase of PoC. With those libraries in place, you don't need to deep dive to the native layer as the work has been done for you in most cases.

Technically, a **native component** is composed of two parts, a **view manager** and a custom native view. The **view manager** works as a proxy for the **native component**. The **view manager** defines the **props** and methods and exposes them to the *JavaScript* layer on behalf of the native view. The *JavaScript* layer can access the native view only through the corresponding **view manager**. After being properly exported, **native components** are no different than ordinary **components**; they can be set with background color and border radius and be incorporated into the layout with **flexbox**. They can also be assigned with **children**, which are populated as subviews of the underlying native views of the **components**.

The layout and other styles of the custom view (e.g., background color) are managed by *React Native*. It is worth noting that the native view returned by the **view manager** is merely a blueprint, which is not the real view rendered. 💣 So please refrain from keeping a reference of a

native view for further manipulation. It is also pointless to attach a gesture handler to the native view for the same reason. ✐ Use a **react tag** (Section 4.3.2) to get the correct **component** instance for such manipulation.

Lastly, a **view manager** cannot be used interchangeably as a **native module**. For example, 💣 on *iOS*, **view managers** cannot be used to send events (Section 4.3.1), while on *Android*, **view managers** cannot expose native methods.

4.2.1 iOS Native Component

4.2.1.1 Setup

The files required by a **native component** are similar to those for a **native module**. Firstly, we need a manager that exports the view to the *JavaScript* layer. Likewise, we right-click the project root group and select a new file. This time, we change its name to HelloViewManager *Swift* (Figure 4-12).

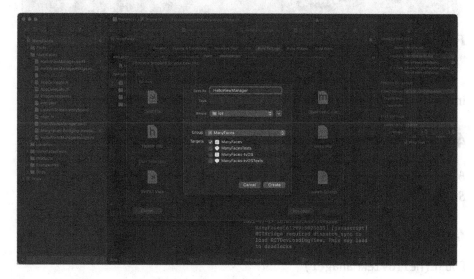

Figure 4-12. *Add HelloViewManager*

We omit the bridge file for **Objective-C** to **Swift** since it has already been created for the native module. And we continue creating the **JavaScript** bridge file for the manager that has to be in **Objective-C**.

This time, the name should be HelloViewManagerBridge (Figure 4-13).

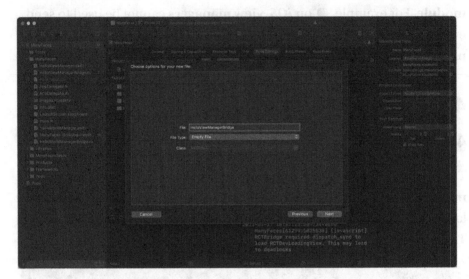

Figure 4-13. *Add HelloViewManagerBridge*

The same as a **native module**, we need three files, one **Swift** implementation and two bridge headers for a **native component**.

4.2.1.2 Implement the View Manager

As usual, firstly, let's see the main logic of HelloViewManager which is in **Swift** (Listing 4-13).

Listing 4-13. HelloViewManager.swift

```
@objc(HelloViewManager)
class HelloViewManager: RCTViewManager { // ---------------> 1)

  @objc(view)
```

```
override func view() -> UIView { // --------------------> 2)
    return UIView() // ------------------------------------> 3)
    let view = HelloView()
    view.backgroundColor = UIColor.purple
    return view
  }
}

class HelloView: UIView { // -------------------------------> 3)

}
```

1) Subclass the RCTViewManager.

2) Override its view() methods.

3) Create a custom view with the **view manager**.

Note   Though it is tempting to return a library native view as is in the view(), it causes chaos in the context of cross-platform. This is because native views always have different interfaces (i.e., properties and methods) on different platforms. 🏛 Hence on **iOS**, it is a good practice to always create a custom native view together with the **view manager** as another layer of abstraction, so as to keep the interface the same to the **JavaScript** layer. We will see it very soon in Section 4.2.1.3.

Directly compiling the preceding source code will give an error that RCTViewManager does not exist in the **Swift** realm. Again, this is where the **Objective-C** to **Swift** bridge header (ProjectName-Bridging-Header) comes into play. We need to expose the required **React Native** class (RCTViewManager) to **Swift** by adding the line shown in Listing 4-14 to the bridge header.

Listing 4-14. Expose the RCTViewManager to Swift

```
#import <React/RCTViewManager.h>
```

Lastly, we bridge the component out to the JavaScript layer in `HelloViewManagerBridge` (Listing 4-15).

Listing 4-15. HelloViewManagerBridge.m

```
#import <Foundation/Foundation.h>
#import <React/RCTViewManager.h>

@interface RCT_EXTERN_MODULE(HelloViewManager,
RCTViewManager)//1)

@end
```

1) Here, we need to export the module as `RCTViewManager`.

4.2.1.3 View Property

The **view manager** is responsible for exporting **view properties** of the **native view** to the *JavaScript* layer. More specifically, properties are made available to the *JavaScript* layer with the macro `RCT_EXPORT_VIEW_ PROPERTY`. After the export, the properties of the **native view** can be passed in with values as an ordinary **prop**. Lastly, the **prop** name exported is the same as the name of the corresponding **view property**.

Now we change the **view manager** a bit to expose a **view property** called `bgColor` to the *JavaScript* layer (Listing 4-16).

Listing 4-16. Export a view property in the view manager

```
@interface RCT_EXTERN_MODULE(HelloViewManager, RCTViewManager)

RCT_EXPORT_VIEW_PROPERTY(bgColor, int) // -----------------> 1)

@end
```

Next, we make a custom native view to respond to the property change (Listing 4-17).

Listing 4-17. Export a view property in the native view

```
...
class HelloView: UIView {
  func setBgColor (color: int) { // -----------------------> 1)
    self.backgroundColor = UIColorFromInt(color) //--------> 3)
  }

  func UIColorFromInt(_ rgbValue: Int) -> UIColor { // ----> 2)
    let red =   CGFloat((rgbValue & 0xFF0000) >> 16) / 0xFF
    let green = CGFloat((rgbValue & 0x00FF00) >> 8) / 0xFF
    let blue =  CGFloat(rgbValue & 0x0000FF) / 0xFF
    let alpha = CGFloat(1.0)

    return UIColor(red: red,
               green: green,
                blue: blue,
               alpha: alpha)
  }
}
```

1) Here, we export the bgColor as int instead of UIColor in order to make the interface consistent with **Android**. As you will see repeatedly in this book, 🏛 keeping the interface consistent by finding the common factor is a good practice in the context of cross-platform.

2) As such, we need another native method to convert the int to UIColor. From the structure, we can see that it extracts *RGB* values from different portions of the int value and assigns them to the UIColor. But for now, we don't have to understand its implementation details.

3) Lastly, we can use the preceding method to convert the int **view property** to the UIColor as required by the backgroundColor.

Note   After being exported, the native view is converted to an ordinary **component** by the React Native runtime. Hence, the background color can be set with the **style props**. So the bgColor here is for demonstration purposes only. In practice, we don't need to export a stand-alone **view property** for the background color.

As mentioned before, 🏛 it is always more desirable to have a customized **native view** designed with the same properties instead of exporting the original native view as is. This is critical to provide a unanimous *JavaScript* interface for different platforms. One example is *AirPlay* and *Chromecast*. The properties of the two native views are completely different. In our example, we use a wrapper view to reconcile the differences. Another approach is to use the RCT_REMAP_VIEW_PROPERTY macro to achieve the same.

One special type of a **view property** is the callback. After the export, this property accepts a *JavaScript* function or closure as the input **props**. The callback then is stored in the **native view** and gets invoked when a certain condition is met. For instance, a video **native view** might need to notify the consumer in the *JavaScript* layer when an exception occurs. We can use `RCTBubblingEventBlock` (not the `RCTResponseSenderBlock` used in the native module) as the property type to make the property callable.

4.2.2 Android Native Component

4.2.2.1 Setup

The files required by **native components** on *Android* are similar to those for **native modules**. Here, we only need to add one additional file, `HelloViewManager.kt`, for the **view manager**. We can reuse the `ManyfacePackage.kt` created before for **view manager** registration (Figure 4-14).

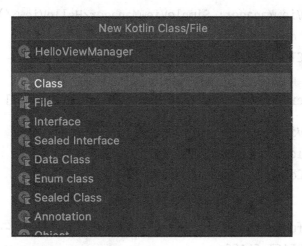

Figure 4-14. *Add HelloViewManager*

4.2.2.2 Implement the View Manager

The way of implementing the **view manager** is very different from that in *iOS*. But the critical points are the same. To recap, we (1) export the module to the *JavaScript* layer with a name, (2) we create a custom **native view** for the unanimity of the API, and (3) we instantiate the **native view** in the **view manager**. See Listing 4-18.

Note   We create a custom **native view** the same as in *iOS* to keep these two examples more comparable. However, this cannot be achieved easily in practice. We could add the abstract layer on setters of view properties to maintain the unanimity of the API if that is the case.

Listing 4-18. HelloViewManager.kt (Android version)

```kotlin
class HelloViewManager: SimpleViewManager<HelloView>() {
  companion object {
    val REACT_CLASS = "HelloView" // ---------------------> 1)
  }
  var mCallerContext: ReactApplicationContext? = null

  fun HelloViewManager(reactContext:
  ReactApplicationContext?) {
    mCallerContext = reactContext
  }

  override fun getName(): String { // --------------------> 1)
    return REACT_CLASS
  }
```

```
  override fun createViewInstance( // --------------------> 3)
  reactContext:ThemedReactContext
  ): HelloView {
    return HelloView(mCallerContext)
  }
}

class HelloView: View { // -------------------------------> 2)
  constructor(context: ReactApplicationContext?):
  super(context)
  {
  }
}
```

Like the **native module**, we also need to register the **native component** with the ManyfacePackage. This time, we populate the list returned by createViewManagers in ManyfacePackage (Listing 4-19).

Listing 4-19. Register the native component

```
...
  override fun createViewManagers(
reactContext: ReactApplicationContext
  ): MutableList<ViewManager<out View, out ReactShadowNode<*>>>
  {
    return mutableListOf(HelloViewManager(reactContext))
  }
```

We have already registered the ManyfacePackage with the MainApplication, so we can omit the step here.

> **Note**   Here, we need to declare the template variables View and
> ReactShadowNode as out. So ViewManager<out View, out
> ReactShadowNode<*>> can be compatible with the returned Simp
> leViewManager<HelloView>.

4.2.2.3 View Property

Next, we export the same bgColor property for the *Android* version of
HelloView. Firstly, in the **view manager**, we export the **view property** and
assign the setter with it (Listing 4-20).

Listing 4-20. Export a view property in the view manager (Android)

```
@ReactProp(name = "bgColor")
fun setBgColor(view: HelloView, color: Int) {
  view.setBgColor(color)
}
```

Next, we implement the setBgColor in the custom native view
(Listing 4-21).

Listing 4-21. Export a view property in the native view (Android)

```
class HelloView: View {
  constructor(context: ReactApplicationContext?):
  super(context)
  {}

  public fun setBgColor(color: Int) {
this.setBackgroundColor(color)
  }
}
```

Unlike *iOS*, we cannot simply indicate the type as Callback to make a callback **view property** on *Android*. Rather, we need to mimic the callback using the event system (Section 4.3.1). For example, if we want to implement an onComplete callback view property, we need to define an event with the same name in the **view manager** (Listing 4-22).

Listing 4-22. Callback view property in the native view (Android)

```
...
override fun getExportedCustomBubblingEventTypeConstants() =
  mapOf(
    "onChange" to // -------------------------------------> 2)
      mapOf(
        "phasedRegistrationNames" to // ----------------> 1)
          mapOf("bubbled" to "onChange")
      )
  )
...
```

1) This is the event name that will be used in the native layer to invoke the callback **view property**.

2) This is the view property name mapped with the event name.

With this setup, the native side can invoke the callback **view property** with the code in Listing 4-23.

Listing 4-23. Invoke the callback view property (Android)

```
...
val event: WritableMap = Arguments.createMap()
event.putString("data ", "Data content") // -------------> 4)
```

```
reactContext?.getJSModule(
  RCTEventEmitter::class.java
)?.receiveEvent( // ---------------------------------------> 5)
  id,
  " onChange", // ---------------------------------------> 3)
  event
)
...
```

3) This is the event name registered in step 1.

4) Here, we can also put the parameters for this callback.

5) Call the JavaScript layer to receiveEvent, which means sending the event from the native layer.

As mentioned, we are going to make use of the callback **view property** when implementing the video **native component** later in Section 4.5. At that time, we are going to see some real and workable code.

4.2.3 Use the Native Component in JavaScript

Let's see how the **native component** we created can be used in the *JavaScript* layer. Next, let's see how it looks.

4.2.3.1 The Easy Way

requireNativeComponent is the method provided by *React Native* to "import" a **native component**. The return value of requireNativeComponent is an ordinary **component** that can be used directly inside the render() method. See Listing 4-24.

Listing 4-24. A modified version of App.js

```
import { requireNativeComponent } from 'react-native';

let HelloView = requireNativeComponent('HelloView'); // --> 1)

const App: () => React$Node = () => {
  return (
    <SafeAreaView style={{width: '100%', height: '100%'}}>
      <HelloView
        bgColor={processColor('red')} // ----------------> 2)
        style={{width: '100%', height: 50}}
      />
    </SafeAreaView>
  );
};
export default App;
```

1) Import directly from the **native component**.

2) Here, we use the processColor to convert the CSS
   style color values to int as defined by the **view
   property**.

4.2.3.2 The Right Way, Abstraction on the JavaScript Layer

In practice, however, it causes confusion when debugging by
using requireNativeComponent directly in the user **component**.
More specifically, in the case where *fast refresh* is enabled, the
requireNativeComponent will be called whenever the user code is
changed, which eventually will give the "Tried to register two views with
the same name" error.

To mitigate this issue, it is better to encapsulate the native **component** in its own file which will not be touched after being created in normal cases.

This wrapper can also serve as another layer of abstraction that eases out any potential differences on the two mobile platforms when necessary (Listing 4-25).

Listing 4-25. A native component in its own file

```
import React from 'react';

import { requireNativeComponent } from 'react-native';

let HelloView = requireNativeComponent('HelloView');

export default HelloView;
```

Then the view can be used unchanged. The only difference is that the **component** should be imported from this file (Listing 4-26).

Listing 4-26. Import from the isolated file

```
...
let HelloView = requireNativeComponent('HelloView');
import HelloView from './HellowView';
...
```

4.2.4 Children of a Native Component

A **native component** can also be added with **children** (Listing 4-27).

Listing 4-27. A native component with children

```
<HelloView style={{
          width: '100%',
          height: 50,
```

```
        flexDirection: 'row',
        bgColor={processColor('red')} // -------------> 1)
      }}
>
  <View style={{flex: 1, backgroundColor: 'green'}}/> // --> 2)
  <View style={{flex: 1, backgroundColor: 'blue'}}/>
  <View style={{flex: 1, backgroundColor: 'yellow'}}/>
</HelloView>
```

1) We use bgColor to dye the **container** component so it's more standout in the view inspector.

2) We add three **children** to the **container** which is essentially a **native component**.

On **iOS**, **children** are added as subviews. This useful characteristic can enable advanced visual effects such as gradient and mask to any ordinary **components** with a customized **native component** (Figure 4-15).

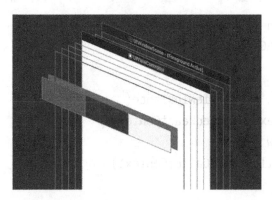

Figure 4-15. *Native view with children*

On *Android*, we need to adjust the **view manager** to support **children** under the **native component**. This is because *Android* differentiates View and ViewGroup, and only the latter can contain subviews. This is how the newer version of the **view manager** looks in order to support **children** (Listing 4-28).

Listing 4-28. Support ViewGroup

```
class HelloViewManager: ViewGroupManager<HelloView> { // --> 1)
  companion object {
    val REACT_CLASS = "HelloView"
  }
  var mCallerContext: ReactApplicationContext? = null

  constructor(reactContext: ReactApplicationContext?):
  super() {
    mCallerContext = reactContext
  }

  override fun getName(): String {
    return REACT_CLASS
  }

  override fun createViewInstance(
    reactContext: ThemedReactContext
  ): HelloView {
    return HelloView(mCallerContext)
  }

  @ReactProp(name = "bgColor")
  fun setBgColor(view: HelloView, @ColorInt color: Int) {
    view.setBgColor(color)
  }
}
```

```kotlin
class HelloView: ViewGroup { // --------------------------> 2)
constructor(context: ReactApplicationContext?):
super(context)
{}

override fun onLayout(changed: Boolean, // ---------------> 3)
                         l: Int,
                         t: Int,
                         r: Int,
                         b: Int) {
  }

  public fun setBgColor(@ColorInt color: Int) {
    this.setBackgroundColor(color)
  }
}
```

1) The view manager needs to inherit from
   ViewGroupManager instead of SimpleViewManager.

2) The **custom native view** needs to inherit from ViewGroup.

3) The **custom native view** needs to override onLayout of
   the ViewGroup. We don't need to do anything for this
   method as *React Native* will handle all the layout for us.

Note   Please always consider using ViewGroupManager first
instead of SimpleViewManager whenever possible since it is
always preferred that **components** can work as **containers**. In
practice, this is not feasible because some stock views on *Android*
are derived from **View** or **SurfaceView**. In such a case, we can
design the wrapper **component** in *JavaScript* (Section 4.2.3.2) if
we need it to work as a **container**.

This way, we can achieve the same view hierarchy as on *iOS* (Figure 4-16).

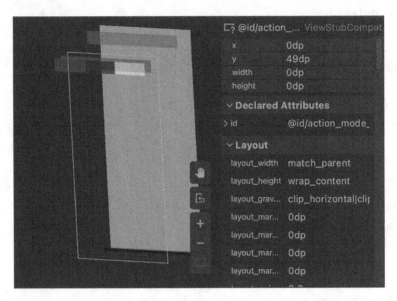

Figure 4-16. Native view with children (Android version)

4.2.5 Key Takeaways

In this section, we looked into **native components**. At the core of each **native component** are **view managers**. We learned that a **view manager** needs three key steps to be fully functional: (1) declare a name to be exported, (2) declare a custom native view, and (3) instantiate and return the **native view**. Moreover, we can define **view properties** to be used in the *JavaScript* layer.

We also saw how the custom native views can be used interchangeably with other ordinary **components**; they can be nested as **children** within **components** or the other way around. Moreover, to enjoy this perk on *Android*, we need to use ViewGroup and ViewGroupManager. It is worth noting again that ViewGroup and ViewGroupManager are always more preferred to be aligned with *React Native* stock **components**.

Table 4-1 provides a quick summary to implement **native components** on both platforms.

Table 4-1. *Summary of native components*

	iOS	Android
Export module name	RCT_EXTERN_MODULE	override fun getName(): String
Custom native view	extends UIView	extends View
Instantiation	override func view() -> UIView	Override fun createViewInstance(reactContext: Themed ReactContext): View
View properties	RCT_EXPORT_VIEW_PROPERTY	@ReactProp
Callback view properties	RCTResponseSenderBlock	getExportedCustom BubblingEventType Constants
Work as container	Naturally supported	extends ViewGroupManager

We have discussed all the basics in **native modules** and **native components**. Next, let's look at some advanced techniques.

4.3 Advanced Techniques

4.3.1 Event

The *JavaScript-to-native* communications we saw in the previous sections are all requests initialized from the *JavaScript* layer, or "pulls." An **event** allows for a "push" from a **native module** to the *JavaScript* layer. There are other ways, such as retained callbacks and set properties, with which **native modules** can send updates to the *JavaScript* layer actively. For example, a **native module** can retain a callback argument and invoke it when an event of interest occurs. Nonetheless, using explicit events is the most intuitive way.

Note   As discussed in Chapter 3, frequent communication (e.g., frame by frame) between *JavaScript* and native is far from ideal and should be avoided at all times. The same principle applies for callback **props** (Sections 4.2.1.3 and 4.2.2.3) which virtually "push" events from a **native component**. As a quick reminder, we resort to native-to-native events for such scenarios.

4.3.1.1 Send Events from iOS

As mentioned, only **native modules** can post events to the *JavaScript* layer. On *iOS*, a **native module** needs to inherit RCTEventEmitter. It is impossible for a **native component** to send an event in that a **native component** has to inherit from RCTViewManager.

To post events to the *JavaScript* layer, a **native module** calls [self sendEventWithName:body:] that is inherited from the base class RCTEventEmitter. Next, let's modify the HelloWorldManager to send back an event (Listing 4-29).

Listing 4-29. Send an event within hello()

```
@objc(HelloWorldManager)
class HelloWorldManager: RCTEventEmitter { // -------------> 1)

  @objc(hello)
  func hello() -> Void {
    print("Hello World")
```

```
  self.sendEvent( // -------------------------------------> 2)
    withName: "HELLO_EVENT", // -------------------------> 3)
    body: ["data": "hello() got called"] // -------------> 4)
  )
}
...

}
```

1) RCTEventEmitter is a special native module that can emit events.

2) We send the event at the end of a native method.

3) We name the event HELLO_EVENT. The *JavaScript* layer can in turn use this identifier to register the listener for the event.

4) We also provide some payload as the event body.

4.3.1.2 Send Events from Android

On *Android*, we use a similar way to send events to the *JavaScript* layer. We can use the following line to send events from anywhere, and it does not require a native module to inherit from a special superclass.

Next, we change the *Android* version of the hello() method the same way as on *iOS* (Listing 4-30).

Listing 4-30. Send an event within hello() (Android version)

```
@ReactMethod
fun hello() {
  Log.d("HelloWorldManager", "Hello World");

  val params = Arguments.createMap() // -------------------> 1)
  params.putString("data", "hello() got called")
```

```
mCallerContext?.getJSModule<
  DeviceEventManagerModule.RCTDeviceEventEmitter
>(
  DeviceEventManagerModule.RCTDeviceEventEmitter::class.java
)?.emit("HELLO_EVENT", params) // ----------------------> 2)
}
```

1) Construct the parameter for the event. This is
   equivalent to the event body of the *iOS* counterpart.

2) Indicate the event name HELLO_EVENT as on
   iOS. And pass in as payload the params constructed
   earlier. This line can be used anywhere to send
   events from the native side.

4.3.1.3 Receive Events in JavaScript

To receive events in the *JavaScript* layer, we need to instantiate a
NativeEventEmitter from the **native module**. And register a callback with
the event name that is of interest (Listing 4-31).

Listing 4-31. Receive events in the JavaScript layer

```
const receiver = new
NativeEventEmitter(NativeModules.HelloWorldManager); // ---> 1)
receiver.addListener('HELLO_EVENT', (params) => { // ------> 2)
  if (params['data'] !== undefined) { // ------------------> 3)
    console.log("received event from native: " +
    params['data']);
  }
})
```

1) Here, we instantiate a `NativeEventEmitter` based on our `HelloWorldManager`.

2) Then we attach a listener to the `NativeEventEmitter` for `HELLO_EVENT`.

3) We process the event payload when it arrives.

Here, the `HELLO_EVENT` and `params` are the first and second parameters of the [`self sendEventWithName:body:`] and `emit()` on *iOS* and ***Android***, respectively.

4.3.2 React Tag

As said, the view returned by the **native component** is not the **UIView rendered**. Although it is tempting to retain the **UIView** instance with a **native component** instance variable, it is futile to change its attributes or to operate on it, for example, change its background color. To manipulate the actual **UIView** instance, we must resort to a **react tag**, a unique identifier allocated by the ***React Native*** runtime to identify a particular **UIView**. We need to get a ***react* ref** before we can fetch a **react tag**. So let's start from there.

4.3.2.1 React Refs

The beauty of ***React*** is found in its extensive adoption of composition and unanimous way to interact with **components**. Nevertheless, in very rare cases, we need to regress to the traditional *Object-Oriented* paradigm and invoke an instance method. One example is `ScrollView.scrollTo()`.

It is not straightforward to fetch the reference of the **component** instance as the instantiation and life cycle are managed by ***React Native***. But we can retrieve a **component** instance from the **VDOM tree** in the `render()` method with `ref` which is a special **callback prop**.

Note 💣 The **ref** is not supported by *functional components*.

Before we dive in, let's take `ScrollView` as an example. Listing 4-32 demonstrates how to retrieve the **react ref** of a `ScrollView`.

Listing 4-32. Retrieve a ref

```
<ScrollView ref={ref => {
  this._scrollViewRef = findNodeHandle(ref)
}}>
</ScrollView>
```

Then `scrollTo()` is ready for use as given in Listing 4-33.

Listing 4-33. Call an instance method of a ScrollView

```
this._scrollViewRef.scrollTo({ x: 0, y: 0, animated: true });
```

`ScrollView` is a stock **component**. Eventually, `scrollTo()` needs to call the native function to complete the action. This step is encapsulated inside the `ScrollView`, and underneath a technique called a **react tag** is used to achieve that.

Note   Sometimes, a **component** is wrapped within an **HOC**(s). This obscures **react tag** fetching in that the ref obtained by the consumer will be the **react ref** of the **HOC** instead of the real component being consumed semantically. This issue can be resolved using **ref forwarding** which we are going to apply in Section 4.5.3.4.

4.3.2.2 React Tags

In the native layer, the instances of *components* are in the form of concrete **UIView**. Again, the instantiation and life cycle of native views are managed by *React Native*. As given in Listing 4-34, this time we use a **react tag**, a unique identifier that is associated with a particular **UIView** to retrieve the instance. A **react tag** can be retrieved in the *JavaScript* layer using findNodeHandle passed with a **react ref** retrieved in the last section.

Listing 4-34. Retrieve a react tag

```
import { NativeModules, findNodeHandle } from 'react-native'

<View ref={ref => {
  this._viewTag = findNodeHandle(ref)
}}>
</View>
```

Now in a native **view manager** (or a **native module**), we can use this **react tag** to retrieve the **UIView** instance for further operations. Listings 4-35 to 4-37 give the implementation on *iOS*.

Listing 4-35. Manipulate UIView with a react tag

```
@objc(setBlue:)
func setBlue(_ reactTag: Int) {
  self.bridge.uiManager.addUIBlock({ // -------------------> 1)
  (uiManager: RCTUIManager?,
viewRegistry: [NSNumber: UIView]?) in
    let view = viewRegistry?[NSNumber.init(value:
    reactTag)] //2)
    view?.backgroundColor = UIColor.blue // ---------------> 3)
  })
}
```

1) Use [RCTUIManager addUIBlock] to execute the logic on the main thread.

2) Retrieve the UIView from viewRegistry which stores all UIView in use.

3) Apply the UI operation on the UIView, for example, set its background color.

Next, we bridge out the setBlue method in HelloViewManagerBridge.m.

Listing 4-36. Add setBlue in HelloViewManagerBridge.m

```
RCT_EXTERN_METHOD(setBlue:(int)reactTag)
```

Lastly, we bridge in the missing dependency ***Objective-C*** class RCTUIManager in ProjectName-Bridging-Header.h.

Listing 4-37. Add the Objective-C dependency in ProjectName-Bridging-Header.h

```
#import <React/RCTUIManager.h>
```

💣 We need a completely different implementation to manipulate a **native view** on ***Android***. Unlike ***iOS***, we don't have an exposed viewRegistry that keeps records of instances of **native views** and their corresponding **react tags**. Moreover, **native components** lack the ability to export methods to the ***JavaScript*** layer. Rather, we need to make use of a *command system* designed on ***Android***. Though the *command system* still relies on the **react tag** implicitly, the use of such a system is completely different and is less elegant compared to that on ***iOS*** when achieving the same end purpose.

Let's explain the *command system*. Basically, the commands are strings defined in **native components** together with their associated procedures. These predefined commands in turn can be sent from the ***JavaScript*** layer.

The command is required to be attached with a **react tag** to indicate which **native view** it is meant for. Then the *command system* translates the **react tag** to the view instance and passes the instance into the mentioned procedure.

Next, we implement the same "set blue" functionality on **Android** to see how this command system looks (Listing 4-38).

Listing 4-38. Add the setBlue as a command in HelloViewManager

```
class HelloViewManager: ViewGroupManager<HelloView> {
  companion object {
    val REACT_CLASS = "HelloView"

    private const val COMMAND_SET_BLUE = "setBlue" // -----> 1)
    private const val COMMAND_SET_BLUE_VAL = 1
  }

...

  override fun getCommandsMap() = mapOf( // ---------------> 2)
    COMMAND_SET_BLUE to COMMAND_SET_BLUE_VAL
  )

  override fun receiveCommand( // ------------------------> 3)
      view: HelloView, // --------------------------------> 4)
commandId: String, args: ReadableArray?)
  {
    when (commandId) {
      COMMAND_SET_BLUE -> {
        view.setBlue() // --------------------------------> 5)
      }
    }
  }
...
}
```

```
class HelloView: ViewGroup {
...

    public fun setBlue() { // ----------------------------> 5)
        this.setBackgroundColor(Color.BLUE)
    }
...
}
```

1) Declare the constant command string.

2) Export the command to *React Native*.

3) Declare the procedures for each command exported. Here, we have only one command, `COMMAND_SET_BLUE`.

4) The command system translates the react tag into the **native view** instance and passes it in.

5) With the instance of the **native view**, we can operate on it.

4.3.2.3 Reconcile React Tag Implementation on JavaScript

The implementation difference we have seen earlier is not well aligned. To reconcile a platform difference, we add a *JavaScript* abstraction layer of the **native component**. As mentioned, the common critical information shared between *iOS* and *Android* is the **react tag**; hence, the arguments taken on both platforms can be made the same. Listings 4-39 and 4-40 give the implementation of such reconciliation.

Listing 4-39. Make a wrapper of the native module

```
class HelloViewManager {
  static setBlue(reactTag) {
    if (Platform.OS === 'ios') {
      NativeModules.HelloViewManager.setBlue(reactTag);
      // --> 1)
    } else {
      UIManager.dispatchViewManagerCommand( // ------------> 2)
        reactTag, 'setBlue', []
      );
    }
  }
};

export default HelloViewManager;
```

1) When the platform is *iOS*, invoke **native method** setBlue in the ordinary way.

2) When the platform is ***Android***, send the corresponding command together with the **react tag**.

Listing 4-40. Call the native method using a react tag

```
class App extends React.Component {
  constructor() {
    super();
  }
```

```
componentDidMount() {
  setInterval(() => {
    if (this._viewTag) {
      HelloViewManager.setBlue(this._viewTag); // -------> 2)
    }
  }, 1000);
}

render() {
  return (
    <SafeAreaView style={{width: '100%', height: '100%'}}>
      <HelloView ref={ref => {
                  this._viewTag = findNodeHandle(ref)
                  // -> 1)
                }}
                bgColor={processColor('red')}
                style={{width: '100%', height: 50}}
      />
...
    </SafeAreaView>
  );
 }
};

export default App;
```

1) Fetch the **react tag** using `findNodeHandle` and **react ref** as discussed.

2) Call the `setBlue()` method exposed from `HelloViewManager`, which eventually call the corresponding native method.

4.3.3 Direct Manipulation

When carrying out UI operations that are out of scope to the *React* rendering process, we want to circumvent rerendering of the **component** tree. This is helpful for use cases where (1) most of the UI logic is offloaded to the native layer and (2) smooth, continuous animation is involved. More specifically, the updates on **props** of an animation **component**, video states (e.g., pause/play) of a pure native video player, and content of a TextInput are considered to belong to the preceding cases. This is where **direct manipulations** come into play.

To carry out such operations, we firstly need to get the **react ref** of the **component** as discussed in the last section. Then we can invoke setNativeProps() of the **component** instance with the **react ref**.

Note   Though a direct manipulation is more lightweight than an ordinary prop update (which triggers a rerender), it still imposes the overhead for *JavaScript-to-native* communication. Please refrain from using it for frequent updating which, again, better be carried out using techniques discussed in Chapter 3.

4.3.4 Synchronous Method Call

The invocations of a native method from *JavaScript* can be made synchronous. More specifically, the binary execution of such method calls is directly on the *JavaScript* thread. This technique is useful when multiple sources of asynchronous events get involved (such as user interaction and network events), and the results for all events are critical to the subsequential logic flows. Using synchronous method calls can significantly reduce complexity and makes the overall logic less error-prone.

The synchronous method call is optimal in that (1) it is executed directly on the *JavaScript* thread; (2) all interthread communication and serialization for data passing between native and *JavaScript* layers have been done away. As we will see in Chapter 6, all synchronous calls are essentially made effective with a *C++* method `nativeCallSyncHook`.

There are some caveats with using it. Firstly, it does not support remote debugging on Chrome. Secondly, since synchronous methods are executed on the *JavaScript* thread, we need to consider race conditions when they need to share resources with other native methods running on the native thread. Other than that, synchronous methods give lower latency than their asynchronous counterparts.

On *iOS*, we use `RCT_EXPORT_BLOCKING_SYNCHRONOUS_METHOD` to export synchronous methods.

On *Android*, we use `@ReactMethod(isBlockingSynchronousMethod = true)` to export methods of such kind.

On the *JavaScript* layer, we can use those methods like ordinary ones exported from **native modules**.

4.3.5 Export Constants

When we want to pass some native-level configuration to the *JavaScript* layer, we can export constants to do so. Those constants are determined during the bootstrap phase and cannot be changed throughout the app life cycle. As we will see in Chapter 6, constants are stored originally in `RCTModuleData` and are gathered when the **native module** is referred to for the first time. 🏛 The scope of constants is the module, so they are more suitable to define module-specific values.

💣 The drawback of **export constants** is that they cannot be used to reflect a configuration that can only be determined during runtime, for example, fetched from remote. In the next section, 🚀 we will use **initial properties** for such use cases.

4.3.5.1 iOS

To export constants from a **native module** or a **view manager**, we simply override the constantsToExport method (Listings 4-41 and 4-42).

Listing 4-41. Export constants by overriding constantsToExport

```
@objc(constantsToExport)
override func constantsToExport() -> [AnyHashable : Any]? {
  return ["Version": "0.0.1"]
}
```

4.3.5.2 Android

Listing 4-42. Export constants by overriding getConstants

```
override fun getConstants(): Map<String, Any>? {
  return mapOf("Version" to "0.0.1")
}
```

4.3.5.3 Access Constants in JavaScript

Constants exported on both platforms can be accessed using the **native module**'s getConstants() method (Listing 4-43).

Listing 4-43. Access the constants exported

```
const { Version } = NativeModules.HelloWorldManager.getConstants();
console.log('Version is: ' + Version);
```

4.3.6 Initial Properties

As said, once determined in bootstrap, constants cannot change afterward. **Initial properties** come into play when we need values that can only be determined during runtime, for instance, feature flags fetched from remote, endpoints that are determined after speed racing, and domain configurations. 🏛 Unlike constants, the scope of **initial properties** is the application, which makes it more suitable for the mentioned tasks.

On *iOS*, **initial properties** are passed from the native layer to the RCTRootView during initialization (Listing 4-44).

Listing 4-44. Pass initial props to the init method of RCTRootView

```
...
let params = ["endpoint": "holmeshe.me/debug"]
let rootView = RCTRootView(bridge: self.bridge, moduleName:
"ManyFaces", initialProperties: params)
...
```

On *Android*, we can pass the initial properties in a similar way. One particularity here is that we use Bundle to populate the key and values this time, and we need to perform the **initial properties** in MainActivity. Next, we pass the same attributes as on *iOS* (Listing 4-45).

Listing 4-45. Pass initial props to the init method of the main activity (Android version)

```
class MainActivity: ReactActivity() {
  override fun getMainComponentName(): String? {
    return "ManyFaces"
  }

  override fun createReactActivityDelegate()
  : ReactActivityDelegate? {
    return object : ReactActivityDelegate(
      this, getMainComponentName()
    ) {
```

```kotlin
override fun getLaunchOptions(): Bundle? {
    val bundle = Bundle()
    bundle.putString("endpoint", "holmeshe.me/debug")
    return bundle
  }
 }
 }
}
```

On the *JavaScript* layer, **initial properties** are received as the **props** of the top-level **component** (normally, App) which is registered with the AppRegistry. As such, using setProperties to update these properties on the native layer is treated as a **prop** update, which triggers rerendering (Listing 4-46).

Listing 4-46. Access initial properties on the JavaScript layer

```javascript
componentDidMount() {
  console.log('initial properties:', this.props);

...
}
```

4.3.7 Dependency Injection

We all know that dependency injection is a million-dollar pattern. It helps decouple the software modules and make tests much easier. This section is not meant to explain dependency injection but to examine how to support dependency injection of **native modules** and **native components** on the *iOS* platform.

The instantiation of **native modules** and **native components** is performed implicitly using the RCT_EXTERN_MODULE, and the life cycle is managed by the *React Native* runtime ever since. This makes the dependency injection not feasible.

Note   We always manually instantiate the **native modules** and **native components** on *Android*; hence, the difficulty only exists on the *iOS* platform.

Luckily, ***React Native*** provides a way to manually control the life cycle of **native modules** and **native components** on *iOS*. In order to do so, we need to rely on the second option of initializing the bridge, that is, instead of initializing the bridge directly, we pass in a RCTBridgeDelegate instance to the bridge init method. This delegate provides the necessary information such as the location of the *JavaScript* bundle. Here, if we implement extraModulesForBridge() of the RCTBridgeDelegate, this delegate becomes responsible for provisioning extra **native modules** and **native components**. At this point, we shall perform proper dependency injection.

Let's look at the implementation details to have a better understanding. The RCT_EXTERN_MODULE (1) turns an ordinary class into a **native module** and (2) registers it with ***React Native***. Here, we only want step 1. As given in Listing 4-47, let's implement a macro to achieve that.

Note   The internal mechanisms of RCT_EXTERN_MODULE will be fully examined in Chapter 6.

Listing 4-47.   Custom macro to create a module

```
#define CREATE_MODULE(objc_name, objc_supername)              \
  objc_name:                                                  \
  objc_supername @                                            \
  end @interface objc_name(RCTExternModule)<RCTBridgeModule> \
  @end                                                        \
  @implementation objc_name (RCTExternModule)                 \
```

```
RCT_EXTERN void RCTRegisterModule(Class);              \
+(NSString *)moduleName                                \
{                                                      \
   return @ #objc_name;                                \
}
```

Next, in Listing 4-48, we use the CREATE_MODULE instead of
RCT_EXTERN_MODULE for the HelloWorldModule.

Listing 4-48. Use the new CREATE_MODULE

```
@interface RCT_EXTERN_MODULE(HelloViewManager, RCTViewManager)

RCT_EXTERN_METHOD(hello)

RCT_EXTERN_METHOD(setBlue:(int)reactTag)

RCT_EXPORT_VIEW_PROPERTY(bgColor, int)

@end
```

Lastly, we need to implement extraModulesForBridge in our
AppDelegate which is also a RCTBridgeDelegate (Listing 4-49).

Listing 4-49. Use the new CREATE_MODULE

```
@objc
func extraModulesForBridge(_ bridge: RCTBridge!) -> NSArray! {
   return [HelloWorldManager()]
}
```

This is how we can gain full control of HelloWorldModule by
instantiating it ourselves.

4.3.8 Key Takeaways

In this section, we covered some of the advanced techniques of **native modules** and **native components**. Firstly, we introduced the event system, a *native-to-JavaScript* communication mechanism. Then we demystify how to adopt a **react tag** to manipulate a specific **component**, which is required when designing advanced **native components**. We also covered some less common practices such as direct manipulation and synchronous method call, which are designed as an escape hatch that is only useful in certain situations. Moreover, we examined two ways to pass a configuration to the *JavaScript* layer, constants and initial properties. The former way is simple, while the latter is more versatile when the configuration can be determined or is required to be changed during runtime. Lastly, we introduced how to manually manage the life cycle of **native modules** and **native components** specifically on *iOS*, which is vital to implement dependency injection on the native layer.

Despite the diverse support of those features on both platforms, we have seen that it is always possible to make unanimous logic on the *JavaScript* layer, which is the key to cross-platform. In each section, we highlighted those differences in implementation and the best practice to mitigate them. Table 4-2 is the summary as a reminder.

Table 4-2. Summary of advanced native techniques

	Native module (iOS)	Native module (Android)	Native component (iOS)	Native component (Android)
Events	Inherits from RCTEventEmitter	getJSModule<>()?.emit()	Not supported	getJSModule<>()?.emit()
React tag	N/A	N/A	Ordinary native method	Command system
Direct manipulation	N/A	N/A	View property + react ref	View property + react ref
Synchronous method call	RCT_EXPORT_BLOCKING_ SYNCHRONOUS_METHOD	@ReactMethod(isBlockingSynch ronousMethod = true)	RCT_EXPORT_BLOCKING_ SYNCHRONOUS_METHOD	N/A
Export constants	Override constantsToExport	Override getConstants	Override constantsToExport	Override getConstants
Initial properties	Naturally supported	Naturally supported		Naturally supported
Dependency injection	Override extraModulesForBridge		Override extraModulesForBridge	

Before we move on to the hands-on, the last missing piece is the exception handling in the native layer. Let's get straight to it.

4.4 Exception Handling

Like on the *JavaScript* layer where all errors are translated into exceptions that need to be captured carefully, in the native layer exists a different set of exceptions. On *iOS*, some of those exceptions cannot be caught locally at all (e.g., *BAD_ACCESS*). Whenever occurring, they crash the app and hence are much riskier. If we enlist a C layer using techniques such as *JNI*, we also introduce another layer of exception flow. Now that we know that exceptions occurring in each layer (i.e., *JavaScript*, native, *C*) cannot be caught by another, we need to handle them separately and notify the upper layer whenever possible. The fact is that inappropriately handling exceptions in the native layer is one of the main causes of crashes.

One of the approaches is presented by `react-native-exception-handler`. Basically, it provides functions that can install a replaceable global exception handler that is responsible for all native exceptions. However, global exception handlers are less preferred than local ones as only the latter can maintain the current app state and can better offer graceful degradation or recovery (the principles of exception handling will be fully discussed in Chapter 6).

Note   `react-native-exception-handler` is among the awesome third-party libraries that are not used in our case studies. We reinvent some wheels for educational purposes. For example, rather than using react-native-video directly, we create a simplified version of a video **component** to better illustrate the critical parts of a **native component**, Here we decided to implement our own solution for exception handling so as to offer fine-grained exception boundaries.

Here, we escalate the responsibility of ErrorBoundary to catch not only UI exceptions but also exceptions from the native layer. To understand this design, let's consider *Manyface* that eventually evolves into a super app. In its ultimate form, *Manyface* includes not only moments but also payment, mini apps, instant messaging, and QR code discovery. Each feature resides in a stand-alone tab. Each tab is backed a full fledged team consisting of front end, back end, PM, testers dedicated to the feature. The last thing we want to see is that exceptions from one feature propagate to another. And we shall consider ErrorBoundary as the key to avoid such cross-module transgression. And we want to capture all exceptions within the native layer if the corresponding module knows how to handle it.

Another way to understand this design is to look at real-time strategy games, for example, *StarCraft* (Figure 4-17). One of the effective defending strategies is called a *wall-in*, in which defensive facilities are placed in the narrowed pass-throughs, a.k.a. critical points. So those reinforced, densified defense lines (or points) can take effect regardless of which directions or dimensions the rush is from. Here, we define ErrorBoundary as those strategic points, and exception rushes could be from both UI rendering in the *JavaScript* layer or from native.

***Figure 4-17.** Wall-in in StarCraft*

> **Note**   In the next chapter, we will see the exception could also be
> from asynchronous calls of slow operations such as network fetch.
> And we are going to introduce patterns to capture those exceptions in
> `ErrorBoundary` as well.

In the next section, we are going to apply the preceding design to the implementation of the video component.

4.5 Case Study – a Video Component

We have covered pretty much everything we need to know about **native modules** and **native components**. Now it's good timing to get back to *Manyface*. This time, we are going to support multimedia moments or video moments. Let's look at the requirements first (Figure 4-18):

1) Video clips are playable within the moment stream.

2) When the video card enters the viewport, the video playback starts automatically. Conversely, when the video card leaves the viewport, the video is paused.

Figure 4-18. *A video feed*

We take a bottom-up approach by implementing the **native components** first. For the second requirement, we rely on the **react tag** (Section 4.3.2) to control the video component.

4.5.1 iOS Implementation of a Video Component

First, let's look at the *iOS* implementation (Listing 4-50).

Listing 4-50. The video component

```
@objc(VideoViewManager)
class VideoViewManager: RCTViewManager {

  @objc(play:)
  func play(reactTag: Int) -> Void { // ------------------> 1)
    self.bridge.uiManager.addUIBlock(
{(uiManager: RCTUIManager?,
viewRegistry: [NSNumber: UIView]?) in
      guard let view =
      viewRegistry?[NSNumber.init(value: reactTag)]
      as? VideoView else {
        print("VideoView is nil in
        VideoViewManager::play()")//8
        return
      }

      view.play()
    })
  }

  @objc(pause:)
  func pause(reactTag: Int) -> Void { // ----------------> 1)
    self.bridge.uiManager.addUIBlock(
{(uiManager: RCTUIManager?,
viewRegistry: [NSNumber: UIView]?) in
      guard let view =
      viewRegistry?[NSNumber.init(value: reactTag)]
      as? VideoView else {
        print(
          "VideoView is nil in VideoViewManager::pause()"
        ) // ---------------------------------------------> 8)
```

```
        return
      }

      view.pause()
    })
  }

  @objc(view)
  override func view() -> UIView {
    let view = VideoView(); // ----------------------------> 2)
    return view
  }
}

class VideoView: UIView {
  var player: AVPlayer?
  var playerLayer: AVPlayerLayer?

  @objc(setSrc:)
  func setSrc(_ src: String) { // ------------------------> 3)
    guard let url = URL.init(string: src) else {
      print("url is nil in VideoView::setSrc()") // -------> 8)
      return
    }

    if player == nil { // ----------------------------------> 4)
      player = AVPlayer(url: url)

      assert(playerLayer == nil)

      playerLayer = AVPlayerLayer(player: player)
      playerLayer!.masksToBounds = true

      self.layer.addSublayer(playerLayer!)
    } else { // --------------------------------------------> 5)
```

```
      assert(playerLayer != nil)

      playerLayer?.removeFromSuperlayer()

      player = AVPlayer(url: url)

      playerLayer = AVPlayerLayer(player: player)
      playerLayer!.masksToBounds = true
      self.layer.addSublayer(playerLayer!)
    }
  }

  func play() { // ----------------------------------------> 6)
    guard let player = player else {
      print("player is nil in VideoView::play()") // ------> 8)
      return
    }
    player.play()
  }

  func pause() { // ---------------------------------------> 6)
    guard let player = player else {
      print("player is nil in VideoView::pause()") // -----> 8)
      return
    }
    player.pause()
  }

  override func layoutSubviews() { // ---------------------> 7)
    super.layoutSubviews()

    guard let layer = playerLayer else {
      print("layer is nil in VideoView::layoutSubviews()") //> 8)
      return
    }
```

```
    layer.frame = self.bounds;
  }
}
```

1) Implement both methods that take a **react tag** as in Section 4.3.2.3, which in turn invoke the customer view's corresponding methods.

2) Return a custom view that wraps the original native view as discussed in Section 4.1.1.2. And we are going to do the same on *Android* and keep a consistent interface and properties.

3) Implement the src property.

4) Initialize the AVPlayer and its AVPlayerLayer counterpart when the src is set the first time.

5) Instantiate new AVPlayer and its AVPlayerLayer and replace the old ones with them.

6) Implement the custom view's play() and pause() methods.

7) layoutSubviews() is invoked when the *React Native* engine has completed the layout of the **native views**. We use this callback to lay out the AVPlayerLayer that is not aware of *React Native*.

8) We leave the exception handling as simple logs for now. Later, they will be replaced with real handling mechanisms.

We also need to remember exporting the **native component** along with its property from the bridge file (Listing 4-51).

Listing 4-51. Export the video component

```
@interface RCT_EXTERN_MODULE(VideoViewManager, RCTViewManager)

RCT_EXPORT_VIEW_PROPERTY(src, NSString)

RCT_EXTERN_METHOD(play:(int)reactTag)

RCT_EXTERN_METHOD(pause:(int)reactTag)

@end
```

4.5.2 Android Implementation of a Video Component

Next, let's continue by implementing the ***Android*** counterpart (Listing 4-52).

Listing 4-52. The video component (Android version)

```
class VideoViewManager: SimpleViewManager<Video> {
  companion object {
    val REACT_CLASS = "VideoView" // ---------------------> 1)

    private const val COMMAND_PLAY = "play" // ------------> 2)
    private const val COMMAND_PLAY_VAL = 1

    private const val COMMAND_PAUSE = "pause" // ----------> 2)
    private const val COMMAND_PAUSE_VAL = 2
  }

  private var mCallerContext: ReactApplicationContext? = null

  constructor(reactContext: ReactApplicationContext?):
  super() {
    mCallerContext = reactContext
  }
```

```
override fun getName(): String {
  return REACT_CLASS // ---------------------------------> 1)
}

override fun createViewInstance(
  reactContext:ThemedReactContext
): Video {
  return Video(mCallerContext)
}

override fun getCommandsMap() = mapOf( // ---------------> 2)
  COMMAND_PLAY to COMMAND_PLAY_VAL,
  COMMAND_PAUSE to COMMAND_PAUSE_VAL
)

override fun receiveCommand(
  view: Video, commandId: String, args: ReadableArray?
) {
  when (commandId) { // ----------------------------------> 3)
    COMMAND_PLAY -> {
      view.play()
    }
    COMMAND_PAUSE -> {
      view.pause()
    }
  }
}

@ReactProp(name = "src") // ------------------------------> 4)
fun setSrc(view: Video, src: String) {
  view.setSrc(src)
}
}
```

```kotlin
class Video: VideoView { // --------------------------------> 5)
  private var mCallerContext: ReactApplicationContext? = null

  constructor(context: ReactApplicationContext?)
  : super(context) {
    mCallerContext = context
  }

  override fun onLayout(
    changed: Boolean,
    l: Int,
    t: Int,
    r: Int,
    b: Int
  ) {}

  fun play() { // ---------------------------------------> 6)
    this.start()
  }

  override fun pause() { // -------------------------------> 6)
    super.pause()
  }

  public fun setSrc(src: String) { // --------------------> 6)
    val uri: Uri = Uri.parse(src)

    this.setVideoURI(uri)
  }
}
```

1) Export the view named VideoView, the same as on *iOS*.

2) Declare all the commands the **native component** supports. This is the equivalent of the native methods on *iOS*.

3) Apply the commands to the concrete custom **native view**.

4) Export the `src` **view property**, the same as on *iOS*.

5) Create the custom native view. We name the class `Video` as `VideoView` is used by the *Android* stock view we want to inherit from. Note that the name exported in step 1 to the *JavaScript* layer is still `VideoView`.

6) Implement the native methods and **view properties** for the custom **native view**, the same as on *iOS*.

You might have noticed here that the **view manager** inherits from `SimpleViewManager`; 💣 hence, the **component** backed by the **native view** exported cannot work as a container. This limitation is caused by the fact that the *Android* `VideoView` is a `SurfaceView` instead of a `ViewGroup`. We are going to mitigate this issue with an abstraction on the *JavaScript* layer (Section 4.2.3.2). And that will be our first task when implementing the *JavaScript* layer of this feature.

4.5.3 JavaScript Layer

4.5.3.1 Native Component Wrapper

As a reminder, a *JavaScript* wrapper of **native components** (Section 4.2.3.2) is recommended for easing out platform discrepancies (Listing 4-53).

Listing 4-53. JavaScript wrapper of the native component

```
let VideoView = requireNativeComponent('VideoView');

class Video extends React.Component {
  constructor() {
    super();
  }

  render() {
    return (
      <View style={this.props.style}> // ------------------> 1)
        <VideoView
          {...this.props} // ----------------------------> 2)
          style={StyleSheet.absoluteFill} // -------------> 3)
          ref={this.props.videoRef} // ------------------> 4)
        />
        {this.props.children} // -----------------------> 5)
      </View>
    );
  }
};

export default Video;
```

1) The container accepts styles passed from the outside. So the consumer can lay out the **component** in design.

2) VideoView accepts the specialized **props**, for example, src, to work properly.

3) VideoView overrides any **styles** accidentally passed down through **props** with StyleSheet. absoluteFill. This makes the **component** a background layer of the **component** in design.

4) Forward any refs passed in using videoRef.

5) Lay out the **children** as always.

4.5.3.2 View Manager Wrapper

Next, we encapsulate the **view manager** (Listing 4-54).

Listing 4-54. JavaScript wrapper of the view manager

```
class VideoViewManager {
  static play(reactTag) {
    if (Platform.OS === 'ios') {
      NativeModules.VideoViewManager.play(reactTag);
    } else {
      UIManager.dispatchViewManagerCommand(reactTag,
      'play', []);
    }
  }

  static pause(reactTag) {
    if (Platform.OS === 'ios') {
      NativeModules.VideoViewManager.pause(reactTag);
    } else {
      UIManager.dispatchViewManagerCommand(reactTag,
      'pause', []);
    }
  }
};

export default VideoViewManager;
```

4.5.3.3 Video Feed

Next, we add a new feed category that is designed to populate video content. Let's create the feed **component** (Listing 4-55) first.

Listing 4-55. JavaScript wrapper of the native component

```
class FeedVideo extends React.Component {
  constructor() {
    super();

    this.videoTag = undefined;
  }

  render() {
    return (
      <>
        <ExpandableText
          style={styles.textPost}
          text={this.props.item.feed.text}
        />
        <Video style={styles.videoPost} // ----------------> 1)
          src={this.props.item.feed.videoUri} // ----------> 2)
          videoRef={(ref) => { // -------------------------> 3)
            this.videoTag = findNodeHandle(ref); // -------> 3)
          }}
        />
      </>
    )
  }

  onVisible() { // -----------------------------------------> 4)
    if (this.videoTag) {
      VideoViewManager.play(this.videoTag);
    }
```

```
  }

  onHidden() { // ------------------------------------------> 4)
    if (this.videoTag) {
      VideoViewManager.pause(this.videoTag);
    }
  }
}

const styles = StyleSheet.create({ // ---------------------> 5)
  textPost: {
    marginBottom: 20,
  },
  videoPost: {
    width: '100%',
    aspectRatio: 4/3,
    marginBottom: 20,
  },
});

export default withErrorBoundary(
  withMetaAndControls(FeedVideo), undefined, undefined
);
```

1) Use the video component created in the previous steps.

2) Apply a different set of **props** as we are creating another layer of abstraction.

3) Hide the videoRef and carry out the actual native method call at this layer.

4) Encapsulate the native method call here. This layer of abstraction transfers the concerns from play/

pause to onVisible/onHidden ones which are more relevant to a feed. Actually, other feeds can implement those same methods when required. Eventually, these two methods are called by the Moment when appropriate.

5)   The rest of the code is the same as an ordinary feed.

Note   Again, we believe that wrong abstraction is more expensive than no abstraction at all. So we only introduce a layer of abstraction when absolutely necessary.

And we add the provisioning logic of the newly created feed type in the FeedFactory (Listing 4-56).

Listing 4-56. Provisioning of a video feed

```
export default function FeedFactory(props) {
  let numOfImages = props.item?.feed?.images?.length;

+ if (props.item?.feed?.videoUri) { // --------------------> 1)
+   return <FeedVideo {...props}/>
+ }

  if (numOfImages > 4 && numOfImages <= 9) { // -----------> 2)
    return <Feed3x3 {...props}/>;
  } else if (numOfImages > 1 && numOfImages <= 4) {
    return <Feed2x2 {...props}/>;
  } else if (numOfImages === 1) {
    return <Feed {...props}/>;
  }

  return null;
}
```

1) Use the existence of `videoUri` as an indicator of a video feed.

2) The rest logic in the `FeedFactory` is kept the same.

4.5.3.4 Ref Forwarding

We hide the `Video` **component** and its corresponding native module inside the `FeedVideo`. This is the correct layer of abstraction. However, this design leads to a challenge; the method of `Video` cannot be called directly in `Moment`. This is because of the several intermediate proxies such as `FeedFactory` and **HOCs** (Section 2.2) that hide the actual **react ref** we want to obtain.

We need to apply the technique called *ref forwarding* to all the intermediate proxies to resolve this issue. The method in use is `React.forwardRef`. It is worth noting that the implementation detail of *ref forwarding* is slightly different for class **components** and functional **components** working as the intermediate proxy. Let's look at `FeedFactory` first which is a functional **component** (Listing 4-57).

Listing 4-57. Enhance FeedFactory with ref forwarding

```
+-const FeedFactory = React.forwardRef((props, ref) => {
// -> 1)
    let numOfImages = props.item?.feed?.images?.length;

    if (props.item?.feed?.videoUri) {
+-      return <FeedVideo {...props} ref={ref} /> // --------> 2)
    }

    if (numOfImages > 4 && numOfImages <= 9) {
      return <Feed3x3 {...props} ref={ref}/>;
    } else if (numOfImages > 1 && numOfImages <= 4) {
      return <Feed2x2 {...props} ref={ref}/>;
```

```
  } else if (numOfImages === 1) {
    return <Feed {...props} ref={ref}/>;
  }

  return null;
});
```

```
export default FeedFactory;
```

1) A functional **component** accepts the ref directly from React.forwardRef.

2) Pass the ref down to the product **components**.

Next, we look at withMetaAndControls which is a **HOC** based on class **components** (Listing 4-58).

Listing 4-58. Enhance withMetaAndControls with ref forwarding

```
export default function withMetaAndControls(Feed) {
  class ElemComponent extends React.Component {
    render() {
      return (
        <View style={[
          {...this.props.style},
          styles.commonPadding]}
        >
          <View style={styles.metaContainer}>
            <LoomingImage
              style={styles.avatar}
              source={{uri: this.props.item.meta.avatarUri}}
            />
            <View style={styles.infoContainer}>
              <Text style={styles.userName}>
                {this.props.item.meta.name}</Text>
```

```
        <Text style={styles.date}>
          {this.props.item.meta.date}
        </Text>
      </View>
    </View>
+-      <Feed {...this.props} ref={this.props.
    innerRef}/> //>2)
    <View style={styles.controlContainer}>
      <NumberedWidget
        style={{flex: 1}} type={widgetTypes.LIKE}
        number={this.props.item.meta.numOfLikes}
      />
      <NumberedWidget style={{flex: 1}}
        type={widgetTypes.COMMENT}
        number={this.props.item.meta.numOfComments}
      />
      <NumberedWidget style={{flex: 1.5}}
        type={widgetTypes.SHARE}
        number={this.props.item.meta.numOfShares}
      />
      <Widget type={widgetTypes.MORE} />
    </View>
  </View>
  )
  }
 }

+ return React.forwardRef((props, ref) => <ElemComponent
+   innerRef={ref} {...props} // --------------------------> 1)
+ />);
}
```

1) Use `innerRef` to avoid conflict with the `ref` **prop** of a class **component**.

2) Pass the `innerRef` down as `ref` to the designated **component**.

The `withErrorBoundary` is enabled with **ref forwarding** in the same way. Hence, we omit the code here.

4.5.3.5 Video Feed in Moment

We need to fetch the **react refs** of all feeds so we can control them in accordance with their visible state as in the third requirement. With **ref forwarding** explained in the last section, we can simply pass the **react ref** as if there are no intermediate proxy. Technically, this is done in the `renderItem` method of `Moment` which is in turn passed in as a **prop** to the `FlatList` (Listing 4-59).

Listing 4-59. Obtain the refs of all feeds

```
class Moment extends React.Component {
...
  renderItem = (entry) => {
    return (
      <FeedFactory
+       ref={(ref) => {
+         this.feedRefs[entry.index] = ref;
+       }}
        item={entry.item}
      />
    );
  }
...
```

We use the onViewableItemsChanged of FlatList to be notified of the visibility state of each feed. Let's have a look at its implementation. The logic is straightforward and hence will not be further explained (Listing 4-60).

Listing 4-60. Provisioning of a video feed

```
...
  onViewableItemsChanged = (result) => {
    let {changed, viewableItems} = result;

    for (item of changed) {
      let visible = false;
      for (i of viewableItems) {
        if (item.index === i.index) {
          visible = true;
          break;
        }
      }

      if (visible){
        if (
          typeof this.feedRefs[item.index]?.onVisible ===
          'function'
        ) {
          this.feedRefs[item.index]?.onVisible();
        }
      } else {
        if (typeof this.feedRefs[item.index]?.onHidden ===
          'function'
        ) {
          this.feedRefs[item.index]?.onHidden();
        }
```

```
        }
      }
    }
...
```

This method is passed as a **prop** of the same name of `FlatList`.

4.5.4 Reinforced Video Component

This is a follow-up of the theoretical part of exception handling of the
native layer (Section 4.4). We are going to use the callback **view properties**
(Sections 4.2.1.3 and 4.2.2.3) to implement the exception flow that is across
JavaScript and native layers.

As usual, now that all visible requirements are implemented, we need
to continue with the hidden requirements. Again, let's recall one of the
most important principles for implementing a robust exception flow: clear
boundary.

In that spirit, we can now derive the end goal. Whenever exceptions
occur in the `VideoView` in the native layer, we want it to trigger the
predefined exception flow of an ordinary feed, that is, to hide it. More
specifically, this design decision is because exceptions thrown in a feed
should be captured by the feed and be treated equally in regard to the
visual and UX. This is regardless of which layer the exception comes from.
After all, the feed **component** processes the best knowledge of the UX of
the feed. Thus, it holds the final call to what should be presented to the
user when an exception occurs within.

After we define the requirements, we need to force the **native
component** throws to the *JavaScript* layer. The best way is to add an
`onException` callback **view property** to the **component** (Sections 4.2.1.3
and 4.2.2.3).

Note   Now the key points discussed throughout the chapter seem to come together.

4.5.4.1 Protect the iOS Component

Let's get into the code directly and see how a well-protected **view manager** looks like.

Firstly, let's add a utility function to throw the exception to the *JavaScript* layer (Listing 4-61).

Listing 4-61.   Provisioning of a video feed

```
+ func throwToJS(_ e: Error) {
+   if self.onException == nil {
+     self.unThrownException = e
+     return
+   }
+   self.onException?(["exception": "\(e)"])
+ }
```

This method temporarily stores the exception if the onException is yet not sent. Otherwise, it simply fires the exception to the *JavaScript* layer using **props**. The stored value will be used in step 5 of when we further the implementation of the VideoViewManager.

Then we can leverage this method to protect the VideoViewManager (Listing 4-62).

Listing 4-62.   Protected view manager

```
+enum VideoViewManagerError: Error { // ------------------> 1)
+    case runtimeError(String)
+}
```

```
@objc(VideoViewManager)
class VideoViewManager: RCTViewManager {
  var player: AVPlayer?
  var playerLayer: AVPlayerLayer?

  @objc(play:)
  func play(reactTag: Int) -> Void {
    self.bridge.uiManager.addUIBlock(
      {(uiManager: RCTUIManager?,
     viewRegistry: [NSNumber: UIView]?) in
        guard let view =
        viewRegistry?[NSNumber.init(value: reactTag)]
              as? VideoView else { // -------------------> 2)
          print("VideoView is nil in VideoViewManager::play()")
          return
        }
+       do { // --------------------------------------------> 3)
+-        try view.play()
+       } catch {
+         view.throwToJS(error) // -----------------------> 4)
+       }
      })
  }

  @objc(pause:)
  func pause(reactTag: Int) -> Void {
    self.bridge.uiManager.addUIBlock(
      {(uiManager: RCTUIManager?,
     viewRegistry: [NSNumber: UIView]?) in
        guard let view =
        viewRegistry?[NSNumber.init(value: reactTag)]
              as? VideoView else { // -------------------> 2)
```

```
        print("VideoView is nil in
VideoViewManager::pause()")
        return
      }

+      do { // -----------------------------------------> 3)
+-        try view.pause()
+      } catch {
+        view.throwToJS(error) // -----------------------> 4)
+      }
    })
  }

  @objc(view)
  override func view() -> UIView {
    let view = VideoView();
    return view
  }
}

class VideoView: UIView {
  var player: AVPlayer?
  var playerLayer: AVPlayerLayer?
+ var onException: RCTBubblingEventBlock?
+ var unThrownException: Error?

+ @objc(setOnException:) // -------------------------------> 5)
+ func setOnException(
+   _ onException: @escaping RCTBubblingEventBlock
+ ) {
+   if let e = self.unThrownException {
+     onException(["exception": "\(e)"])
+     return
```

```
+   }
+
+   self.onException = onException
+ }

  @objc(setSrc:)
  func setSrc(_ src: String) {
    do { // ---------------------------------------------> 6)
      guard let url = URL.init(string: src) else {
+-        throw VideoViewManagerError.runtimeError("url is nil in
          VideoView::setSrc()")
      }

      if player == nil {
        player = AVPlayer(url: url)

        if (playerLayer != nil) {
+-          throw VideoViewManagerError.runtimeError("playerLayer
            is not nil while player is in VideoView::setSrc()")
            // ------> 6)
        }

        playerLayer = AVPlayerLayer(player: player)
        playerLayer!.masksToBounds = true

        self.layer.addSublayer(playerLayer!)
      } else {
        if (playerLayer == nil) {
+-          throw VideoViewManagerError.runtimeError("playerLayer
            is nil in VideoView::setSrc()") // --------------> 6)
        }

        playerLayer?.removeFromSuperlayer()

        player = AVPlayer(url: url)
```

```
          playerLayer = AVPlayerLayer(player: player)
          playerLayer!.masksToBounds = true
          self.layer.addSublayer(playerLayer!)
        }
+     } catch {
+        self.throwToJS(error) // --------------------------> 4)
+     }
   }

+-func play() throws {
     guard let player = player else {
+-       throw VideoViewManagerError.runtimeError("player is nil
         in VideoView::play()") // -------------------------> 6)
     }
     player.play()
   }

+-func pause() throws {
     guard let player = player else {
+-       throw VideoViewManagerError.runtimeError("player is
         nil in VideoView::pause()") // ---------------------> 6)
     }
     player.pause()
   }

   override func layoutSubviews() {
     super.layoutSubviews()

     guard let layer = playerLayer else {
+-       self.throwToJS(VideoViewManagerError.runtimeError("layer
         is nil in VideoView::layoutSubviews()")) // ---------> 4)
         return
     }
```

```
    layer.frame = self.bounds;
  }
...
}
```

1) Define the Error type for this **view manager**.

2) Log and do nothing for now since even the **native view** is not available. In practice, this is also an unrecoverable system error when a view cannot be retrieved using a **react tag**. This kind of error could be treated the same as a BAD_ACCESS that aborts the app.

3) Wrap every entry point of our own logic in the **view manager**.

4) Call the throwToJS of the corresponding native view whenever an exception occurs.

5) Implement the callback **view property**. Here, if an exception occurs prior to this point, for example, in the setter of other **view properties**, fire the exception immediately.

6) Throw the exception whenever unexpected conditions are met. And the logic eventually flows to step 4 which is handled by throwToJS.

4.5.4.2 Protect the Android Component

Next, we implement the *Android* version (Listing 4-63).

Listing 4-63. Protected view manager (Android version)

```
class VideoViewManager : SimpleViewManager<Video> {
  companion object {
    val REACT_CLASS = "VideoView"

    private const val COMMAND_PLAY = "play"
    private const val COMMAND_PLAY_VAL = 1

    private const val COMMAND_PAUSE = "pause"
    private const val COMMAND_PAUSE_VAL = 2
  }

  private var mCallerContext: ReactApplicationContext? = null

  constructor(reactContext: ReactApplicationContext?) :
    super() {
    mCallerContext = reactContext
  }

  override fun getName(): String {
    return REACT_CLASS
  }

  override fun createViewInstance(
reactContext: ThemedReactContext
  ): Video {
    return Video(mCallerContext)
  }

  override fun getCommandsMap() = mapOf(
    COMMAND_PLAY to COMMAND_PLAY_VAL,
    COMMAND_PAUSE to COMMAND_PAUSE_VAL
  )
```

```
  override fun receiveCommand(
view: Video, commandId: String, args: ReadableArray?
  ) {
+   try { // ---------------------------------------------> 2)
+     throw Exception()
+     when (commandId) {
+       COMMAND_PLAY -> {
+         view.play()
+       }
+       COMMAND_PAUSE -> {
+         view.pause()
+       }
+     }
+   } catch (e: Exception) {
+     view.throwsToJs(e) // --------------------------------> 3)
+   }
  }

+ override fun getExportedCustomBubblingEventTypeConstants() =
+   mapOf( // --------------------------------------------> 1)
+     "onException" to
+             mapOf(
+               "phasedRegistrationNames" to
+                     mapOf("bubbled" to "onException")
+             )
+   )

  @ReactProp(name = "src")
  fun setSrc(view: Video, src: String) {
+   try { // ---------------------------------------------> 3)
      view.setSrc(src)
+   } catch (e: Exception) {
```

```
+      view.throwsToJs(e) // ------------------------------> 3)
+    }
  }
}

class Video : VideoView {
  private var mCallerContext: ReactApplicationContext? = null

  constructor(context: ReactApplicationContext?):
  super(context) {
    mCallerContext = context
  }

  override fun onLayout(
changed: Boolean, l: Int, t: Int, r: Int, b: Int
  ) {}

  fun play() {
    this.start()
  }

  override fun pause() {
    super.pause()
  }

  public fun setSrc(src: String) {
    val uri: Uri = Uri.parse(src)

    this.setVideoURI(uri)
    this.start()
  }
+ public fun throwsToJs(e: Exception) { // ----------------> 3)
+    val event: WritableMap = Arguments.createMap()
+    event.putString("exception", e.localizedMessage)
```

```
+    mCallerContext?.getJSModule(
+    RCTEventEmitter::class.java)?.receiveEvent(
+      id,
+      "onException",
+      event
+    )
+  }
}
```

1) Declare the onException callback **view property** (Section 4.2.2.3).

2) Wrap every entry point of the **view manager** with try catch. Call the throwsToJs of the corresponding **native view** to notify the *JavaScript* layer that something went wrong.

3) Implement the throwsToJs using the command system on *Android* (Section 4.2.2.3).

4.5.4.3 JavaScript Layer

The last piece is the *JavaScript* layer. Here, we simply throw an exception that can be caught by the ErrorBoundary with the predefined behaviors (Listing 4-64).

Listing 4-64. Throw the exception to ErrorBoundary

```
let VideoView = requireNativeComponent('VideoView');

class Video extends React.Component {
  constructor() {
    super();
  }
```

```
+ onException = (e) => {
+   this.setState(() => { // ----------------------------> 1)
+     throw {
+       name: 'Video Error',
+       description: e?.nativeEvent?.exception
+     }
+   });
+ }

  render() {
    return (
      <View style={this.props.style}>
        <VideoView
          {...this.props}
          style={StyleSheet.absoluteFill}
          ref={this.props.videoRef}
+         onException={this.onException}
        />
        {this.props.children}
      </View>
    );
  }
};

export default Video;
```

1) Rethrow the native exception with the message
   populated.

Now we have connected the exception flow from the native layer to the *JavaScript* layer, and all the nice redefined behaviors of `ErrorBoundary` can now be activated to also account for native exceptions. As a reminder, for feeds, whenever an exception occurs within its boundary, the feed card will be made invisible to not bother the user while applying the silent logging in the meantime.

4.6 Summary

We have covered everything you need to know about native development. Though a typical *React Native* team should work mostly on *JavaScript* for business logic and UIs, the fluid part. It is still desired for you, or some mates on your team, to dominate the hardcore mobile development and to clear the technical blockers on the path to a **05 app**.

In this chapter, we went through discrete points spanning from basics to topics that are quite advanced. We firstly learned how to create **native modules** and **native components** and got to know some particularities on each platform. Based on that, we continued examining some of the advanced topics of **native modules** and **native components** as well as the bidirectional communication between *JavaScript* and native layers. Then, with a dedicated section, we expanded our exception handling pattern by including the native layer in the picture, and we found it a cool name, *wall-in*.

And, oh! *Manyface* supports video feeds now. Yeah!!!

CHAPTER 5

Network Programming

Most modern apps would be useless without a network. This is true for *Manyface* and other real-world apps alike. A network, on the other hand, is complex and is rough at times. This is especially true for a mobile network where even the connectivity could be nondeterministic and intermittent. This scenario of weak connection continuously challenges mobile apps, and the solution logic flow cannot be easily tested, verified, or validated. A network also contributes a large bulk of waiting time, and anxiety, to the users. This is because network latency (approximately tens to hundreds of milliseconds for WAN RTT (round-trip time)) is by magnitude greater than that imposed by logic or the UI (~16.6 milliseconds). Without the content fetched from a network, any discussion on rendering time optimization is futile. To make peace with the network, we need to understand its nature, and this is the purpose of this chapter.

Note   Always checking using the network conditioner is a good practice to make sure the app is working well in critical network conditions.

Network programming is a broad topic. Covering everything in such an area is neither the best interest of nor feasible for this book. In the meantime, network programming is sophisticated. It's hard to grasp the "why" of practical techniques without the understanding of its basic building blocks, the fundamentals. In order to make the best out of it,

© M. Holmes He 2022
M. H. He, *Creating Apps with React Native*, https://doi.org/10.1007/978-1-4842-8042-3_5

we take an approach by only striking through the critical points of network programming that are directly related to app development. In terms of network fundamentals, we are going to emphasize two protocols, TCP and HTTP, throughout our discussion.

This chapter is divided into four parts: (1) TCP/IP 101, (2) network programming in *JavaScript*, (3) network programming on the native layer, and (4) new updates on the modern Internet.

The first few sections start with a refreshment on the basics of network protocols. Those have been around since the good old days. Based on that, we discuss some of the new updates of network protocols and practices aiming to improve performance and/or versatility. In the meantime, we are going to equip ourselves with diagnostic tools such as tcpdump, tcptrace, and mitmproxy. Another goal we set for this section is to help you to fully understand some of the frequent albeit enigmatic network terms used in various tech talks such as bufferbloat.

The second section focuses on the *JavaScript* layer. In particular, we are going to focus on the asynchronous operations in *JavaScript* and one of its instances, `fetch`, which is the major *JavaScript* method for fetching network resources. We conclude the second part with a case study by moving all the data used for *Manyface* online. So, from that point on, *Manyface* will need to fetch *feeds* from an endpoint.

The third part is the native layer. Again, native programming is needed for critical tasks such as big file downloading and connectivity detection. For the latter task, we are going to introduce and examine another third-party library, *react-native-netinfo*. This section concludes with a cross-platform download module for videos.

Let's march forward.

5.1 A Very Brief Introduction to TCP/IP

Note   As the name of TCP/IP implies, there are two major purposes for network engineering: (a) to identify a node on the network (IP) and (b) to deliver data (TCP). Combined with network types (i.e., WAN and LAN), we can derive the metrics of protocols that are currently in use on today's Internet.

In the sense of software engineering, a network stack is a software module, and protocols are its submodules. From the network communication point of view, protocols define sets of rules so that the sender and receiver can talk to each other. It's like you fill this field with a magic number, and I know what you mean. So, we can think of protocols as the "black speeches" in the network world.

A network stack is designed in layers. A network layer is an abstract concept, and each of them is assigned with a general purpose. For instance, layer 4 is assigned with transmitting data on WAN; layer 3 is to identify a node on WAN; and layer 2 is designed to both identify a node and to transmit data on LANs. The following are the layers in the TCP/IP stack:

1) Physical layer

2) Ethernet layer

3) IP layer

4) Transport layer

5) Application layer

A layer might consist of one or more protocols. A protocol defines a concrete way or "how" to achieve the "purpose" assigned to the layer the protocol belongs to. For instance, in layer 2, ARP is responsible for node identifying, and Ethernet is for packet delivery. Both protocols

243

work on LANs. In layer 3, we have a sole protocol, IP, that is used for node identifying in WAN; and in layer 4, TCP and UDP are the two main protocols for packet delivery in WAN. Although belonging to the same layer, TCP and UDP achieve the purpose of data delivery in completely different ways. TCP tries its best to deliver packets in order as a stream. Meanwhile, it accounts for network congestion and retransition in case of packet loss. On the other hand, UDP tries its best to send packets, and then ¯_(ツ)_/¯.

Due to the seemingly unreliability of UDP, it has been dwarfed by its accountable brother TCP. However, everything has a flip side to it. This time, the flip side is performance overhead. For years, the industry has been exploring UDP for reliable connection while demanding less system resources than TCP. And we will see soon in this chapter such an initiative from Google.

Layers 2–4 are all general-purpose layers. Based on that foundation, layer 5 (a.k.a. the application layer) thrives in vast diversity. The most important one is HTTP. Based on TCP, HTTP is designed to transmit text-based data between the server and web browsers. Due to its simplicity, HTTP is also one of the most commonly used protocols that facilitates traffic not only for the Web but for many apps like *Manyface*. Another important application layer protocol is DNS which provides a domain name to IP address translation. DNS is based on UDP. SSH is another commonly used protocol based on TCP. It is designed to offer secured communication for administrators to operate network servers and devices.

All the data transmitted on the network needs to go through the network stack, or, more specifically, layers of protocols. So the network stack also works as a pipeline that decorates and dismantles data that are either received from the previous layer or sent to the next.

Each protocol is a processing unit on this pipeline. Programmatically, protocols are defined in headers which are attached to the data payload layer by layer. The structure and information embedded in protocol headers varies a lot due to the different tasks each protocol is designed for. For example, an ID (MAC address) is required to identify a machine on a LAN, so the ID is included in the layer 2 ARP header. Similarly, an IP address, another ID, is included in layer 3 IP to identify a machine on a WAN. Like data structures in any other program, protocol header fields can reflect how a packet is organized and transmitted (logically and physically) and how it is processed by each protocol.

Next, let's follow a trip of a pseudo packet. As illustrated in Figure 5-1, when an outbound packet is sent by an application, it goes downward to the network stack. Each time the packet reaches a layer, it is selectively processed by a certain protocol and is filled with the protocol header. Then the header is attached to the packet before it is pushed down to the next layer. All the involved protocols concatenate their respective headers during the process and form the final outgoing data frame that is eventually transmitted on the physical medium. To recap, the headers are attached to the front of the packet in a top-down manner in the order of layers. That means the header of layer 4 is attached first, and that of layer 2 is attached last.

When an inbound packet arrives, it travels from the NIC hardware upward through layers. As depicted in Figure 5-1, protocols in each layer (1) read the headers that are populated by the same protocol on the sender side, (2) process them using the information extracted, (3) strip the header that has been processed, and (4) push the packet upward to the next layer. This occurs for every layer until the payload reaches the application layer.

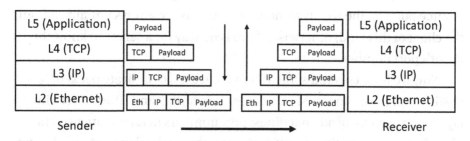

Figure 5-1. *Processing of protocol headers*

For each of the layers beneath the application layer, the operating system (or libraries) is responsible for handling packets sent from/received by the host. So the IDs in those layers are used to identify the host itself (in different networks). In the application layer, however, there are multiple executable instances (i.e., applications such as postfix, nginx, ssh server, *Manyface*, etc.), so we need yet another ID to identify them.

In order to deliver packets meant for a specific app, that is, an incoming email to postfix, an HTTP request to an Nginx, an ssh prompt message to an Xshell client, and a feed to *Manyface*, we use port numbers that are agreed on between the clients and servers. Because a network stack needs to know the destination process of a packet before it reaches the application layer (layer 5), port numbers are defined in layer 4.

There are default port numbers for common servers, and all clients that want to talk to those servers implicitly include the predefined port numbers in the outbound packets (dest port) sending to the server process running in a remote host. For example, 80 is used for HTTP, 22 is used for SSH, and 25 for SMTP (email). A process, either a server or a client, can listen to any port number provided the number has not been bound by another. Otherwise, a "port conflict" exception will be raised by the port binding API so the process should fail.

Because of the ephemeral nature of client side, apps use temporal port numbers (of very big numbers to avoid port conflict). The port is allocated when a client process initializes and is released when the process terminates. The client tells a server its temporal port in the first packet (source port) on the run as all network sessions are always initialized from the client of this kind; otherwise, there is no way for a server to know the client's port number.

Now we have covered some IDs that are used to indicate packets' destination. In summary, MAC addresses in layer 2 and IP addresses in layer 3 are used to locate machines; port numbers in layer 4 are used to identify processes within a host. This is pretty much all the network IDs we need to know. Easier than thought, eh?

In the following, we are going to go through in detail each of the important protocols one by one. To deepen the understanding of the core concepts, we also prepare some hands-on experiments by inspecting the packets. It is highly recommended to set up the tools for network inspecting and carry on those experiments.

5.1.1 TCP

The purpose of TCP is to provide continuous and reliable data delivery between two nodes. Let's take an example; the data is sent as "abc" (in reality, it is binary instead of ASCII) from one side, and somehow it is received as "bac." This is a case of out-of-order packets. Another example, the data is sent as "abc," and it is received as "abbccc." It is called duplication. Last one, the same "abc," then only "ac" is received. This is a packet loss. Worse, all the preceding cases could compound due to the unpredictable temperament of the network. The purpose of TCP is to recover the received data back to "abc" regardless of the situation.

The solution of TCP is straightforward – to tag packets. In doing so, each packet is marked with an ordered unique number, a.k.a. a sequence number. With those numbers, TCP can recover the original data by reordering the out of order, deduplicating the duplicates, and asking for retransmission in packet loss. To agree on those numbers, the three-way handshake comes into play. The sequence number is contained in the TCP header which is attached to every TCP segment.

Offset Octet		0									1									2									3							
Octet	Bit	7	6	5	4	3	2	1	0	7	6	5	4	3	2	1	0	7	6	5	4	3	2	1	0	7	6	5	4	3	2	1	0
0	0	Source Port																Destination Port															
4	32	Sequence number (SEQ)																															
8	64	Acknowledgement number (ACK)																															
12	96	Data offset				Reserved			...	...	...	...	A C K	P S H	R S T	S Y N	F I N	Window size (Sliding window)															
16	##	Checksum																...															

Figure 5-2. *TCP header*

The TCP header is given in Figure 5-2. We have covered very briefly what (source and destination) ports are. The other fields that are of interest are the acknowledgment number, SYN, ACK, FIN, and Window size. We will cover them in the following sections.

5.1.1.1 Three-Way Handshake (Opening Connection)

The three-way handshake is the preamble of all TCP connections. As mentioned, the major purpose of the three-way handshake is to agree on the sequence number attached to the segments from both sides. Let's observe a real network request. In the process, we will also map the output of *tcpdump* and the corresponding fields in the TCP header.

Firstly, we open two command-line windows and execute `curl holmeshe.me` and `sudo tcpdump -ntS host holmeshe.me` on each window, respectively. Listing 5-1 gives the tcpdump output.

Listing 5-1. Three-way handshake

```
IP 10.10.0.194.64608 > 104.248.189.33.80: Flags [S], seq
271799524, win 65535, options [mss 1360,nop,wscale 6,nop,nop,TS
val 907211967 ecr 0,sackOK,eol], length 0 // -----------
-----> 1)

IP 104.248.189.33.80 > 10.10.0.194.64608: Flags [S.],
seq 417121955, ack 271799525, win 65160, options [mss
1336,sackOK,TS val 4054341923 ecr 907211967,nop,wscale 7],
length 0 // -----> 2)
```

```
IP 10.10.0.194.64608 > 104.248.189.33.80: Flags [.], ack
417121956, win 2048, options [nop,nop,TS val 907212224 ecr
4054341923], length 0 // ------------------------------
-----> 3)
```
...

The first three segments are the three steps of the three-way handshake. They are SYN, SYN-ACK, and ACK. SYN and ACK are flags in the TCP header that mark the type of the segment. Next, we explain each step in detail to understand the mechanism. To give a concrete idea of the setup, we have two endpoints involved: a client, the laptop on which this text is written, and a server which is hosting the author's personal blog.

The three-way handshake is normally initialized from the client side:

1) The first step is called SYN. This request is issued by the client to initialize the connection by announcing its initial sequential number, that is, seq 271799524, which is the sequence number filed in the TCP header. This step is indicated by the Flags [S] in the tcpdump output, which means the SYN flag in the TCP header is set.

2) The second step is called SYN-ACK, a response from the first SYN by the server. This step (a) acknowledges the first SYN request by increasing the sequential number by 1 (i.e., ack 271799525) and sending it back and (b) announces the sequential number of the server (i.e., seq 417121955). Here, the Flags [S.] means both SYN and ACK flags have been set in the TCP header, which indicates a SYN-ACK segment.

3) The last step is called an ACK. This is issued again
from the client to acknowledge the last SYN (from
the server). Again, this is done by increasing
the received sequential number by 1 (i.e., ack
417121956) and sending it back. This time, only the
ACK flag is set (Flags [.]).

After the exchange of sequential numbers, both sides can set the
expectation to the coming packets and, with that information, can take
action on the mentioned abnormal network behavior properly. In doing
so, the application layer can be always delivered with a reliable stream of
packets in sequential order.

Computer science is full of trade-offs. TCP is one of them, and the
trade-off for reliable delivery is latency. The operations for reordering and
deduplicating take time. The retransmission and three-way handshake
take more time due to the Internet RTT, that is, again, tens to hundreds
of milliseconds. Actually, the three-way handshake is one of the most
noticeable performance hits in that (1) it multiplies the RTT by 3, and (2) it
blocks the first screen experience. Table 5-1 lists some empirical values.

***Table 5-1.** Latency and its consequences*

100–200 milliseconds	Noticeable
> 200 milliseconds && < 1 second	Lagging
> 1 second	Approaching failure

❋ The three-way handshake needs to complete before everything
else can even happen. Now let's do a simple math; within a continent, the
latency could be somewhere between 30 and 100 milliseconds. ❋ Latency
introduced by the three-way handshake alone exceeds the first threshold,

which gives a lagging impression to the user instantly after they open the app. No, not instantly, with a delay of about 90 ~ 300 milliseconds, which doesn't make it any better.

We have two ways in general to mitigate this performance bottleneck: (1) optimize the protocol itself; (2) optimize the app (e.g., using offline content). We are going to discuss some of those protocol heuristics in Section 5.1.5. The offline mode will be implemented in Section 5.3.1.

5.1.1.2 Sliding Window

In the *tcpdump* output, `win` is called a sliding window. Basically, a sliding window is an indicator of the server's load; the larger this number, the lesser the load and hence the better. A zero in `win` means the server is fully loaded, and all clients should stop sending any packets.

Technically, a sliding window is the size of the available buffer. This buffer works as an intermediate place that holds the incoming packets. When the server process is active, it reads the packets from the buffer and processes them. This action gradually depletes the buffer. Thus, if the server process is under high load and cannot pick up the packet in the buffer in time, the available buffer size will decrease. This scenario, in turn, is reflected in the decreasing `win`, and clients will slow down the request sending speed after picking up this signal in the response TCP header.

Bufferbloat is one of the common misconfigurations of the buffer size potentially on all hops on the routes and all layers on the network stack. This includes the TCP buffer. Sometimes, bufferbloat is a mistake with good intention, that is, 💣 to reduce packet loss and to make the performance data look good. Bufferbloat effectively exaggerates the processing power which leads to overcommitment of the server. This causes unstable latency and, sometimes worse, a complete service collapse. Let's elaborate a bit.

We consider the server process(es) now is being overloaded with an elephant flow, hence not being able to respond to any newly arriving packets in time. In the setting of bufferbloat, this situation is covered by the exaggerated buffer size; hence, the client will continue sending requests.

> *Some of the hardest challenges in network programming are caused by the inconsistent perception of the same situation between client and server.*

> —Holmes

This causes latency spikes. In the worst scenario, when the server is in a very high load, at a certain point all packets in the buffer will time out, and so are all successive requests sent from clients, causing the mentioned service collapse which is, basically, 0 availability, the complete opposite of our goal of **0 crash**.

♡ So if your app has any of the preceding scenarios, remind your devops to check bufferbloat first.

5.1.1.3 Congestion Control

> *It's like reversing your car and only stopping when you hear the collision.*

> —Holmes

A sliding window is designed to throttle the client request so as to avoid overloading the server; congestion control is to throttle the client request so as to avoid overloading the network. Technically, congestion control adopts another window called congestion window (CWND). Unlike a sliding window, the congestion window exists only in the algorithm, the state of which is not reflected in the TCP header. Basically, this algorithm (1) sends packets very slowly in the beginning, (2) increases the request speed gradually, and (3) slows down on certain signals such as packet loss, then repeats from 1. This is how the bottleneck of the network is being tested iteratively.

The first step is called a slow start. For a payload that is relatively large, ✳ a slow start imposes some extra RTTs for the initial few requests. We give the congestion control in Figure 5-3.

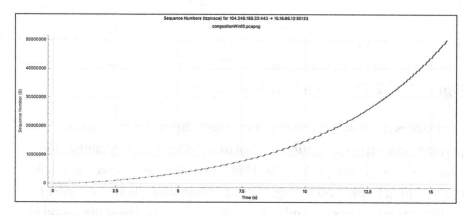

Figure 5-3. *TCP flow under initcwnd 10*

If we increase the congestion window manually by running the following commands:

```
sudo ip route change default via 104.248.176.1 dev eth0  proto
static initcwnd 150
```

it gives a more steep curve and better initial velocity in terms of throughput. The graph is given in Figure 5-4.

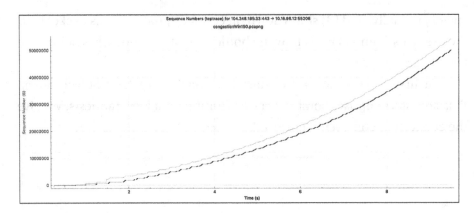

Figure 5-4. *TCP flow under initcwnd 150*

Besides the slow start that inflicts some initial RTTs, ❋ another
performance hit of congestion control inherits from its mechanism for
congestion detection, packet loss. This is because packet loss is a signal
of something already occurring, instead of something is about to occur.
It's like reversing your car and only stopping when you hear the sound of
collision.

5.1.1.4 Four-Way Handshake (Closing Connection)

A four-way handshake is the counterpart of the three-way handshake,
which severs a TCP connection. In this process, one side (a) when done
sending data should issue a FIN segment, and the other side (b) needs
to acknowledge it after receiving it. Then at some point, (b) sends FIN
when its sending also completes, and lastly (a) should acknowledge it to
completely finalize the connection. A four-way handshake is shown in
Listing 5-2.

Listing 5-2. Four-way handshake

```
IP 10.10.0.194.51255 > 104.248.189.33.80: Flags [F.], seq
1181238171, ack 331510598, win 2048, options [nop,nop,TS val
2437516076 ecr 4174449536], length 0

IP 104.248.189.33.80 > 10.10.0.194.51255: Flags [F.], seq
331510598, ack 1181238172, win 509, options [nop,nop,TS val
4174449792 ecr 2437516076], length 0

IP 10.10.0.194.51255 > 104.248.189.33.80: Flags [.], ack
331510599, win 2048, options [nop,nop,TS val 2437516325 ecr
4174449792], length 0
```

First, like SYN and ACK, FIN is also among the flags in the TCP header to indicate the packet type.

As described earlier, the textbook version of the four-way handshake is (1) FIN, (2) ACK, (3) FIN, (4) ACK. This leaves the option half-closed where the passive closing side can send more data even after receiving a FIN. However, in the real world, the *tcpdump* output looks something like the ones given earlier, where the ACK and FIN are aggregated, rendering it's effectively a three-way handshake exactly symmetric to the three-way handshake for opening a connection.

5.1.1.5 Miscellanies

Next, we briefly cover some other header flags:

1) PSH means bypass the buffer and deliver the segment directly to the receivers (could be either a server or a client) process.

255

2) RST is similar to FIN. The difference is that it stands for abnormal closing of a connection. Situations include no process listening to the port indicated, sending packets to a closed connection, duplicated FIN, etc.

3) Data offset means from where the payload of the TCP segment starts.

Lastly, we look at the "stream" nature of TCP. In case you need to write a socket in your app, please note that TCP traffic sometimes aggregates individual segments, meaning 💣 the size each read() returns could vary from that by send(), which could be caused by various intermediate factors. As a result, all TCP-based application protocols are required to indicate the length for each of its request segments, just like HTTP has a Content-length header (HTTP headers will be discussed in Sections 5.1.2.2 and 5.1.2.3). Let's look at one example of TCP aggregation in Figure 5-5. Note that HTTP will be discussed in the next section.

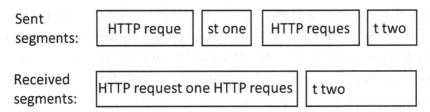

Figure 5-5. *TCP packet aggregation*

In the preceding fictional example, the receiver should (1) read HTTP request one for the first read() with the Content-length header, (2) save the HTTP reques in the application buffer and wait for the next segment, and (3) concatenate the saved value with t two when the last segment arrives.

5.1.2 HTTP/1.1

Simplicity wins. It's that simple.

—Holmes

HTTP/1.1 is an application layer built on top of TCP (in the following section, HTTP will be used for simplicity). It was originally designed as a plain text-based protocol for a very simple purpose – hypertext web page presentation. Thus, it is text based and hence less performant than binary-based network transmission such as raw TCP and Protocol Buffers. However, due to its extreme simplicity and versatility, the use of HTTP and its derivative protocols (HTTPS, HTTP 2.0, etc.) has been extended from websites, its original territory, to almost all parts on today's Internet; video streaming, mobile, and desktop apps of all sorts are all using it.

Note   *JavaScript* is yet another example of primary albeit extremely simple and flexible technology that succeeds. *React Native* is another.

5.1.2.1 HTTP Is Text Based

In HTTP, the client sends requests to the server to fetch resources. In general, there are two types of resources, static and dynamic. Texts and images are examples of static resources that can be located with a resource identifier, a.k.a. URI. On the other hand, dynamic resources are more complex. They could be an HTML rendered from the server side or a JSON response composed from a database. So a client normally needs to attach the request with additional information, so the server can respond with the data in demand. That additional information is called query parameters.

Let's observe an HTTP request in action using our old friend *tcpdump*. This time, we add -A to observe the full payload (Listing 5-3).

Listing 5-3. An HTTP request

```
... // 3-way handshake is omitted
IP 10.10.0.194.57805 > 104.248.189.33.80: Flags [P.], seq
2941389973:2941390048, ack 1652671737, win 2048, options
[nop,nop,TS val 1347624543 ecr 3297846], length 75: HTTP: GET /
HTTP/1.1
....E.....@.@.        .

..h..!...P.R..b.......K......
PS._.2R6GET / HTTP/1.1 // ----------------------------------> 1)
Host: holmeshe.me
User-Agent: curl/7.64.1
Accept: */*

// ----------------------------------------------------------> 2)
IP 104.248.189.33.80 > 10.10.0.194.57805: Flags [.], ack
2941390048, win 509, options [nop,nop,TS val 3298098 ecr
1347624543], length 0
....E..4i.@.'..Dh..!

...P..b....R.............
.2S2PS._
IP 104.248.189.33.80 > 10.10.0.194.57805: Flags [P.], seq
1652671737:1652672135, ack 2941390048, win 509, options
[nop,nop,TS val 3298098 ecr 1347624543], length 398: HTTP:
HTTP/1.1 301 Moved Permanently
....E...i.@.'...h..!

...P..b....R.......s.....
.2S2PS._HTTP/1.1 301 Moved Permanently // ----------------> 3)
Server: nginx/1.14.0 (Ubuntu)
Date: Mon, 04 Oct 2021 11:18:48 GMT
Content-Type: text/html
```

```
Content-Length: 194
Connection: keep-alive
Location: https://holmeshe.me/// ------------------------> 4)

<html> // ----------------------------------------------> 5)
<head><title>301 Moved Permanently</title></head>
<body bgcolor="white">
<center><h1>301 Moved Permanently</h1></center>
<hr><center>nginx/1.14.0 (Ubuntu)</center>
</body>
</html>
... // 4-way handshake is omitted
```

1) The beginning of the HTTP header of the request. We can see that it is a GET request under HTTP 1.1. Note that in the TCP header, a PSH flag is set, which means this packet needs to bypass the buffer and be handled immediately.

2) The end of the HTTP request header. In HTTP, new lines are used to mark the header end. We are going to examine the HTTP request header very soon in Section 5.1.2.2.

3) The beginning of the HTTP response header (Section 5.1.2.3).

4) The end of the HTTP response header, which is also marked with new lines.

5) The body of the HTTP response. We can see that it is HTML in plain text.

As shown in the preceding example, the most common HTTP request method is called a GET. In this method, parameters are attached directly to a resource identifier (URI). A typical HTTP dynamic request looks like this: `https://holmeshe.me/05apps/feeds?count=5&by=lily`.

And let's examine its parts:

1) `https://` is called a schema.

2) `holmeshe.me` is the domain name.

3) `/05apps/feeds` is called a path, or an API.

4) `count` and `by` are the query parameters.

Another method is POST. In POST, parameters are attached in the request body after the HTTP headers. This can effectively avoid parameters that are too long to be populated inside a URI. Other types of HTTP requests are PUT and DELETE that are used for requests modifying the server's state.

Certain characters in a URI are reserved. For instance, the new line is used as a separator between the HTTP header and the body, / is used as a separator for components in a path, ? is the separator between a path and parameters, = is the connector of a parameter key and its value, & is the separator among parameters, and so forth. So we need a way to escape those characters when they appear in a parameter value as an ordinary string. In *JavaScript*, we can use `encodeURIComponent` for this purpose.

It is also possible to use binary data in the request. Say, send the content of an image in a PUT request. An easier way is to use the Base64 algorithm which can transfer a binary blob into a piece of plain text in an efficient way. Besides Base64, HTTP by design supports using a binary as its body, which will be briefly discussed in Section 5.1.2.3. We can also attach the binary directly after the HTTP header which is less common practice.

HTTP headers are also text based and hence are directly readable. However, it is still a bit clumsy to read from *tcpdump* the HTTP payload which is mixed with binary output. For a web developer, a browser is all they need to inspect the traffic when debugging a web application. For us app developers, we can use utilities such as Fiddler or Charles to proxy the HTTP traffic in order to conveniently inspect the traffic. In this text, we are going to use *mitmproxy*, an open source HTTP proxy and inspector.

Let's observe a typical HTTP request with *mitmproxy* and use it to discuss some of the header fields to better understand this protocol (Figures 5-6 to 5-8).

```
Flow Details
2021-10-03 18:26:04 GET https://holmeshe.me/
                    ← 200 OK text/html 11.27k 204ms
             Request                      Response                      Detail
Host:                         holmeshe.me
Connection:                   keep-alive
Cache-Control:                max-age=0
sec-ch-ua:                    "Google Chrome";v="93", " Not;A Brand";v="99",
                              "Chromium";v="93"
sec-ch-ua-mobile:             ?0
sec-ch-ua-platform:           "macOS"
Upgrade-Insecure-Requests:    1
User-Agent:                   Mozilla/5.0 (Macintosh; Intel Mac OS X 10_15_7)
                              AppleWebKit/537.36 (KHTML, like Gecko)
                              Chrome/93.0.4577.82 Safari/537.36
Accept:                       text/html,application/xhtml+xml,application/xml;q=0.9,i
                              mage/avif,image/webp,image/apng,*/*;q=0.8,application/s
                              igned-exchange;v=b3;q=0.9
Sec-Fetch-Site:               none
Sec-Fetch-Mode:               navigate
Sec-Fetch-User:               ?1
Sec-Fetch-Dest:               document
Accept-Encoding:              gzip, deflate, br
Accept-Language:              en-NZ,en;q=0.9,zh-CN;q=0.8,zh;q=0.7,en-GB;q=0.6,en-US;q
                              =0.5
Cookie:                       _ga=GA1.2.677349877.1633090242;
                              _gid=GA1.2.384090364.1633090242; __gads=ID=3b3b5a1b6d99
                              8a21-224e7f6b0dcc005a:T=1633090242:RT=1633090242:S=ALNI
                              _Mb7TQCuqXNiwZNuD7Oc3NFfxCgSjQ; _gat=1
No request content                                                       [ :auto]
```

Figure 5-6. *A typical HTTP request*

```
Flow Details
2021-10-03 18:26:04 GET https://holmeshe.me/
                     ← 200 OK text/html 11.27k 204ms
            Request                    Response                    Detail
Server:              nginx/1.14.0 (Ubuntu)
Date:                Sun, 03 Oct 2021 10:26:05 GMT
Content-Type:        text/html
Last-Modified:       Mon, 01 Feb 2021 12:45:48 GMT
Transfer-Encoding:   chunked
Connection:          keep-alive
ETag:                W/"6017f7fc-f26a"
Content-Encoding:    gzip
[decoded gzip] HTML                                                   [ :auto]
<!DOCTYPE html>
<html>
<head>
  <meta name="generator" content="Hexo 3.9.0">
  <meta charset="utf-8">
  <title>Holmes He</title>
  <meta name="viewport" content="width=device-width, initial-scale=1,
maximum-scale=1">
  <meta name="viewport" content="width=device-width, initial-scale=1,
maximum-scale=1">
  <meta property="og:type" content="website">
  <meta property="og:title" content="Holmes He">
  <meta property="og:url" content="https://holmeshe.me/index.html">
  <meta property="og:site_name" content="Holmes He">
  <meta property="og:locale" content="default">
  <meta name="twitter:card" content="summary">
  <meta name="twitter:title" content="Holmes He">
  <link rel="icon" href="/gallery/air-balloon.svg">
  <link href="//fonts.googleapis.com/css?family=Source+Code+Pro" rel="stylesheet"
type="text/css">
  <link href="https://fonts.googleapis.com/css?family=Open+Sans|Montserrat:700"
rel="stylesheet" type="text/css">
  [4/22]                                                              [*:8080]
```

Figure 5-7. *A typical HTTP response (first part)*

```
Flow Details
2021-10-03 18:26:04 GET https://holmeshe.me/
                     ← 200 OK text/html 11.27k 204ms
            Request                    Response                    Detail
Server Connection:
    Address          holmeshe.me:443
    Resolved Address 104.248.189.33:443
    HTTP Version     HTTP/1.1
    ALPN             http/1.1
```

Figure 5-8. *A typical HTTP response (second part)*

From the traffic inspected, we can see that the requests and responses are populated with key-value contents, for example, Host: holmeshe.me. Those are HTTP headers. The values of the headers are called directives that define certain properties of or behaviors for the traffic.

Next, we go through some of the common headers and their associated directives.

5.1.2.2 Common Request Headers

We look at some of the common request headers first:

1) The foremost information we should care about is 200 OK. This is called an HTTP status code, and 200 means success. We are going to discuss more about status code very soon in Section 5.1.2.4.

2) HTTP Version HTTP/1.1 indicates the current version of HTTP. We are going to talk about the drawbacks of this version and introduce briefly HTTP 2.0. in Section 5.1.5.

3) Host means the hostname being requested.

4) User-agent is the signature of the client (browser).

5) Accept is the format that this client is expecting, such as HTML and XML.

6) Cookie is where to store the cross-request data. These data are sent back and forth using the same header, hence cross-requests. In common practice, a user session is represented by the Cookie on the client side.

7) Another very common header that is not included in this request is X-Forwarded-For, a.k.a. XFF. This header can only be observed from the server side as it is attached by a non-anonymous HTTP proxy (or a reverse load balancer) to indicate the original IP address.

8) Another interesting header is Connection: keep-alive. In the traditional HTTP paradigm, each request initiates a new TCP connection, each of which, as said, imposes a three-way handshake and is subject to the slow start. By indicating Connection: keep-alive, all requests to the same hostname will share a single connection, which saves a few RTTs for the successive requests. For sure, the server needs to support persistent connections to enable this optimization. As shown in Figure 5-7, servers declare it can accept persistent connections by including the same header in the HTTP response.

Note   Here, if you run tcpdump at the same time, you will notice that the FIN will not be observed even after the last response. We can observe FIN only when killing the browser (or the nginx server). This is the side effect of Connection: keep-alive. Note that sending FIN on behalf of a terminated process is the behavior of major operating systems.

5.1.2.3 Common Response Headers

Next, we look at the HTTP response:

1) Server is the web server signature that serves the response. Here, we are using Nginx.

2) Content-type is the actual format of the response body that conforms to one of the expecting formats in the request header, Accept. It is also called a MIME type. As said, HTTP is highly versatile. Besides text/html, it even supports a binary payload as an HTTP body as briefly mentioned. To adopt this, we firstly set application/octet-stream as the Content-type. Then we can use our favored binary format, for example, Protocol Buffer, as the payload. This way, we can enjoy the easy setup of an HTTP server and the efficiency of a binary data transportation. Best of the two worlds.

3) Content-encoding means the content has been compressed using gzip so the client will know it needs to unzip it before reading the response body.

4) We have covered Connection: keep-alive in the last section.

5) Another interesting header is Transfer-Encoding: chunked. This is an optimization in HTTP 1.1. to divide a single big request into chunks. Thus, less buffer is required for both sides when processing the request. In an otherwise situation, the mentioned Content-Length is required in the header.

Note   For chunked requests, the size of each chunk is included in the HTTP request so the Content-length that is for the whole request size can be omitted.

5.1.2.4 HTTP Status Code

We have seen the 200 that means a success. However, most of the status codes are used to indicate the reason when something goes wrong. We categorize the status code as follows. Here, we only list the common ones in practice, and things related to teapot or coffee machines are omitted.

2xx series means "all good":

1)   200 Ok (seen before).

2)   201 Created means "created," a success of a PUT request.

3xx series are a redirection:

Note   A web page can also return a *JavaScript* file to carry out the redirection. So we don't always expect a 3xx status code when observing a redirection.

---

1)   301 Moved Permanently means the resource in request has been moved permanently. All successive requests should use the new URL indicated in the response header Location. 301 could be the most common 3xx series code that is used for the purposes such as standardizing domain name, forcing HTTPS, migrating old domain to a new one, etc.

2)   302 Found is less common than 301. It means the resource in request has been moved temporarily. Upon receipt of this status code, successive requests could still use the old URL.

3) 304 Not Modified means the resource has not been unchanged since last fetching; hence, the client could use the cached value. We are going to discuss cache control in detail in Section 5.1.2.5.

4xx series are client-side errors:

1) 400 Bad Request means the request format failed the sanity check.

2) 401 Unauthorized means unauthorized.

3) 403 Forbidden is similar to 401. It could mean the authorized permission is not sufficient.

4) 404 Not Found.

5) 429 Too Many Requests means the number of requests sent by a client exceeds the threshold.

5xx series are server-side errors:

1) 500 Internal Server Error is a generic status (error) code. All unknown exceptions occurring on any layers of the server side could be surfaced by this status code.

2) 502 - 504 These errors are more relevant to the server-side debugging. They occur when the worker processes behind the proxy crash or are overloaded. For the app side, we can only retry the failed request after receiving this status code. We are going to examine the retry mechanism in Section 5.4.

5.1.2.5 Cache Control

RTT is the most critical bottleneck for network performance. So, it's better to bring the content close to the users so as to reduce or completely eliminate RTT. A cache is one of the most efficient ways to do so.

HTTP generally enlists two layers of caches, local and remote. The local cache holds the data requested by the user, so successive requests from the same user for the same data can benefit from it by retrieving the data directly from the cache. For example, a browser cache may save an image that has been requested before and display it directly whenever this image is referenced from the same or other web pages.

Remote caches, on the other hand, are running on servers that are normally deployed very close to the users. The most prominent remote cache is CDN that is deployed on the edge network. Each CDN server is responsible for a group of users within the same geoproximity and is populated with data requested by any of the users in the group. So all successive requests from all other users in the same group can benefit from it. Besides CDN, HTTP proxies can enlist a cache that serves the users using the same proxy. Generally speaking, a cache shortcuts the requests which would hit on the remote server(s) in an otherwise situation.

Note   A cache gives simultaneously two benefits: (1) it reduces latency by bringing the content closer to the users, and (2) it reduces the server load by shortcutting the requests. For that matter, utilizing cache systems is one of the most worthy topics in a server-side architecture as server capacity is always a scarce resource. A drawback of a cache is that it can only serve static content.

The cache control headers affect both local cache and CDN. It can be included in both request and response HTTP headers. The following are some common derivatives for cache control:

1) `private` means the content should only be saved in local caches and not in intermediate caches such as CDN. Normally, this indicates privacy-sensitive data.

2) `public` means the content can be saved anywhere.

3) `no-cache` is quite misleading by its name 💣. It does not mean "forbid cache," but "read from cache but always check with the server for the validity." That means the request marked with `no-cache` is still sent to the server which, in turn, could return a 304 response if the content is not changed. This can spare some RTTs for the payload of the server response. One of the cache validity flags is ETag.

4) `ETag` is not a cache control directive but a stand-alone HTTP header. This tag is given by the origin server when the resource is fetched. And it is changed when the resource is updated. `ETag` can be used to validate the content in the cache. More specifically, the server returns a full response with content only when the `ETag` embedded in the request and that on the server do not match.

5) `no-store` is the actual "forbid cache" flag. When set, all requests will always hit the origin server. This flag could only be of good use in the debugging phase.

6) `max-age` indicates how long the content will be considered stale and must be refetched from the origin server.

5.1.2.6 HTTP API Design

Eventually, the network tech stack is surfaced to app developers in the form of web APIs. Technically, a web API is a predefined HTTP request and response with which the app communicates with the server. As a reminder, the HTTP request and response are a composite of a URI, the payload, and HTTP headers.

REST is one way to structure the HTTP-based API. The idea of REST is to utilize the different building blocks of HTTP to further separate the concerns in an HTTP request: the URI is used to indicate the resource (noun); the request method (Section 5.1.2.1) is used to indicate the action (verb). Moreover, the HTTP status code (Section 5.1.2.4) can indicate the result by nature.

In terms of the resource, we need to use `https://holmeshe.me/05apps/feeds` to indicate the resource. Adding any verb to the URI, for example, `https://holmeshe.me/05apps/getFeeds`, could be inappropriate.

On the other hand, actions should be represented by HTTP methods. In REST, GET is used to indicate a fetch request, and POST is for creating entry requests. DELETE and PATCH are used for deleting and updating requests, respectively.

Instead of putting constraints on the HTTP protocol itself, GraphQL works on only the payload to optimize the API structure. GraphQL defines a graph query language that is comparable to SQL. The HTTP query is categorized into *query, mutation,* and *subscription,* which are marked in the payload. The names are self-explained. The major improvement GraphQL gives over traditional APIs (REST or not) is its dynamic granularity in terms of response payload. In GraphQL, the data response is dynamically constructed catering for the requests in an on-demand manner.

GraphQL introduces another dimension of partition between the client and the server, which is agnostic to how services are grouped. The layer provides great potential in engineering flexibility as well as performance improvements. As frequent demands can be met with GraphQL with low cost, (1) to aggregate multiple requests into one to save RTTs or (2) to remove unused fields by the app to save bandwidth.

Versioning is another important aspect in a web API. An HTTP protocol gives three places where we can put version information: HTTP header, URI path, and parameters. We shall choose one which we think is the coolest. What's more important in versioning is actually two scenarios, that is, when releasing and when deprecating. Let's examine them one by one.

When releasing a new API support from the app side, the server side should have the API 100% released. Then what we do is to (1) embed supports of the two versions (current and the target) both inside the app executable, (2) make the newer version inactive, and (3) resort to a remote config (i.e., Firebase) to gradually release the newer version.

When deprecating an old API, the server might have been running multiple versions simultaneously to support users who are reluctant to upgrade. At some point, the user population of the oldest API reduces to a threshold, and the server side decides to free the computing and devops resource for the API. At this point, we (1) turn off the API support from the remote config, and (2) the users running on this API will be forced to upgrade. Then we can sunset the API from the server side safely.

5.1.3 DNS

DNS is an application layer protocol. DNS is responsible for translating the easy-to-remember domain name to the actual IP address. Let's see the DNS query in action.

Firstly, we need to clear the DNS cache:

```
sudo dscacheutil -flushcache; sudo killall -HUP mDNSResponder
```

Next, we run the tcpdump on port 53:

```
sudo tcpdump -nt -s 502 port 53
```

On another terminal, visit holmeshe.me using curl:

```
curl holmeshe.me
```

Then the output is printed on the terminal running tcpdump (Listing 5-4).

Listing 5-4. Inspect the DNS query result

```
IP6 2404:f801:10:102:8000::223.58923 > 2001:4898::1050:5050.53:
1001+ A? holmeshe.me. (29)
IP6 2404:f801:10:102:8000::223.56909 > 2001:4898::1050:5050.53:
60392+ AAAA? holmeshe.me. (29)
IP6 2001:4898::1050:5050.53 > 2404:f801:10:102:8000::223.58923:
1001 1/0/0 A 104.248.189.33 (45)
```

DNS is across the data center. This trait gives it an advantage over other protocols when it comes to system resilience design. So it is very useful for geolocation distribution for disaster recovery. Basically, we can set multiple values for a DNS record and remove the ones selectively for data centers that are malfunctioning. More specifically, data centers with dedicated cables broken by incidents such as construction activities or earthquakes can be inactivated using DNS. With this mechanism, clients can fail over to the healthy data center automatically and hence survive in those unexpected events.

DNS has three major drawbacks, ✳ initial latency similar to that in TCP three-way handshake, 💣 DNS hijacking, and 💣 single (or very few) point(s) of failure. The third one is the most disastrous since failure of the DNS could lead to massive outage of Internet services.

🚀 One solution in practice is to, well, do away with DNS completely by using direct IP address(es). This is not an easy task in that we need (1) to maintain an IP list file both in the app bundle and remotely, (2) to sync versions of this list in the app cache and remote using certain rules, and (3) to apply a speed racing algorithm for available data centers, so the app side can selectively connect to the ideal data center while imposing the least overhead to all other data centers.

We will also discuss some modern improvements on DNS in Section 5.1.5. Since most of the heavy lifting is applied on the system level for those improvements, they are much less involved than the custom roll direct IP mentioned earlier.

5.1.4 TLS

TLS is on the application layer. The purpose of TLS is to encrypt the data transition so it cannot be either read or modified by any proxy in the middle of the two communicating endpoints. When combined with HTTP, we get HTTPS running on port 443.

Working on top of TCP, TLS imposes more RTTs for handshakes which are used to establish a secure communication tunnel between two endpoints, more specifically, to agree on a secret with which all the data transmission post handshakes can be encrypted. These handshakes are also called a key exchange.

For performance reasons, the fast symmetric key cryptography is used for the encryption of data itself which is in high volume and is in the long term, while the slow asymmetric key cryptography is for the one-off encryption of the symmetric key during the key exchange. A simplified version of key exchange is illustrated (in roundtrips) as follows:

1) A client asks for a public key (asymmetric).

2) A server sends a public (asymmetric) key to
the client.

3) A client uses the public key (asymmetric) to encrypt
a session key (symmetric) and send it to the server,
and the server uses the private key (asymmetric) to
decrypt the session key (symmetric).

Then all the successive communication can be carried out with the
session key (symmetric) agreed on.

A TLS handshake is a bit more complicated and hence more robust
and secure. For example, instead of sending the session key directly in
roundtrip 3, the client and the server can exchange some random numbers
in roundtrips 1 and 2 and generate the session key altogether based on
those random numbers.

One critical SSL step not included in the simplified version of key
exchange is authentication. The client needs to make sure the server is
who it claims to be; otherwise, important information could be sent to
malicious entities. This is achieved in roundtrips 2 and 3. In roundtrip
2, the server sends a certificate together with the public key mentioned
earlier; and in roundtrip 3, the client needs to verify the certificate with the
information embedded in the client (browser or operating system) before
any of the following steps could be carried out.

More specifically, the information embedded in the client is the
public key of a handful of root certificate authorities (CA). To verify the
information, the client needs to compare the signature generated from
the base information using the public key. This process can be chained so
signatures of trusted certificate authorities by root certificate authorities
can be verified too.

5.1.4.1 Pinning

CA pinning is a practice of embedding the server certificate in the client side. In doing so, the client will rigidly trust only the certificate pinned. This is not a suggested practice because 💣 certificate verification failure causes zero availability. We don't want this to happen regardless of the causes whenever updating certificates intentionally or passively.

5.1.5 The Modern Internet

In facing the physical limit, which is speed of light, the Internet keeps on evolving on qualities like latency, resilience, continuity, and the ability of multiplexing, which leads to better user experiences. This section will focus on those improvements, and please make the best use of them when making your next awesome app.

HTTP/2

HTTP/2 is the enhanced version of HTTP/1.1. Multiplexing is one of the major optimizations in HTTP/2.

We recommended enabling `Connection: keep-alive` in the request header (Section 5.1.2.2) to save some RTTs for handshakes for new requests. However, this is at the cost of concurrency because `keep-alive` has an intrinsic drawback called head-of-line blocking (HOL blocking). For instance, when a client requests three resources, a PNG graphic, a CSS stylesheet, and an HTML file, the requests of the latter two need to wait for the first one to fully complete. Often than not, in the network system design, a wait means a waste in resources such as computing power and bandwidth. Those resources could be otherwise put in better use to provide more responsive services (Figure 5-9).

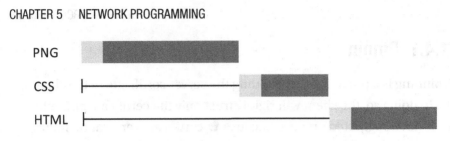

Figure 5-9. *HOL blocking in HTTP/1.1*

Note   To better understand the issue, please consider you are waiting in a queue in a fast food restaurant. And some guy in the front takes ages to contemplate what to eat for lunch, which causes a HOL blocking.

Alternatively, a client can initiate multiple connections simultaneously to mitigate the HOL blocking, but at the cost of (1) the handshakes and (2) the superfluous press on the server for those additional connections.

Note   One way to solve the preceding HOL issue is to add more counters. This is at the cost of the restaurant's operational expense and of the press on the management for the additional employees. It is a common trade-off scenario which is happening all the time.

HTTP/2 multiplexing enables the parallel processing of network requests over a single connection. Instead of waiting for HOL blocking, the network responses are served in an interleaved manner. This also opens the opportunity to serve the prioritized resources such as the HTML file first, which gives better perceived overall performance (Figure 5-10).

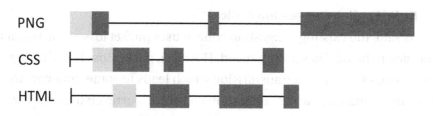

Figure 5-10. *Multiplexing in HTTP/2*

Note   Let's get back to the fast food restaurant. Another way to solve the HOL problem is to use a QR code which is part of an online ordering system. Now each person is ordering simultaneously so you don't have to wait for the guy in front of the queue anymore. This is a breakthrough scenario which occurs rarely only for a brilliant mind combined with determined execution.

Other optimizations introduced by HTTP/2 include header compression and a binary protocol, which make HTTP/2 way better than HTTP/1.1.

Note   They say everything is a trade-off in the world of computer science. Nevertheless, there are exceptions that make breakthroughs. Good designs such as HTTP/2 make use of both low overhead of keep-alive and high throughput of parallelism. As mentioned throughout this book, ***React Native*** is yet another good example of breakthroughs of this kind.

ECN (Explicit Congestion Notice)

As said, the existing congestion control uses packet loss as the signal to slow down the packet sending speed. However, packet loss is both a signal and a cost, as it causes retransmission which leads to some unnecessary RTTs and overall latency. If congestion control is like reversing your car and only stopping when you hear a collision, ECN is the reverse radar.

In ECN, the bottleneck gateway will notice the sender ahead of time by setting a flag in the IP header. Moreover, gateways that enable ECN will benefit from the more sophisticated queuing algorithm that can minimize bufferbloat.

IPV6

IPV6 is the replacement of IPV4 on the network layer. Unlike IPV4, IPV6 has almost unlimited address space. It gives better performance by removing the NAT. In fact, Apple has been enforcing the support of IPV6 for many years. For servers that do not support IPV6, we can use NAT64 to test the client's IPV6 capacity. Nonetheless, it's better to get both the client and the server to support it.

Multipath TCP

In the world of mobile networks, the absence of a network is a routine rather than an exception. Multipath TCP is a mechanism to mitigate the issue by simultaneously establishing multiple "subflows" and sharing the connectivity and bandwidth between both Wi-Fi and cell networks. This is useful in scenarios where Wi-Fi is fading out such as when the user is walking away from a Wi-Fi range. In an otherwise situation, the mentioned DNS query, TCP handshake, and TLS handshake are imposed by network switching, and the user will experience excessive latency.

QUIC and HTTP/3

QUIC is another level above all the optimizations based on the existing TCP network stack. In fact, it has the potential to replace the existing TCP/HTTP stack completely and makes the Internet much more responsive:

1) QUIC is based on UDP and could be implemented in user space.

2) QUIC aggregates the handshakes of transport and key exchange, which were conducted by TCP and TLS, respectively. This aggregation reduces RTTs required and hence is faster.

3) QUIC also takes the preceding optimizations such as header compression, explicit congestion notice, and, more importantly, multiplexing into account.

5.1.6 Key Takeaway

In this section, we have gone through the critical path in the network stack that is directly related to app development. Firstly, we briefly introduced the basic idea of TCP/IP. Then we examined in detail and by hand the essential protocols in the network stack, namely, TCP, HTTP, DNS, and TLS. During the discussion, we also highlighted important features of each protocol such as congestion control, bufferbloat, keep alive, cache control, HOL, etc. Lastly, we connected the dots by relating those textbook protocols to today's new updates in network engineering.

You might have noticed that we emphasized on latency and RTTs while rarely mentioning bandwidth whenever discussing the performance aspect of each protocol. This is because in most cases, bandwidth is not the bottleneck, unless you are developing a service that is bandwidth hungry like streaming. Nonetheless, it is always nice to reduce unnecessary bandwidth consumption whenever possible.

You might also notice that we did not emphasize on concrete practice as in other sections. This is because some of the modern Internet attributes, such as IPV6 and HTTP/2, involve a server-side setup which is not the best interest of this book. Moreover, some features such as QUIC are not in production yet at the time when this book is being written.

The good news is the *iOS* and *Android* ecosystems are following closely and naturally support, from the client side, some of those. For instance, NSURLSession supports multipath, HTTP/2, and IPV6 out of the box. As you will see very soon (Section 5.2.2), the *React Native* fetch() benefits from those features too as it is implemented on top of NSURLSession.

This section is far from a complete guide to network programming. Rather, we have achieved three major goals: (1) to know what the building blocks in the network stack are, (2) to understand what critical network bottlenecks are, and (3) to leverage new Internet heuristics in network programming.

Network programming is an interesting topic where there exist a lot of opportunities and huge potentials to make our app more performant and more responsive while demanding less bandwidth in the meantime. In the background of the Internet, the best practices of network programming are not yet defined for cross-platform mobile development. One of the major purposes of this and the following sections is to establish the foundation for you to explore such best practices.

Let's be hungry and continue hunting.

5.2 Network Programming on the JavaScript Layer

5.2.1 Asynchronous Operations

Generally, asynchronization has two layers of meaning: (1) unblocking of slow operations and (2) triggering events nonlinearly. In OS terms, the event is also called an interruption that can represent an incoming network packet, a clock tick, or simply a mouse click. Technically, the event interrupts the current process, puts the next CPU instruction on hold, and calls a predefined code block (a.k.a. an event handler) "asynchronously."

The concept is essentially the same at the application level.

In a narrow sense, asynchronization solves a fundamental difficulty in application development: blocking operation on the UI thread (mostly I/O). No matter what kind of app (with a UI) you are working on (an embedded system, a mobile app, a game, or a web page), there is an underlying "loop" that is used to calculate screen rendering. If the "loop" is blocked by a slow operation, say, a network interaction, the UI will be frozen. So the common practice is to offload the waiting operations to other threads. This is where asynchronous operations come into play.

5.2.1.1 Promise

In *JavaScript*, asynchronous operations are carried out using an object called a **promise** which literally reflects a promise of the future.

The Promise object takes as a parameter a closure which runs the slow operation, which is in turn passed in with two closure parameters resolve and reject. resolve and reject are called at the end of the operation depending on whether it was a success or a failure. Listing 5-5 shows a typical usage of Promise.

Listing 5-5. Use the Promise object

```
var theFuture = new Promise((resolve, reject) => {
    setTimeout(() => { // -----------------------------------> 1)
        resolve("The future is now"); // ------------------> 2)
    }, 250);
});

theFuture.then((message) => { // --------------------------> 3)
  console.log(message); // --------------------------------> 3)
});
```

1) Simulate a slow operation using setTimeout.

2) The callback of the timer asynchronously invokes resolve() which effectively resolves the **promise**.

3) The then block is invoked and passed in with the same parameter after the **promise** resolves. In fact, then takes two callbacks instead of just one. The second closure is linked to the reject() which belongs to the exception flow in asynchronous operations. Since we use a timeout in this simple example, the exception flow is omitted for now. We will bring this topic back in Section 5.4.

A **promise** provides catch() as the shortcut for reject of then(). catch() is normally attached as the end step of a typical *promise chain*.

Note   A traditional callback paradigm is notoriously bad. 💣 When the logic becomes more and more complicated, it could cause a phenomenon called a callback hell which is barely readable and is difficult to be debugged. 🏛 A **promise** keeps logic linear regardless of its complexity – so it can be always read from top down. This technique is referred to as a *promise chain*.

Next, we look at a promise chain in Listing 5-6.

Listing 5-6. Promise chain

```
let promiseA = ....
somePromise.then(() => {
  let promiseB = ...
  return promiseB
}).then(() => {
  let promiseC = ...
```

```
    return promiseC
})
```

We can also use `Promise.all()` to combine multiple **promises** into one that can resolve only when all of the combined ones are resolved (Listing 5-7).

Listing 5-7. Promise.all()

```
let promiseA = ...
let promiseB = ...
Promise.all([promiseA, promiseB]).then(() => {
...
})
```

Similar to `Promise.all()`, `Promise.race()` takes multiple `Promises` and combines them into one. The difference is `Promise.race()` resolves when one of the `Promises` resolves (Listing 5-8).

Listing 5-8. Promise.any()

```
let promiseA = ...
let promiseB = ...
Promise.any([promiseA, promiseB]).then(() => {
...
})
```

5.2.1.2 Await

A **promise** is a step forward to the linear logic flow compared to a callback. **await** takes a step more.

Await is designed to mimic the programming style that is plain linear; hence, it is highly intuitive. Even the exception flow can be achieved using ordinary `try catch` blocks. In practice, the keyword `await` is used together with `async` which is a method name decorator. The `async` keyword makes a method "awaitable." Under the hood, **await** is built on top of a **promise**, so they are completely compatible. In Listing 5-9, we use await on the Promise object created in the last section.

Listing 5-9. Use the Promise object in await

```
await theFuture;
console.log(message); // ----------------------------------> 1)
```

1) Please do keep in mind that the line followed by the await keyword is executed in an asynchronous manner, in other words, in another iteration of the *JavaScript* run loop.

As you can see, this version is much simpler than the **promise**-based one. **await** also accepts advanced **promise** combinations such as Promise.all() and Promise.race() as input, which we will see very soon in Section 5.4.1.

Note   *async/await* is not unique to **JavaScript**. A similar programming paradigm called *coroutine* has been well used on the server side for ages. A comparable *async/await* syntax now is available in *Swift* as well.

Nonetheless, **await** has drawbacks too. One of those is that it is so intuitive that sometimes programmers forget they are dealing with asynchronous blocks when using it. Another issue is that a cancel operation is not as explicit as in techniques such as NSOperation. Hence, we need to manually deal with cancel semantics when multiple competing *promise chains* are involved.

🏛 When using **await**, we need to always be clear whether the asynchronous operation is in a critical path or not. And only operations that are part of the critical path should be "awaited." What is a critical path and under what criteria we can distinguish operations? A rule of thumb is if the result of an operation is essential to the following UX, it should be part of the critical path. For instance, fetching the feed list belongs to the critical path, while refetching images (for speeding up UX) and telemetry (totally UX irrelevant) do not.

Note   Similar concepts can be found in the *iOS* development discipline, where *QoS* is defined to categorize the concurrent operations in *GCD*.

🏛 The same criteria should be applied to the exception flow. We only capture the exception for critical paths and eventually reflect it to UX in some forms. If exceptions occurred in peripheral paths (a.k.a. *orphan operations*), *silent logging* should be applied.

Note   We can call asynchronous operations not within the critical path *orphan operations* (similar to orphan processes in the operating system terminology). They are simply "unleashed"; neither the return value nor the exception is of interest to the main logic flow. As a result, *orphan operations* need to be self-contained and take care of the full logic including exceptions within themselves.

💣 When using **await**, one frequent mistake is that programmers are not aware that exceptions will not be caught within an asynchronous method that is not explicitly "awaited." This happens either for *orphan operations*, or the programmer simply forgot adding the **await** keyword. Please do note that bugs in the exception flow (a.k.a. second fault) take enormous time, energy, and intuition to debug, so ♡ better to avoid such faults beforehand in the first place with vigilance.

In the following text, we are going to use the **await** primarily so we can get used to the more advanced technique.

5.2.2 fetch( )

Now it's time to discuss fetch( ), the standard way in *JavaScript* to make HTTP requests. fetch( ) takes two parameters: the first one is the URI of the resource; the second one is an object that can further customize the request, such as changing the query method, adding an HTTP header, attaching an HTTP body in the request, etc. The return value of fetch( ) is a **Promise** object. Listing 5-10 gives a quick example.

Listing 5-10. Fetch

```
let rsp = await fetch('https://holmeshe.me/05apps/
feeds'); //> 1)
let feeds = await rsp.json(); // -------------------------> 2)
console.log(feeds);
```

1) We fetch the feeds from remotely. In the next section, we are going to integrate the API call and replace all local data files.

2) In *JavaScript*, response.json( ) is also an asynchronous operation.

Note   Though fetch( ) looks like pure *JavaScript* from the surface, it's actually native code that takes effect under the hood. We have seen this pattern several times for other *React Native* components, so it's not a surprise. The good thing is that we can upgrade to, free of cost, all the modern network improvements (e.g., HTTP 2.0) provided they have been supported by the platform.

5.2.3 Case Study, Move Everything Online

It's time to get some work done for *Manyface*. First things first, here are the requirements:

1) The API for all feeds is located from `https://holmeshe.me/05apps/feeds`.

2) Display a loading page when the first screen (i.e., feed) is being loaded.

3) When the user pulls down, reload the data.

Listings 5-11 to 5-14 show a complete overhaul of `Moment` to support network fetching.

Listing 5-11. Add the state to the component

```
class Moment extends React.Component {
  constructor() {
    super();

    this.pullDownPos = new Animated.Value(0);
    this.autoScrolling= new Animated.Value(0);
    this.userPulling = new Animated.Value(0);

    this.scrollViewRef = undefined;

    this.feedRefs = [];

    this.state = {
      loading: false,
+     data: [] // ----------------------------------------> 1)
    }
  }
}
```

1) First, we add a **state** in the constructor for the feeds.
   It is now fetched from the remote API and hence
   becomes a variable that affects the UI.

Listing 5-12. Fetch the feed list in Moment

```
+ async loadData() { // --------------------------------------> 1)
+   try {
+     let rsp = await fetch('https://holmeshe.me/05apps/feeds',
+       __DEV__ ? { // --------------------------------------> 2)
+         headers: {
+           'Cache-Control': 'no-cache'
+         } : undefined
+     });
+     let feeds = await rsp.json();

+     let feedsModel = feeds.map((obj) => {
+       return new FeedModel(obj);
+     });

+     this.setState({data: feedsModel}); // ---------------> 3)
+   } catch(e) {
+     // do nothing for now
+   }
+ }
```

1) Add a new method for feed fetching and add
   an `async` annotation to the method name, so
   `loadData()` can be awaited.

2) Add `no-cache` to the HTTP header to deprecate the
   stale cache entry when debugging.

3) Invoke `setState()` and update the UI after the
   fetching completes.

Listing 5-13. Use the loadData()

```
+ componentDidMount() {
+   this.loadData(); // ----------------------------------> 1)
+ }

  renderItem = (entry) => {
... // not irrelevant
  }

  onViewableItemsChanged = (result) => {
... // not irrelevant
  }

  beginDrag = () => {
... // not irrelevant
  }

+-endDrag = async (evt) => { // --------------------------> 2)
    this.userPulling.setValue(0);
    this.autoScrolling.setValue(1);

if (
  evt.nativeEvent.contentOffset.y < -loadingIndicatorOffset
) {
      this.setState({loading: true});

+     await this.loadData(); // ---------------------------> 3)
      setTimeout(() => {
      this.scrollViewRef.scrollToIndex({
        index: 0,
        animated: true
      });
      }, 1000);
  }
}
```

```
  onReset = (evt) => {
... // not irrelevant
  }
  getScrollViewRef = (ref) => {
... // not irrelevant
  }
```

1) Invoke the loadData() in componentDidMount() life cycle callback. This is the fresh fetch.

2) Invoke the loadData() in endDrag(). This fetch is invoked by pulling down the action of the user. Note that endDrag() is now marked with async as the semantic is passed down from loadData().

3) The bouncing back is now invoked by the fetching complete event, implemented with await.

Listing 5-14. Change the conditional rendering

```
render() {
  if (this.state.data.length === 0) { // ----------------> 1)
    return <Skeleton style={{flex: 1}}/>
  }

  return ( // --------------------------------------------> 2)
    <View style={{flex: 1}}>
      <Animated.FlatList
        data={this.state.data}
        renderItem={this.renderItem}
        onViewableItemsChanged={this.onViewableItemsChanged}
        contentInset={{
          top: this.state.loading ?
              5: 0
```

```
    }}
    scrollEventThrottle={1}
    onScroll={
      Animated.event([{
        nativeEvent: {
          contentOffset: { y: this.pullDownPos }
        }
      }], { useNativeDriver: true })
    }
    onScrollBeginDrag={this.beginDrag}
    onScrollEndDrag={this.endDrag}
    ref={this.getScrollViewRef}
    onMomentumScrollEnd={this.onReset}
  />
  <View style={styles.overlay}>
    <LoomingSpinningEnvelope
      color={'#6291f0'}
      size={45}
      style={{
        opacity:
          Animated.add(
            Animated.multiply(
              this.userPulling,
              this.pullDownPos.interpolate({
                inputRange: [-loadingIndicatorOffset, 0],
                outputRange: [0.5, 0]
              })
            ),
            Animated.multiply(
              this.autoScrolling,
              this.pullDownPos.interpolate({
```

```
                    inputRange: [-loadingIndicatorOffset, 0],
                    outputRange: [1, 0]
                  })
                ),
              )
          }}
        />
      </View>
    </View>
  );
 }
};

...// styles
```

1) Shortcut the render() and return the skeleton view (made in Chapter 3) when fresh fetching is undergoing.

2) Return the normal feed list UI in an otherwise situation.

Note   The action of fetching data from online and updating the UI is also called a side effect. Instead of componentDidMount(), sometimes it is tempting to introduce the side effect in the **component's** constructor to save a couple of milliseconds. However, this could lead to race conditions in theory as the network response could be faster than componentDidMount(); in such case, the setState() will not be effective. 💣 So in general, this practice is considered an antipattern.

5.3 Network Programming on the Native Layer

Now we know how to use fetch() to fetch network resources. Next, let's take a step more forward with two critical questions regarding UX: (1) What if the app is offline? (2) When the app cold starts, can we display something from the local cache instead of waiting for the initial RTTs? A local cache is the key to answer both questions. Basically, we read data directly from it in critical situations as mentioned earlier.

An HTTP cache can answer only partial of this question as we only use fetch() for the feed list. Multimedia such as videos and graphics are requested and rendered in their specific logic flows, by their respective **components**, without using direct HTTP fetch(). So we need to consider different offline strategies for each of them:

1) Feed list: HTTP cache.

2) Image: Leverage *react-native-fast-image* (*Fast Image*), the best **React Native** image cache system so far. It is based on *SDWebImage* and *Glide* on **iOS** and **Android**, respectively.

3) Video: Enhance the VideoViewManager we created in the last chapter by enabling the download capability.

Note   The mechanism of an image cache is also an interesting and sophisticated topic. In fact, *SDWebImage* and *Glide* are go-to open source projects worth reading on their respective platforms. However, we have to compromise on this topic to better focus on our main goal.

5.3.1 Case Study, Enable Local Caching

Here are the requirements:

1) When the app starts offline, we display the user content fetched last time instead of a blank skeleton view.

2) When the user cold starts with an Internet, we display the user content fetched last time instead of a blank skeleton view, during the fresh fetch.

Let's start from image cache which is a simple one. As said, we need to install the *Fast Image* by executing the following two commands:

```
npm i react-native-fast-image
./pod install
```

Then we need to replace all <Image> occurrences with <FastImage>. FastImage provides extra **props** for cache control (Section 5.1.2.5), so we shall provide those **props**. Luckily, we have a nice encapsulation of the raw <Image> in our LoomingImage **component**, so we need to change only this place to enable an offline cache of all image contents for feeds and avatars (Listing 5-15).

Listing 5-15. LoomingImage with an offline cache

```
const AnimatedFastImage = Animated.createAnimatedComponent
(FastImage); // ------------> 1)

class LoomingImage extends React.Component {
  constructor() {
    super();

    this.opacity = new Animated.Value(0);
```

```
    this.state = {loaded: false};
  }

  render() {
    return (
      <View style={[{
        ...this.props.style
      }, {
        backgroundColor
      }]}>
        {this.state.loaded === false &&
        <View style={styles.overlay}>
          <RotatingCircle size={28}/>
        </View>
        }
        <Animated.Image
+       <AnimatedFastImage // ------------------------------> 2)
          style={{
            width: '100%',
            height: '100%',
            opacity: this.opacity
          }}
          source={this.props.source} // ------------------> 3)
          onLoad={this.onLoad.bind(this)}
        />
      </View>
    );
  }

  onLoad() {
    this.setState({loaded: true});
    Animated.timing(this.opacity, {
      toValue: 1,
```

```
      duration: 300,
      useNativeDriver: true
    }).start();
  }
}
```

1) Use `Animated.createAnimatedComponent()` to enable the **component** with the animation **HOC**.

2) Replace the raw `Image` with `FastImage`, well, without any change in **props**. Note that cache control will be set as a default value, `FastImage.cacheControl.immutable`, which is what we want for the offline cache.

3) Add a cache policy. Different from a general-purpose HTTP cache, this policy is applied to and managed by the **component** specific for image contents.

Note   By running the code through *Xcode*, you might not be able to browse the feed list offline. This is because the HTTP cache control is set to `no-cache` for develop. Removing the cache control then you will see the correct behaviour.

Next, we enable the offline cache for video (Listing 5-16). This time, the task is a bit more involved because we will need to program in the native layer again.

Note   The download does not belong to the critical path; hence,
the exceptions are swallowed by the component and are not related
to the *JavaScript* layer. So the exception flow we set up in the last
chapter is basically unchanged. We are going to discuss the matter of
exceptions more in Section 5.4.

Listing 5-16. VideoView with download

```
class VideoView: UIView {
... // unchanged code

  @objc(setSrc:)
  func setSrc(_ src: String) {
guard let doc = FileManager.default.urls( // -------------> 1a)
  for: .cachesDirectory, in: .userDomainMask
).last else {
      print("doc is nil in setSrc")

      self.setup(src)
      return
}

    guard let url = URL.init(string: src) else { // ------> 1b)
      print("Parsed url is nil for \(src) in setSrc")

      self.setup(src)
      return
    }

let dest = doc.appendingPathComponent(
url.lastPathComponent) // -------------------------------> 1c)
```

```
if FileManager.default.fileExists(
  atPath: dest.relativePath
) {
      self.setup(dest.absoluteString) // ------------------> 2)
    } else {
      self.setup(src) // ------------------------------------> 3)

      self.download(url, dest, {dest in // ----------------> 5)
      }, {dest in
        // in production this should be real log uploaded
        print(dest) // ------------------------------------> 5)
      })
    }
  }

... // unchanged code

  private func setup(_ src: String) { // ------------------> 4)
    do {
      guard let url = URL.init(string: src) else {
        throw VideoViewManagerError.runtimeError("url is nil in
        VideoView::setSrc()")
      }

      if player == nil {
        player = AVPlayer(url: url)

        if (playerLayer != nil) {
          throw VideoViewManagerError.runtimeError("playerLayer
          is not nil while player is in VideoView::setSrc()")
        }

        playerLayer = AVPlayerLayer(player: player)
        playerLayer!.masksToBounds = true
```

```
    self.layer.addSublayer(playerLayer!)
  } else {
    if (playerLayer == nil) {
      throw VideoViewManagerError.runtimeError("playerLayer
      is nil in VideoView::setSrc()")
    }

    playerLayer?.removeFromSuperlayer()

    player = AVPlayer(url: url)

    playerLayer = AVPlayerLayer(player: player)
    playerLayer!.masksToBounds = true
    self.layer.addSublayer(playerLayer!)
  }
} catch {
  self.throwToJS(error)
}
}

private func download( // ------------------------------> 5)
_ src: URL,
_ dest: URL,
_ onSuccess: @escaping (_ dest: String) -> Void,
_ onError: @escaping (_ desc: String) -> Void)
{
  let request = URLRequest.init(url: src) // ------------> 6)
  let session = URLSession.init(configuration:
  URLSessionConfiguration.default)
  let task = session.downloadTask(with: request) {(source:
  URL?, _, error: Error?) -> Void in
```

```
    guard error == nil, let source = source else {
      onError("Download failed with error:\
      (String(describing: error)) source:\(String(describing:
      source))") // -----------> 7)
      return
    }

    do {
      try FileManager.default.copyItem(at: source, to: dest)//8)
    } catch (let error) {
      onError("Download failed when copying file: \(error)")//7)
      return
    }

    onSuccess(dest.relativePath) // --------------------> 8)
  }

  task.resume() // -------------------------------------> 6)
}
```

1) Prepare the download by (a) fetching the document
   directory; (b) convert the URL string to the URL
   object; (c) combine the preceding two information
   to get the cache directory.

2) Set up the video view hierarchy using the cached
   video URL if it exists.

3) Otherwise, set up the video hierarchy using the
   remote URL string as in the last chapter, and start
   the download.

4) setup() is equivalent to the old version of setSrc() without the downloading capability. The logic has been moved to this method to make setSrc() more clear.

5) download() is the new method created. It takes the source and destination URLs as inputs. The source URL indicates the location of the video online; and the destination URL indicates the local file that stores the downloaded video. The two closure parameters are called when the download completes and fails, respectively.

6) Prepare components for the download task and start the task.

7) Invoke the error block whenever the error occurs. For now, we simply print a log when an error occurs. In production code, we might need to also upload those logs for the debugging of field failure.

8) Copy the downloaded file from the file buffer to the destination location and invoke the block for success.

Note   This download module is not the most optimal solution though it can work well. For industrial-level video downloading services, we need to employ advanced streaming technologies such as HLS or Dash.

5.4 Exception Handling

In general, we are still going to follow the discussed *wall-in* strategy (Section 4.4) for network operations. As a brief reminder, this strategy pivots around the error boundary and converges error handling code only on critical points where decisions can be made. Normally, those critical points are also entry points in **components** from where the logic of a submodule is entered. This time, the difficulty is another level higher than that in Section 4.4 due to the extensive complexity introduced by the network. Let's analyze it before jumping to the code directly.

The scope is the first thing we need to consider. Now we have two sources of network requests: (1) requests sent from the *JavaScript* layer to fetch the feed list and (2) requests sent from the native layer to fetch the multimedia content, that is, images and videos. We have mentioned in Section 5.3 that image and video downloading does not belong to the critical path. This is because *Manyface* can still proceed with the UX, though degraded, in situations such as missing one or two images or the video of one feed doesn't load. As such, we consider the current exception flow for the native level is sufficient.

Note   As mentioned before, it is so important that it is worth repeating: being degradable (a.k.a. flexible) is the key to **0 crash**.

We have narrowed down our scope to the *JavaScript* layer. The next thing we need to consider is network connectivity. More specifically, how should *Manyface* react when the user device is offline? Let's look at what the potential design options are:

1) Treat the offline state as an ordinary exception and give the user a default error page. This is suboptimal in that the mobile network is intermittent by nature, and we don't want the offline state to be drastic.

Moreover, we just implemented the offline cache (Section 5.3) to handle this situation, which renders the error page even less relevant as *Manyface* is in good shape when offline.

2) Always check the network state and start the fetch() only when connectivity is assured. This can be done using *react-native-netinfo* (a.k.a. *Net Info*). This is actually an antipattern. The moment we check connectivity is a couple of milliseconds ahead when we call the fetch(), so the result is irrelevant for this external state change could occur in between.

3) Not to couple *Net Info* and network fetch(). Use *Net Info* simply to trigger a UI hint to the user. The network fetch() will throw when offline. However, we can catch this exception within and retry the same request later when the network is back. This sounds like the best option so far.

Now let's look at the request timeout. A timeout could be caused by a weak network connection or an overloaded server that cannot respond in time. In such a case, retry is still a plausible option. However, since the server could be already in high load, a flood of retry could exacerbate the problem. So we need to slow it down and set a limit counter for it.

Lastly, let's think about HTTP status code. Should we retry too for abnormal HTTP code? Yes and no. Only for certain codes that represent recoverable errors. For instance, 429 too many request, 500 Internal Server Error, and other 5xx status code belong to this category. And we definitely don't want to retry on 400 bad request or 401 unauthorized, etc. For those unrecoverable exception codes, we translate them into exceptions and throw them to the **error boundary** which will make a final call about the UI and logic on exceptions.

5.4.1 Case Study, Reinforce the Network Components

Let's make an abstract of the preceding discussion in the form of requirements:

1) For offline fetch(), we save the request and retry after coming back online.

2) For a request timeout (3 seconds), 401 and 5xx, we retry at most three times. We set the first retry to be after 3 seconds, the second to be 10 seconds, and the third to be 30 seconds. We consider after 30 seconds the user will leave *Manyface* anyway, so if all retries fail, we throw the exception.

3) For HTTP code other than the ones listed earlier, we throw the exception representing the error.

To get started with this case study, we need to install the *Net Info* package by running the following two commands:

```
npm install --save @react-native-community/netinfo
./pod install
```

Next, we create a service that encapsulates the vanilla fetch() together with the retry logic discussed earlier (Listing 5-17).

Listing 5-17. The network service

```
export default class NetWorkService {
  retryTimes = 0;
  retryIntervals = [0, 3, 10, 30];

  async robustFetch(url, config) { // --------------------> 1)
    await this.throttle(); // ------------------------------> 2)
```

```
try {
  const controller = new AbortController();
  let timer;
  let timeout = new Promise((resolve, reject) => { // ---> 4)
    timer = setTimeout(() => {
      controller.abort();

      reject({message: 'Timed out'});
    }, 3000);
  });

  const response = await Promise.race([fetch(url, { // --> 4)
    ...config,
    signal: controller.signal
  }), timeout]);

  if (!!timer) {
    clearTimeout(timer);
  }

  if (!response.ok) {
    if (response.status === 401 || response.status > 500) {
      return this.robustFetch(url, config); // --------> 5)
    }

    reject({message: 'Netowrk failed with HTTP code:' +
    response.status}); // ----------------------------> 6)
  }

  return response;
} catch (e) {
  if (e?.message?.includes?.('Network request failed')) { //7)
    await this.waitForNetwork()
    return this.robustFetch(url, config);
  }
```

```
      if (e?.message?.includes?.('Timed out')) { // -------> 8)
        return this.robustFetch(url, config);
      }

      throw('Unkown network issue'); // --------------------> 9)
    }
  }

  async throttle() {
    return new Promise((resolve, reject) => {
      if (this.retryTimes >= this.retryIntervals.length) { //> 2)
        reject('Network Failed After 3 Retries');
      }

      const interval =
      this.retryIntervals[this.retryTimes++]; // ----------> 3)

      setTimeout(resolve, interval *1000); // -------------> 3)
    });
  }

  async waitForNetwork() { // -----------------------------> 7)
    return new Promise((resolve, reject) => {
      const unsubscribe = NetInfo.addEventListener(state => {
        if (state.isConnected) {
          unsubscribe();
          resolve();
        }
      });
    });
  }
}
```

1) Create a robust version of `fetch()` with the same signature.

2) `throttle()` implements the retry logic. As per the discussion, if the retry times exceed three, the whole fetch should simply reject.

3) Get the throttle interval based on the number of retry times. And carry out the throttle using this number. As per the requirement, they are 3 seconds, 10 seconds, and 30 seconds each time the retry occurs.

4) Set up the timeout and execute the `fetch()` with `Promise.race()`. As mentioned, this method is passed with an array of `Promises` and resolves/rejects if any of the `Promises` resolve/reject. Note that a timeout throws an error with the corresponding message which will be checked later in the catch block.

5) Retry for recoverable HTTP status code that is exceptional.

6) Reject for all other exceptional HTTP status code.

7) Wait for the network to reconnect when offline. And retry straight after. Here, we use *Net Info* to monitor the connectivity change.

8) Retry for a timeout.

9) Throw all other exceptions. They could be programmatically exceptions or other network exceptions not being accounted for explicitly.

Lastly, we can modify the Moment and connect the dots and complete the exception flow (Listing 5-18).

Listing 5-18. Hook up the exception flow with Moment

```
async loadData() {
  try {
    let service = new NetWorkService();
    let rsp = await
    service.robustFetch(
      'https://holmeshe.me/05apps/feeds', // --> 1)
      true ? {
        headers: {
          'Cache-Control': 'no-cache'
        }
      } : undefined
    );

    let feeds = await rsp.json();

    let feedsModel = feeds.map((obj) => { return new
    FeedModel(obj); });

    this.setState({data: feedsModel});
  } catch(e) {
    setState(() => { throw e }); // ----------------------> 2)
  }
}
```

1) Replace the vanilla fetch() with our robustFetch().

2) Throw the same exception in setState() so the exception can be caught by the well-defined **error boundary** which will make the final call in terms of the UI and behavior for *all* exceptions within.

5.4.2 Case Study, Offline Mode

We use *Net Info* as a trigger to retry the failed requests. It can be also used to manage the user expectation when the device is offline. Basically, we display a bar on top of the screen so the user will be less surprised if something is not working (Listing 5-19). Note that this feature does not affect any logic flow for network requests.

Listing 5-19. Offline indicator for the app

```
class App extends React.Component {
  constructor(props) {
    super(props);

    this.state = {
      offline: false // ------------------------------------> 1)
    };
  }

  componentDidMount() {
    NetInfo.addEventListener(state => { // ----------------> 2)
      if (!state.isConnected) {
        this.setState({offline: true});
      } else {
        this.setState({offline: false});
      }
    });
  }

  render() {
    return (
      <SafeAreaView style={{width: '100%', height: '100%'}}>
        <Moment/>
        {this.state.offline && // -------------------------> 3)
```

```
        <View style={{
          position: 'absolute',
          top: 0,
          left: 0,
          width: '100%',
          height: 60,
          backgroundColor: '#4ea4eb',
          justifyContent: 'center',
          alignItems: 'center',
          paddingTop: 20
        }}
        >
          <Text style={{
            fontSize: 16,
            fontWeight: "bold",
            color: 'white'
          }}>No Network</Text>
        </View>
        }
      </SafeAreaView>
    );
  }
}

export default App;
```

1) Add a new **state** to mark the network status.

2) Use *Net Info* to listen to the network status. Switch the **state** created earlier accordingly.

3) Display the offline tag when losing connectivity.

This is how it looks after completion (Figure 5-11).

Figure 5-11. *Offline mode*

5.5 Summary

Comprehensive skills and knowledge are required to achieve **05 apps**. One of the essentials is a network. In this chapter, we went through the essential network knowledge and techniques directly related to app development.

In the theory part of this chapter, we made a vertical trip through the network stack and visited some of the critical points. Along the path, we also watched the network traffic in action with various tools. Then we conclude the theory part by introducing some of the heuristics of the modern Internet.

For the practical part, we first introduced asynchronous programming in *JavaScript*, followed by the usage of the fetch() method. Then we enhanced *Manyface* with common network-related capabilities including API calls, large file download, local cache, as well as offline mode.

Lastly, we implemented a network-related exception flow in the light of the *wall-in* pattern. The difficulty for a network exception is that it is triggered externally, and we need to account for various scenarios by respecting HTTP error code in different ways, considering the retry strategy, and defining the behavior in offline mode.

CHAPTER 6

Advanced Topics

Believing the dots will connect down the road, will give you the confidence to follow your heart.

—Steve Jobs

This is the last chapter of this book. In this chapter, we are going to better fulfill our knowledge body, as well as our curiosity, in **React Native**, mostly by looking back at what we have learned throughout the previous chapters.

6.1 Revisit Rendering

React employs a **virtual DOM tree (VDOM tree)** to facilitate rendering (Section 1.2.6). A **virtual DOM tree** is an in-memory representation of the **components** being rendered with each **VDOM** as a **component**. What is returned by render() is a blueprint (an element) that is in turn used to construct a **VDOM** by the *React* runtime. The cascading calls of render() eventually provide the fragment of elements that are used to complete **VDOM tree** of the app. When it comes to updates, *React* uses a *diffing algorithm* (reconciliation) on the **VDOM tree** to collect the changes before any rerendering actually takes place. The *diffing algorithm* makes a layer-by-layer comparison of the **virtual DOM tree** and (1) unmounts and remounts the subtree if the types of the old and new versions' root node are different and (2) updates nodes using the new **props** if they are the same.

© M. Holmes He 2022
M. H. He, *Creating Apps with React Native*, https://doi.org/10.1007/978-1-4842-8042-3_6

Note   That means the setState() is heavy. When inappropriately used, ❄ it could trigger excessive rerendering of the whole **VDOM tree**.

This algorithm is expensive when the **VDOM tree** grows. So *React* provides majorly three measures to make the algorithm more efficient at scale: (1) 🚀 shouldComponentUpdate(), (2) 🚀 **pure component**, and (3) 🚀 *Redux*. Technically, all three methods reduce the number of nodes needed to be compared for the diffing algorithm. 🏛 More specifically, the first and second methods undercut the tree by preventing the diffing algorithm from being executed for an entire subtree, and the third uppercuts the tree by making the diffing algorithm only to start from a certain subtree (Figure 6-1). In this section, we are going to cover the first two methods. *Redux* will be covered in Section 6.2.

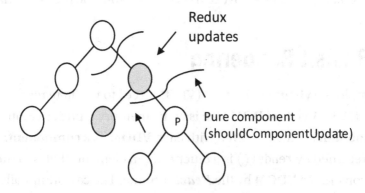

Figure 6-1. Constrain the rerendering

shouldComponentUpdate() gives you a chance to decide whether a **component** and the rooted subtree should be updated in the rendering event. Again, this event could be triggered from a setState() occurring somewhere on the upper layer in the **virtual DOM tree** hierarchy. 🚀 With this method, you make a **component** only listen to certain **props**, which effectively reduce the number of nodes involved in the *diffing algorithm*. ☀ The caveat is that `shouldComponentUpdate()` could block valid updates to the **subcomponents** unintentionally.

To make the updating flow more explicit and predictable, ♡ a general practice is to shallow compare all the **props** passed in – in other words, (1) to compare the value of the **props** if they are of primitive types and (2) to compare the reference of the **props** if they are objects (reference type). This practice has been generalized into a stock **component**, `PureComponent`. As we will see very soon, the principle of *Redux* (Section 6.2) is also established around the same principle of shallow comparison.

As said, the *diffing algorithm* compares the **VDOM tree** layer by layer. For each layer, it simply compares the nodes from left to right. This has a bad performance implication for one layer that is rendered as a list using `map()` or a `FlatList` (Section 6.3). ✳ More specifically, when the list is mutated, the diffing algorithm cannot infer the corresponding **components** to be compared in the new and old **VDOM tree**, which incurs unnecessary rerendering. ✂ To address this issue, it is recommended to attach keys to each **component** within the list.

Note   ☀ Using a list index as the key is an antipattern. This is because using a list index is equivalent to the no-key situation, where a list mutation could change the key of the same entry. ✂ So always use explicit keys for the list entries.

6.2 Redux

Redux is a go-to global state management framework. **States** are basically view modals, which are supposed to be local. A global view modal seems to be counterintuitive and overengineering. Nonetheless, it is a nirvana rising from a prolonged period of confusion, turmoil, and debating. It solves a fundamental difficulty of cross-**VDOM tree** communication, that is, when an event comes from one **component** on the tree and the update should be carried out on another.

To understand this difficulty, let's consider a typical video player **component** (Figure 6-2) where a click event on a play/pause button **component** should change the state of a screen **component** which might be located in a completely different subtree.

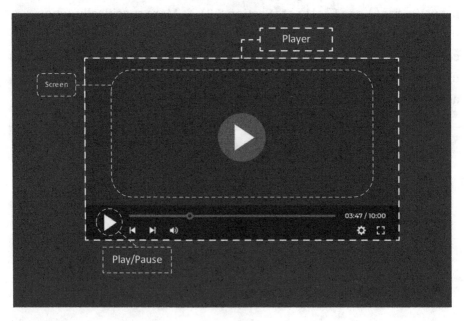

Figure 6-2. *A video player*

With the vanilla *React* local state management that relies purely on the local **state**, we need to pass some callbacks from the screen **component** all the way to the play button. When there are a lot of them, we have the callback hell problem in the context of the **VDOM tree** (Figure 6-3).

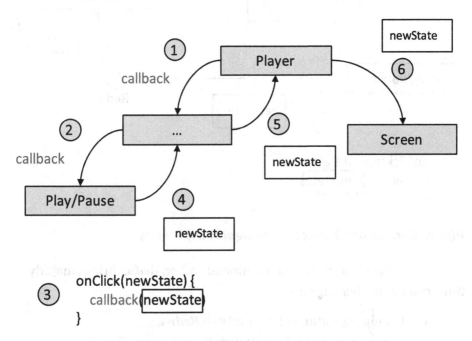

Figure 6-3. Using callbacks to propagate click events

Redux provides a direct way to communicate an event occurring in a **component** to other arbitrary **components** on the **VDOM tree** which are listening to the event. A successful delivery of an event could cause a **state** change and rerendering of the destined **component** (Figure 6-4).

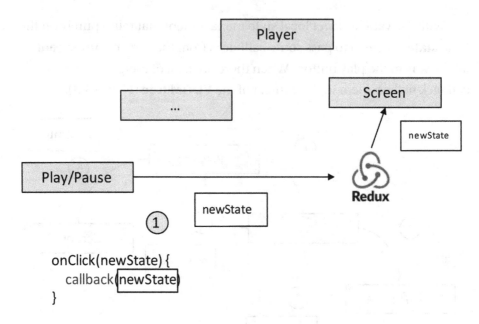

Figure 6-4. *Using Redux to propagate click events*

Besides the obvious benefit mentioned earlier, ***Redux*** brings majorly three collateral advantages:

1) Diffing algorithm efficiency: With ***Redux***, a change can always be sent directly to the specific **component**, so a diffing only on the subtree is required.

2) Unidirectional data change flow: This makes the state changes more reasonable and traceable, especially in the setting where a slice of a state (number of likes) could be changed by multiple sources (network fetch from the server and user interaction).

3) It adopts a semantic called *action* that aggregates by nature the meaningless, sometimes interdetermined, setters of individual properties with meaningful, easier-to-manage logic units.

To summarize:

Redux is an event system hooked up with global UI state updates.

Redux introduces basic concepts such as *store, reducer, dispatcher, action,* and *subscriber*:

1) The global states are managed in a *store* which is associated with a *reducer*.

2) We use a *dispatcher* to send *actions* to the *reducer* modifying the states in the *store*.

3) *Actions* contain all the information (payload) to carry out the change.

Redux follows the principle of immutability, which means, instead of modifying the content of the **global states**, we need to always create new instances of the changed **state** and set the modified version of the **state** back to the *store* (much like copy on write, aye ☺). For instance, if we have a nested **state** of three layers, and the field in the lowest layer got changed, then we need to create new instances top down along the chain and shallow copy the rest. This is how the **components** listening to the specific state change got updated. 🏛 It's better to keep the **Redux** state flatten and make the state directly usable by the UI as much as possible.

Note   *Redux* is a very powerful toolkit for managing global **states**. Nonetheless, the local **state** still has its seat on the table. This is true for UI- and animation-related **states** that are specific to a single **component**. 🏛 So it is suggested to manage in *Redux* only **states** that are changed/listened to by multiple entities, basically global **states**.

💣 One misuse of *Redux* is to copy a business model or service response directly as a *store*. In its essence, *Redux stores* define the view model, so using a business model is not optimal as they are separate concerns. More specifically, it could cause complex calculations during rendering. Simply put, it is better to be simple and direct for UI logic, so it is better to push the convolution out to the parsing and deserialization process or a dedicated adapter layer.

Note   That said, the preceding claim is not true if the client-to-service protocol is defined in a way that the view model is fully respected, which means the view model is returned directly by the service in an end-to-end manner, and the abstraction of the view model happens on the server side. GraphQL could be a good technical candidate to achieve that.

💣 Another misuse is to define a single *reducer* and object for the whole *store* or to bind a state directly on the root **component**. This causes an issue of thunder herding where all trivial updates hit on the complete **VDOM tree** that listens to the root object. 🏛 So it's better to spread the *reducers* and its associated objects out in accordance with different concerns. Besides the methods of separating by UI and domain logic, which are intuitive, here are some general principles:

1)   🏛 Separation of light and heavy

2)   🏛 Separation of important and trivial

3)   🏛 Separation of frequent and seldom

At the end of the day, (software) architecture is about how to converge and to separate.

—Holmes

Next, let's see how to use **Redux** in action.

6.2.1 Case Study, Like

This time, we are going to implement one of the most important features in a social network. To focus on the client side, we are not going to send any requests to the network and change the service state. First things first, here are the requirements:

1)   When a feed is liked, the like number should be increased with one.

2)   When a feed is liked by the user, the style of the like button should be changed to fill.

3)   When a feed is liked, it cannot be liked again and the button will be disabled.

Before everything, we need to install **Redux**:

```
npm install redux
npm install react-redux
```

6.2.1.1 *Reduxfy* Feeds

We need to *Reduxfy Feeds*-related **states** by creating the three mentioned elements, firstly, the *store and reducer* (Listing 6-1).

Listing 6-1. Store and reducer

```
import { createStore, combineReducers } from 'redux';
const INITIAL_STATE = {
  feeds: [], // ---------------------------------------------> 1)
};
const feedsReducer = (state = INITIAL_STATE, action) => {
  let newState = state;
  switch (action.type) { // ------------------------------> 2a)
    case 'UPDATE_FEEDS': // ------------------------------> 2a)
      if (!action?.payload?.feeds) {
        console.error(
          'action?.payload?.feeds is null in [UPDATE_FEEDS]'
        );
        return state;
      }
      newState = { // --------------------------------------> 3)
        ...state,
        feeds: action?.payload?.feeds // -----------------> 2b)
      };
      break;
    case 'LIKE':
...
    default:
      break;
  }
```

```
  return newState;
};

export default createStore(combineReducers({
  moment: feedsReducer // --------------------------------> 1)
})));
```

1) Define the *reducer* (feedsReducer) together with its root object (moment) in the store.

2) A *reducer* could encompass multiple *actions*. Each *action* modifies the object in the *store* in its own way. In the **Redux** paradigm, an *action* should include two important aspects, the type and the payload. The first determines its route in the logic branches; the second contains the information to carrying out the change.

3) In the **Redux** paradigm, we should always create new instances for the *store* objects rather than modifying it directly.

Next, we define *actions* that update the *store*, and we connect the *actions* with the *dispatch* in the form of **props**. Again, we only implement list updating and wait for the next section (Section 6.2.1.2) to implement the like. The following changes are made on Moment to make it listen to **Redux** (Listing 6-2).

Listing 6-2. Actions and dispatch

```
const mapDispatchToProps = dispatch => (
  bindActionCreators({
    updateFeeds: (feeds) => { // --------------------------> 1)
      return {
        type: 'UPDATE_FEEDS',
```

```
      payload: { feeds }
    }},
  }, dispatch)
);
```

1) Use inline closure to implement the *action*. If the
   actions will be reused by other **components**, they
   could be extracted into a dedicated file or folder for
   action creators.

Note   💣 One caveat of using an *action* is not to make a side effect
in it. In general principle, *actions* are supposed to be pure.

This dispatch could be used within `loadData()` of the same
component as shown in Listing 6-3.

Listing 6-3. Use dispatch

```
async loadData() {
...
--this.setState({data: feedsModel});
++this.props.updateFeeds(feedsModel);
...
}
```

Lastly, we connect the *dispatch* and the *store* with the **props** of Moment
and make it a subscriber (Listing 6-4).

Listing 6-4. Connect subscriber

```
const mapStateToProps = (state) => {
  const { moment } = state
  return { feeds: moment?.feeds }
};
```

```
const mapDispatchToProps = dispatch => (
...
);

export default withErrorBoundary(
  connect(mapStateToProps, mapDispatchToProps)
  (Moment), ErrorPage, undefined
);
```

6.2.1.2 Implement Like

Let's look at how the logic branch in the *reducer* for the like *action* looks like (Listing 6-5).

Listing 6-5. Reducer for like

```
const feedsReducer = (state = INITIAL_STATE, action) => {
  let newState = state;
  switch (action.type) {
    case 'UPDATE_FEEDS':
...
    case 'LIKE':
      if (action?.payload?.feedIndex === undefined ||
          action?.payload?.feedIndex === null ||
          action?.payload?.feedIndex < 0 ||
          action?.payload?.feedIndex >= state.feeds.length
      ) {
        console.error('action?.payload?.feedIndex is not valid
        in [LIKE]:' + action?.payload?.feedIndex);
        return state;
      }
      newState = { // ------------------------------------> 1)
        ...state,
```

```
      feeds: state.feeds.map((feed, index) => { // ------> 1)
        if (index === action.payload.feedIndex) {
          feed.meta.numOfLikes += 1; // ----------------> 2)
          feed.meta.liked = true; // -------------------> 2)
          feed.meta = Object.assign({}, feed.meta); // --> 1)
          return Object.assign({}, feed); // ------------> 1)
        } else {
          return feed;
        }
      })
    };
    default:
      break;
  }

  return newState;
};
```

1) As discussed in the beginning of Section 6.2, **Redux**
   follows the principle of immutability. Hence, we
   create new instances for each layer that contains the
   change. 💣 Without this step, the rendering will not
   be triggered at all.

2) Modify the relevant fields to be properly used
   by the UI.

Next, we implement the like with all the preparation of **Redux**.
More specifically, we are going to connect *dispatch* to the **HOC**
withMetaAndControls that contains the like button. Since we have bound
the *subscriber* to Moment that manages the feed list, the change carried out
in the *reducer* will be propagated down naturally to each *Feed* entry. Thus,
we don't need to bind any other *subscriber* again.

Listing 6-6 gives an enhanced version of withMetaAndControls.

Listing 6-6. Action and dispatcher for like

```
export default function withMetaAndControls(Feed) {
  class ElemComponent extends React.Component {
    render() {
      return (
        <View style={[
          {...this.props.style}, styles.commonPadding
        ]}>
          <View style={styles.metaContainer}>
            <LoomingImage
              style={styles.avatar}
              source={{uri: this.props.item.meta.avatarUri}}
            />
            <View style={styles.infoContainer}>
              <Text style={styles.userName}>
                {this.props.item.meta.name}
              </Text>
              <Text style={styles.date}>
                {this.props.item.meta.date}
              </Text>
            </View>
          </View>
          <Feed {...this.props} ref={this.props.innerRef}/>
          <View style={styles.controlContainer}>
            <TouchableOpacity // ------------------------> 3)
              disabled={this.props.item.meta.liked} // ----> 5)
              style={{flex: 1}}
```

```
          onPress={ // ------------------------------> 3)
            this.props.like.bind(this, this.props.feedIndex)
          }
        >
          <NumberedWidget
            type={
              this.props.item.meta.liked ? // ---------> 4)
              widgetTypes.LIKED :
              widgetTypes.LIKE
            }
            number={this.props.item.meta.numOfLikes}
          />
        </TouchableOpacity>
        <NumberedWidget
          style={{flex: 1}}
          type={widgetTypes.COMMENT}
          number={this.props.item.meta.numOfComments}
        />
        <NumberedWidget
          style={{flex: 1.5}}
          type={widgetTypes.SHARE}
          number={this.props.item.meta.numOfShares}
        />
        <Widget type={widgetTypes.MORE} />
      </View>
    </View>
  )
 }
}
```

```
  const mapDispatchToProps = dispatch => ( // -------------> 1)
    bindActionCreators({
      like: (feedIndex) => {
        return {
          type: 'LIKE',
          payload: { feedIndex }
        }},
    }, dispatch)
  );

  const ConnectedElemComponent = connect( // -------------> 2)
null, mapDispatchToProps)(ElemComponent
  );

  return React.forwardRef((props, ref) =>
<ConnectedElemComponent
    innerRef={ref} {...props}
  />);
}
```

1) Establish the *dispatch* with an inline *action* as in
   Section 6.2.1.1.

2) Connect the *dispatch* with the **HOC** ElemComponent
   in production.

3) Wrap the like button with a TouchableOpacity
   and attach the newly created *dispatch* with it. As
   mentioned, the changes in steps 4 and 5 and the like
   count will occur naturally after the execution of the
   reducer.

4) Change the button style according to the liked state.

5) Disable the button when liked.

6.3 Long List

Let's be clear, a long list is not an issue for **React Native**, not anymore. We know that the official **component** for long lists is FlatList which is the equivalent of *TableView* (*iOS*) and *recyclerview* (**Android**). As described in Section 2.3, the basic idea is to always render an area (*window*) larger than the viewport, while significantly smaller than the whole list. This gives an illusion that the complete list has been completely rendered while scrolling at a minimal cost in terms of the memory footprint.

Performance wise, it is sufficient to just go with the default configuration in most cases. If not, FlatList exposes some parameters which can be further fine-tuned to achieve a better perceived performance. The official document has done a great job; here, we summarize those optimization points and categorize them into basic and advanced ones.

Note   In the case where FlatList eventually cannot meet the performance bar, we have third parties like *RecyclerListView* in our hands, which are designed to further increase the performance potential.

Let's start from the basic optimization points that can be applied directly:

1) As mentioned in Section 6.1, adding a key to list entries can reduce the overhead of the diffing algorithm.

2) Use shouldComponentUpdate or a **pure component** (Section 6.1) to avoid rerendering of the complete list.

3) Use getItemLayout to precalculate the item height so the list doesn't need to carry out the calculation.

4) Use an image cache such as *react-native-fast-image*.

Then here are the advanced ones which require some fine-tuning of the FlatList rendering behaviors:

1) initialNumToRender defines the number of initial items to be rendered. Those items are never dismounted throughout the FlatList life cycle.

2) windowSize defines the *window* area in which items are required to be rendered.

3) maxToRenderPerBatch and updateCellsBatchingPeriod: These two parameters are used to control the rendering batch volume and frequency. Small batch and longer batching period could give better *TTI*, while large batch and lower batching period could avoid a blank area. So it's a trade-off on a 2 x 2 matrix.

6.3.1 Case Study, Apply Basic Heuristics

We will apply basic optimization to the list entries: (1) adding keys and (2) applying shouldComponentUpdate.

Firstly, let's add keys to the list entries. Here, we can simply use the feed ID as the key by using the built-in keyExtractor **props** of the FlatList (Listing 6-7).

Listing 6-7. Add a key to the FlatList item

```
<FlatList
...
  keyExtractor={(item) => item.feed.id}
...
/>
```

This removes the following warning message:

```
ManyFaces[19949:1694125] [javascript] Warning: Each child in a
list should have a unique "key" prop.

Check the render method of `VirtualizedList`. See https://
fb.me/react-warning-keys for more information.
```

Next, we look at the second optimization: shouldComponentUpdate and **pure component**. More specifically, we are going to implement shouldComponentUpdate to all *Feeds* **components**, to avoid unnecessary run passes of the *diffing algorithm*.

Note   A **pure component** cannot be applied here in that the *Feeds* are all encapsulated with **HOC** which introduces **prop** changes that are not controllable.

We know that all *Feeds* are listening to one critical **prop** which is item. So shouldComponentUpdate could compare only the item **prop** to determine whether there is an actual update request for the *Feed*. withMetaAndControls provides a single point of change since all *Feeds* are encapsulated using the **HOC**. Let's tune up the **HOC** (Listing 6-8).

Listing 6-8. Apply withMetaAndControls to the HOC

```
export default function withMetaAndControls(Feed) {
  class ElemComponent extends React.Component {
    shouldComponentUpdate(nextProps, nextState) {
      if (nextProps.item === this.props.item) { // --------> 1)
        return false;
      }

      return true; // ------------------------------------> 1)
    }

    render() {
      return (
...
      );
    }

    like = () => {
      this.props.like(this.props.feedIndex);
    }
...
  }
}
```

1) Update the *Feeds* only when the item passed in got
changed. This gives performance gain. For example,
when the user likes a *Feed*, only the render() of the
component that got liked will be invoked. In an
otherwise situation, the render() of all **components**
got called.

6.4 0 Crash, Design Exception Flow

One of the vital differences between an amateur and a professional is a systematic way of fallback.

—Holmes

Problem-solving is one of the most important qualities of a good developer. It takes skill, intuition, and sometimes luck to pinpoint and resolve an elusive bug. This is sometimes hard for even ACE programmers. An exception flow is vital in system design. One that helps discover a bug early and treat it early will definitely make your life easier even if you are one of those ACE programmers. Unfortunately, the exception flow is often out of focus. I have heard a few times the phrase "fail fast" and have seen the situation where exceptions are thrown to no one knows where. There are many ways to understand the phrase "fail fast." In my opinion, "fail fast" reflects the principle of reacting to bugs at the earliest possible chance. For example, if we can unveil a potential exception in compiling time, don't leave it at runtime; if we can discover an exception at the arrival of response data, don't leave it until it causes problems at the UI layer. The bottom line is we don't let our app crash in front of the users.

In this section, we are going to reexamine the low-end exception handling techniques we have learned so far and to derive general principles out of them.

The major difference between the exception flow and the feature flow is that the requirements of the exception flow could come from developers. Since developers know better than anyone else what exact error could happen, it is the developers' responsibility to define or to propose the exception experience. More specifically, we need to know what we want and do not want:

1) We want all exceptions to be properly directed to the intended location. We don't want exceptions being thrown to an arbitrary upper layer of the call stack, or being uncaught at all and crashes the app.

2) We want recoverable exceptions to be treated silently, which has to be transparent to the user.

3) We want unrecoverable exceptions to be defined with explicit behaviors and UI presentation, which should find the best way to express apology to the user.

4) We want to log all logic flows that are out of expectation. This includes both recoverable and unrecoverable exceptions. Even though the exception is minor and is not even noticeable (like Covid-19 no symptoms), it should be logged. The logging, in turn, serves as another bug reporting source besides bug bashing.

5) We want to know what exactly happens when a crash occurs in the field, so we can fix it efficiently and report it precisely to the upper chain.

With the requirements in mind, let's take a closer look at types of exceptions and think about ways to treat them separately. Exceptions can be categorized in four different ways.

In terms of severity, they can be divided into recoverable and unrecoverable exceptions. The difference is that the first one does not block the critical path, while the latter does. Take an example from *Manyface*; an exception thrown by one of the Feed **components** is recoverable by simply hiding the *Feed*, while an exception thrown by the *Moment* is not as it potentially leads to a complete blank screen.

From another dimension, it can be categorized into controlled exceptions and uncontrolled exceptions. Controlled exceptions are those thrown on purpose or protective early returns with an error indicator value. Uncontrolled exceptions are those completely out of our expectation, basically a bug that is too vicious and noticeable and, hence, is thrown out by the runtime.

We can also categorize exceptions into external exceptions and internal exceptions. For instance, a network error falls into external exceptions, and a logic fault falls into internal exceptions.

Lastly, there are global and local exceptions. Global exceptions can be only handled with a global handler; examples are a BAD_ACCESS and a segmentation fault. Local exceptions are those that can be captured in a local catch block or **error boundary**.

Here, we give the principles to handle each exception category:

1) 🚀 For unrecoverable exceptions, we need to throw them all the way to the UI and give feedbacks to the user, such as displaying a "something went wrong" page, popping up a toast, or resetting the state and jumping back to login.

2) 🚀 For recoverable exceptions, we apply a technique called "silent log." Basically, we log it so we know, while we make the UX flow continuous so the users don't know.

3) 🚀 For controllable exceptions, we log them with all information we need.

4) 🚀 We minimize uncontrollable exceptions by transferring them to controllable ones in best efforts. This is achieved again by meticulously logging.

5) 🚀 External exceptions are not completely within the control of client logic, so "retry" logic could be involved to mitigate it, while we normally don't retry on internal exceptions.

6) 🚀 Global exceptions are not recoverable by nature. Hence, it is the last resort when all local exception handlers fail.

Note 🏛 Intentional, controlled, and meticulous logging is generally better than an uncontrolled crash dump. When an uncontrolled crash dump occurs, the root cause might have been obscured. For example, a BAD_ACCESS in sendMsg in **Cocoa** could be caused by a released object which is very hard to be discovered with the information in the crash report.

JavaScript has an inherent advantage. That is, unlike most other programming languages like *C++* and *Objective-C*, we can make all exceptions local in *JavaScript*. That means all exceptions, including null pointers, can be caught in the form of an exception using a catch block or **error boundary**. Let's summarize what we have done to make *Manyface* maintain the minimal bar of crash free:

1) 🚀 Always apply a top-level error boundary which catches an exception from within.

2) 🚀 Always apply a top-level catch block of the entry points of the method calls. And potentially redirect those exceptions to the error boundary.

6.4.1 Robustness Built in Software Architecture

To properly design the exception handling mechanism, we need to define the **bubble** (think about the bubble in the context of Covid-19). More specifically, we need to define two points that are critical. (1) **The entry points** are basically the boundary of a **bubble**, from where the potential risky raw data comes in hence should be transferred to data that is absolutely legit and expectable. (2) **The crash points** represent the high risky parts within the **bubble** that should be taken care of in particular. Programmatically, those are the lines of code that could cause a crash.

6.4.1.1 Entry Points

This is where external data is received and processed. In *React Native*, we have two such places, that is, (1) when the data comes from the server side and (2) when the data comes from the native layer to the *JavaScript* layer. Technically, when interdomain communication is involved, we need to deserialize a general, untyped JSON into a typed model object. At this point, we need to carry out null checks, to gracefully fall back, and to throw exceptions when necessary.

In this process, it's important to be explicit about which is optional, which is compulsory, and which is critical. The first two types are negotiated with the server side, while the last one is decided solely by the client side. Let's look at one way to treat them respectively:

1) Null in optional fields: This is a logic flow rather than an exception flow since no protocol is broken. Hence, we can simply give the field a default value as fallback.

2) Null in compulsory fields: This time the protocol is broken. When identifying such a case, we carry out the same fallback by setting it with a default value and log it so we will know some transactions are broken, but we recover it secretly to not bother the user.

3) Null in critical fields: This time, not only the
    protocol has been broken, but also the missing field
    belongs to the critical path. And the UX cannot
    continue. In such cases, we throw the exception the
    first chance we have. This is the only case where we
    throw an exception which effectively interrupts the
    whole model processing and should be handled by
    the UI layer (a **component**).

Note   95% of crashes come from inappropriately treating illegal
responses from the server, an unofficial, empirical value.

6.4.1.2 Crash Points

Let's be more concrete; we should be careful of **null pointer exceptions**
and **out of boundary exceptions**, by looking at . and [ ].

Note   Out of bound is not an instant exception in *JavaScript*.
However, it should be treated explicitly in my opinion. Here, the
principle of "react at the earliest chance" comes into play.

The preceding two exceptions and any other uncommon exceptions
could occur in three places, within (1) a **component**, (2) a global function,
and (3) a native layer. We have seen how to use an **error boundary** to
deal with exceptions in a **component** in Section 2.4, how to channel
asynchronous exceptions to an **error boundary** in Section 5.4, and how
to channel native exceptions to an **error boundary** in Section 4.4. And we
call this approach a *wall-in*. When handling exceptions, we should also be
clear about recoverable and unrecoverable exceptions. And we only throw
on critical paths for unrecoverable ones where the UX cannot continue;

other exceptions occurring in non-essential logic passes are treated as recoverable exceptions and should be swallowed by their respective module. Again, logging is always desired, especially when something happens in production.

Note   Again, the last thing we want to see is that an exception of a trivial supplementary subsystem jeopardizes the core, much like a glitch in the stereo system crashes a car.

The only place that hasn't been covered is the global function. A good practice is to not put any critical path in global functions. This is because it is too involved to communicate exceptions between a global function and a **component** which should in turn reflect the exception on the UI correspondingly. By applying only optional paths (e.g., update flow), all exceptions should be swallowed within as discussed earlier.

6.4.2 Last Resort, Global Error Handler

At last, exceptions could still occur even with the fully defensive code in place. Those exceptions should be treated as failures and can be only covered by a global error handler. There are majorly three ways of carrying out global error handling:

1) An **error boundary** that wraps around the root **component** of the app, which displays "something went wrong."

2) Install a RCTExceptionManager, and bind a delegate with it.

3) *react-native-exception-handler.*

Exceptions hit on these handlers are uncontrolled and unrecoverable exceptions. Normally, they are uncaught exceptions in the *JavaScript* layer or fatal exceptions in the native layer. Global handlers can be used to carry out tasks such as crash reporting which could provide another invaluable information source directly from the field. Nonetheless, it's much more desired to hunt down those issues early in the development and testing phases.

Much like handrails on a cliff, it's better not to rely on them.

6.4.3 Wrap Up

A disaster is inevitable. In fact, experiencing a disaster, better at scale, is one key ingredient to develop an ACE programmer. This is the next level from a feature implementer (level 1) and a problem solver (level 2). Being exposed to large scale system where disaster is inevitable, these programmers display two key qualities in their everyday development activities:

1) The willingness and capability to deep dive into problems that occur in the production phase

2) The willingness and capacity to design the system up front to be resilient and to provide as much information as possible in disaster to facilitate 1

Good role models are kernel programmers. Without the modern tools discussed in this book, they can design and develop an exception flow that defends hypercomplicated systems mostly using pure goto. So, in the opinion of the author, it might be more important to develop such a mindset than the excellence in tooling. Anyway, it is in our best interests to approach a 0 crash app.

Lastly, please bear in mind that exception experience is an essential part of user experience. We need to work closely with the product team to work out a good plan.

6.5 Native Modules Inside Out

Afterall, a bridge is all we need to cross platforms.

—Holmes

In this section, we will guide you through what happens next after the app initialization. We will first examine the *Objective-C* layer and the *JavaScript* layer of *React Native*. Then we will deep dive into the *C++* layer. In general, it helps you understand how pieces of *React Native* come together and work as a solid unit.

The purpose of **native modules** is to export native functionalities. Technically, functions written in native can be injected to the *JavaScript* runtime and be used by *JavaScript* code directly. This is enabled by engines such as **JavaScriptCore**. The exporting of native methods is built on top of this capability with some adjustment.

Rather than concrete method invocation, calls to **native modules** are translated into messages that are sent through a bridge. ✳ In the past, the parameters passed through are required to be serialized and deserialized when crossing the bridge, which imposes performance penalties. This was a toll for cross-language communication. ✂ The **JSI**-based optimization removed the need for this serialization and deserialization.

Let's have a look at the big picture (Figure 6-5). Here, we need to pay attention to the three different dimensions for the same flow: (1) the dimension of call hierarchy, which is the main flow of the diagram; (2) the dimension of the thread model and lock, which is marked with rectangles and a lock symbol; and (3) the dimension of the storage of **native module** metadata, which is marked with a soft disk.

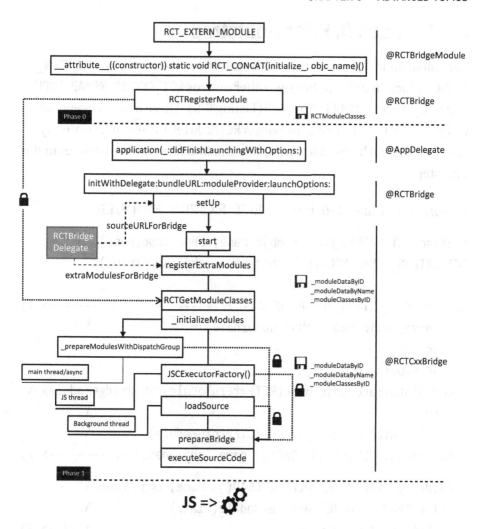

Figure 6-5. *React Native bootstrap (phase 0-1)*

The initialization flow is divided roughly into three phases, prior bootstrap, bootstrap, and initialization on the *JavaScript* layer. They are discussed in the respective sections. Note that we have a dedicated section to explain the thread and locking mechanism, so please don't feel frustrated when something does not look clear in the beginning.

Now, let's start the journey.

6.5.1 Phase 0, Prior Bootstrap

The initialization of a native module starts from the macro RCT_EXTERN_
MODULE which in turn applies two other macros RCT_EXTERN_REMAP_MODULE
and RCT_EXPORT_MODULE_NO_LOAD (Listing 6-9). These macros eventually
will populate the module class within RCTModuleClasses in a very early
stage, which will be used to instantiate the **native module** instances in the
next step.

Listing 6-9. Phase 0-0, behind RCT_EXTERN_MODULE

```
#define RCT_EXTERN_MODULE(objc_name, objc_supername)
RCT_EXTERN_REMAP_MODULE(, objc_name, objc_supername)


#define RCT_EXTERN_REMAP_MODULE( // ----------------------> 1)
  js_name, objc_name, objc_supername)                 \
  objc_name:                                          \
  objc_supername @                                    \
  end @interface objc_name(RCTExternModule)<RCTBridgeModule> \
  @end                                                \
  @implementation objc_name (RCTExternModule)         \
  RCT_EXPORT_MODULE_NO_LOAD(js_name, objc_name) // --------> 2)

#define RCT_EXPORT_MODULE_NO_LOAD(js_name, objc_name)\
  RCT_EXTERN void RCTRegisterModule(Class);          \
  +(NSString *)moduleName                            \ // -> 3)
  {                                                  \
      return @ #js_name;                             \
  }                                                  \
  __attribute__((constructor))
```

```
static void RCT_CONCAT(initialize_,
                       objc_name)()                    \ // -> 4)
{                                                       \
    RCTRegisterModule([objc_name class]);               \ // -> 5)
}
```

1) Define the @interface using the module name passed in.

2) Define its @implementation straight after.

3) Implement moduleName. This is the exact equivalent of getName() in *Android* **native module** implementation.

4) Use __attribute__((constructor)) to make the module registration before everything else.

5) Call RCTRegisterModule to register the module.

Note   RCT_EXTERN_MODULE is primarily used by *Swift*-based native modules where the load() method is not allowed. For vanilla *Objective-C*, we can use the simpler version RCT_EXPORT_MODULE to achieve the same.

At the end of this phase, let's look at how the RCTRegisterModule is implemented (Listing 6-10).

Listing 6-10. Phase 0-1, RCTRegisterModule@RCTBridge

```
void RCTRegisterModule(Class moduleClass)
{
  static dispatch_once_t onceToken;
  dispatch_once(&onceToken, ^{
```

```
        RCTModuleClasses = [NSMutableArray new]; // ------> 1)
        RCTModuleClassesSyncQueue = dispatch_queue_create(
        "com.facebook.react.ModuleClassesSyncQueue",
        DISPATCH_QUEUE_CONCURRENT
        );
});

RCTAssert(
        [moduleClass conformsToProtocol:@protocol
        (RCTBridgeModule)],
        @"%@ does not conform to the RCTBridgeModule
        protocol",
        moduleClass);

// Register module
dispatch_barrier_async(RCTModuleClassesSyncQueue, ^{
        [RCTModuleClasses addObject:moduleClass]; // -----> 2)
});
}
```

1) Instantiate the singleton entities, RCTModuleClasses and RCTModuleClassesSyncQueue.

2) Add the class object to RCTModuleClasses.

At the end of this phase, the **native modules** are in the form of their respective classes and are stored in RCTModuleClasses.

6.5.2 Phase 1, Bootstrap

Next, let's look at the bootstrap of a **React Native** app, more specifically, the initialization of **the bridge**.

RCTBridge offers two approaches for initialization:

1) Direct initialization: This way, the initialization is facilitated with initWithBundleURL:moduleProvider:launchOptions: which accepts the bundle URL and **extra modules** (Section 4.3.7) directly as parameters.

2) Delegate initialization: This way, the initialization is facilitated with initWithDelegate:launchOptions:, where the bundle URL and extra modules are provided by a delegate.

We are going to use the second approach which is more flexible and is more conforming to the general design pattern on *iOS* (Listing 6-11).

Note   When both bundle URL and delegate are provided using the designated initializer (initWithDelegate:bundleURL:moduleProvider: launchOptions:), the information provided by the latter (i.e., delegate) will prevail.

Listing 6-11. Phase 1-0, app bootstrap logic in AppDelegate

```
@UIApplicationMain
class AppDelegate: UIResponder, UIApplicationDelegate,
RCTBridgeDelegate {
  var window: UIWindow?
  var bridge: RCTBridge!

  func application(
    _ application: UIApplication,
    didFinishLaunchingWithOptions
```

```
    launchOptions: [UIApplication.LaunchOptionsKey: Any]?
  ) -> Bool { // --------------------------------------> 1)
    self.bridge = RCTBridge( // ---------------------------> 2)
      delegate: self, launchOptions: launchOptions
    )

    let rootView = RCTRootView( // ------------------------> 3)
      bridge: self.bridge,
      moduleName: "ManyFaces",
      initialProperties: nil
    )

    self.window = UIWindow(frame: UIScreen.main.bounds)
    let rootViewController = UIViewController()

    rootViewController.view = rootView // ----------------> 4)

    self.window!.rootViewController =
rootViewController; // > 4)
    self.window!.makeKeyAndVisible() // -------------------> 4)

    return true
  }

  func sourceURL(for bridge: RCTBridge!) -> URL! { // -----> 5)
#if DEBUG
    return RCTBundleURLProvider.sharedSettings().
    jsBundleURL(forBundleRoot:"index", fallbackResource: nil)
#else
    return Bundle.main.url(
      forResource:"main", withExtension:"jsbundle"
    )
#endif
  }
}
```

1) The initialization all happens within the `application:`
`didFinishLaunchingWithOptions:` callback.

2) Use the second approach to initialize the bridge.
This is the critical line from where we can go deeper.

3) Use the bridge to initialize the root view.

4) Attach the root view to the `window.rootView`
`Controller`, and make it visible.

5) Override the `sourceURL(for bridge: RCTBridge!)`
to provide the bundle. More specifically, when it's in
debug mode, use RCTBundleURLProvider to load
the bundle from the metro server; otherwise, read
the bundle file directly from the asset. Here, the
DEBUG macro is defined under `Build Settings`
➤ `Swift Compiler` ➤ `Custom Flags` ➤ `Other`
`Swift Flags`.

Then let's examine what's going on within RCTBridge (Listing 6-12).

Listing 6-12. Phase 1-1, set up the RCTBridge

```
- (instancetype)initWithDelegate:(id<RCTBridgeDelegate>)
delegate
                    bundleURL:(NSURL *)bundleURL
                    moduleProvider:(RCTBridgeModuleList
                    Provider)block
                    launchOptions:(NSDictionary *)
                    launchOptions
{
  if (self = [super init]) {
    _delegate = delegate; // ----------------------------> 1)
    _bundleURL = bundleURL;
```

```
  _moduleProvider = block;
  _launchOptions = [launchOptions copy];

  [self setUp]; // -------------------------------------> 2)
}
return self;
}

...

- (void)setUp
{
... // perf log

  Class bridgeClass = self.bridgeClass;

  // Only update bundleURL from delegate if delegate bundleURL
    has changed
  NSURL *previousDelegateURL = _delegateBundleURL;
  _delegateBundleURL =
  [self.delegate sourceURLForBridge:self];// --------------> 3)

  if (_delegateBundleURL &&
    ![_delegateBundleURL isEqual:previousDelegateURL]
  ) {
    _bundleURL = _delegateBundleURL; // ------------------> 3)
  }

  // Sanitize the bundle URL
  _bundleURL = [RCTConvert NSURL:_bundleURL.
  absoluteString];//>3)

// ... for debug mode
```

```
self.batchedBridge = [[bridgeClass alloc] // ------------> 4)
initWithParentBridge:self];

[self.batchedBridge start]; // ------------------------> 5)
// ... perf
}
```

1) Set the delegate (an AppDelegate instance) in step 0 to **the bridge**.

2) Move on.

3) Call the delegate sourceURLForBridge implemented in phase 0 to obtain the bundle URL.

4) Instantiate the RCTCxxBridge which is another layer below RCTBridge that deals directly with the *C++* layer. RCTCxxBridge is the layer we are going to stop for this section.

5) Move on to RCTCxxBridge.

As mentioned, the RCTCxxBridge is the cutting point between *Objective-C* and *C++*. In React Native, there are four major C++ entities: Instance, JSIExecutor, JsToNativeBridge, and NativeToJsBridge. Their names are very self-explained. JSIExecutor executes *JavaScript* loaded in the form of bundle or string literals. The JsToNativeBridge and NativeToJsBridge facilitate the two-way communication between *JavaScript* and **native layers**. And Instance is their container that provides the interfaces to the upper layer. The major task of the next phase in RCTCxxBridge is to initialize Instance and the associated entities (Listing 6-13).

Listing 6-13. Phase 1-2, start the RCTCxxBridge

```
- (void)start
{
... // profiling

  // Set up the JS thread early
  _jsThread = [[NSThread alloc] initWithTarget:[self class]
  selector:@selector(runRunLoop) object:nil]; // ----------> 1)
  _jsThread.name = RCTJSThreadName;
  _jsThread.qualityOfService =
  NSOperationQualityOfServiceUserInteractive;

#if RCT_DEBUG
  _jsThread.stackSize *= 2;
#endif

  [_jsThread start];

  dispatch_group_t prepareBridge = dispatch_group_create();

... // perf log

  [self registerExtraModules]; // ------------------------> 2)
  // Initialize all native modules that cannot be loaded lazily
  (void)[self _initializeModules:RCTGetModuleClasses()
  withDispatchGroup:prepareBridge lazilyDiscovered:NO]; // --> 3)

  [self registerExtraLazyModules]; // --------------------> 4)

... // perf log

  // This doesn't really do anything.  The real work happens in
    initializeBridge.

  _reactInstance.reset(new Instance); // ------------------> 5)
```

```
__weak RCTCxxBridge *weakSelf = self;

// Prepare executor factory (shared_ptr for copy into block)
std::shared_ptr<JSExecutorFactory> executorFactory;
if (!self.executorClass) {
...

   if (!executorFactory) {
     executorFactory =
     std::make_shared<JSCExecutorFactory>(nullptr); // ---> 6)
   }
} else {
...
  }


// Dispatch the instance initialization as soon as the
initial module metadata has
// been collected (see initModules)
dispatch_group_enter(prepareBridge); // ----------------> 7)
[self ensureOnJavaScriptThread:^{
  [weakSelf _initializeBridge:executorFactory]; // ------> 7)
  dispatch_group_leave(prepareBridge);
}];

// Load the source asynchronously, then store it for later
   execution.
dispatch_group_enter(prepareBridge); // ----------------> 8)
__block NSData *sourceCode;
[self
  loadSource:^(NSError *error, RCTSource *source) { // --> 8)
    if (error) {
      [weakSelf handleError:error];
    }
```

```
      sourceCode = source.data;
      dispatch_group_leave(prepareBridge);
   }

... // for debug

  // Wait for both the modules and source code to have
     finished loading
  dispatch_group_notify(prepareBridge, // ----------------> 9)
  dispatch_get_global_queue(QOS_CLASS_USER_INTERACTIVE, 0),
  ^{
    RCTCxxBridge *strongSelf = weakSelf;
    if (sourceCode && strongSelf.loading) {
      [strongSelf executeSourceCode:sourceCode sync:NO]; // -> 9)
    }
  });
...
}
```

1) Init the *JavaScript* thread. All JavaScript code will
   be executed on this thread. Inside runRunLoop,
   a technique using *iOS* run loop is used to start a
   persistent thread.

2) Use the **native module** instances provided by
   the delegate to initialize their corresponding
   RCTModuleData which stores all metadata of a **native
   module** (Section 4.3.2). This step is effective if the
   delegate implements the extraModulesForBridge
   in phase 0. More specifically, this step could be used
   for dependency injection on *iOS* (Section 4.3.7).

3) Use native module classes stored in RCTModuleClasses to initialize their corresponding RCTModuleData (Section 4.3.2). RCTModuleClasses is populated with the RCT_EXTERN_MODULE that we used very often to export **native modules** in previous sections. We are going to examine this step very soon in Section 4.3.2.1. This step leads to the next critical phase (1-3).

4) This method is not used for production.

5) Instantiate Instance.

6) Initialize JSCExecutorFactory which is the provider of JSIExecutor.

7) Initialize the four entities. Note that this step is carried out asynchronously on the *JavaScript* thread.

8) Load the *JavaScript* bundle.

9) Execute the *JavaScript* bundle loaded after steps 3, 7, and 8 are completed. Note that this is guaranteed with the prepareBridge.

Next, let's examine the initializeModules in step 3. This is actually the most relevant step to this chapter as it is where all **native modules** (and **view managers**) are instantiated. Again, all unrelated code is removed for clarity (Listing 6-14).

Listing 6-14. Phase 1-3, initialize modules

```
- (NSArray<RCTModuleData *> *)
_initializeModules:(NSArray<Class> *)modules
 withDispatchGroup:(dispatch_group_t)dispatchGroup
  lazilyDiscovered:(BOOL)lazilyDiscovered
```

```
{
  // Set up moduleData for automatically-exported modules
  NSArray<RCTModuleData *> *moduleDataById =
  [self _registerModulesForClasses:modules
                 lazilyDiscovered:lazilyDiscovered]; // --> 1)

  if (lazilyDiscovered) {
// ----------------------------------------------------------> 2)
  } else {
    for (RCTModuleData *moduleData in _moduleDataByID) {
      if (moduleData.hasInstance &&
          (!moduleData.requiresMainQueueSetup || RCTIsMainQueue())
      ) {
        (void)[moduleData instance]; // -------------------> 3)
      }
    }
...
    _moduleSetupComplete = YES;
    [self _prepareModulesWithDispatchGroup:dispatchGroup]; //> 4)
  }
// ... profiling
  return moduleDataById;
}
```

1) Transform the raw classes of native modules to
   RCTModuleData with _registerModulesForClasses.
   This step is similar to that of registerExtraModules
   (phase 1-2, step 2). The difference here is that **native
   modules** are not instantiated in this step. We look at
   the implementation of this method in Listing 6-15.

2) `lazilyDiscovered` is set to no for ordinary **native modules** that are not passed in with `registerAdditionalModuleClasses`.

3) Initialize the **native modules** that require the main queue setup and have been already instantiated, that is, **native module** instances provided by `registerExtraModules` are under this category (phase 1-2, step 2).

4) Initialize and instantiate the **native modules** that require the main queue setup and are provided otherwise (using `RCT_EXTERN_MODULE` macros). The implementation of `_prepareModulesWithDispatchGroup` is shown in Listing 6-16.

Let's look at the `_registerModulesForClasses` (Listing 6-15).

Listing 6-15. Phase 1-4, initialize modules (continue)

```
- (NSArray<RCTModuleData *> *)
  _registerModulesForClasses:(NSArray<Class> *)moduleClasses
          lazilyDiscovered:(BOOL)lazilyDiscovered
{
...
  NSArray *moduleClassesCopy = [moduleClasses copy];
  NSMutableArray<RCTModuleData *> *moduleDataByID =
  [NSMutableArray arrayWithCapacity:moduleClassesCopy.count];

  for (Class moduleClass in moduleClassesCopy) {
    if (RCTTurboModuleEnabled() &&
        [moduleClass conformsToProtocol:
        @protocol(RCTTurboModule)]
    ) {
```

357

```
    continue;
  }

  NSString *moduleName =
  RCTBridgeModuleNameForClass(moduleClass);

// Check for module name collisions
...
    moduleData = [[RCTModuleData alloc]
    initWithModuleClass:moduleClass bridge:self]; // ------> 1)
    _moduleDataByName[moduleName] = moduleData; // --------> 2)
    [_moduleClassesByID addObject:moduleClass]; // --------> 2)
    [moduleDataByID addObject:moduleData]; // -------------> 2)
  }

  [_moduleDataByID addObjectsFromArray:moduleDataByID]; // --> 2)

...

  return moduleDataByID;
}
```

1) Instantiate the RCTModuleData.

2) Save it to the corresponding data structures.

Listing 6-16 gives a simplified version of the previously used _prepareModulesWithDispatchGroup that is removed with all the noncritical logic. As you can see, it is another iteration that invokes an instance of RCTModuleData. Note that this is where the prepareBridge dispatch queue group (prepared in phase 1-3, step 2) is applied.

Listing 6-16. Phase 1-5, initialize modules (continue)

```
- (void)_prepareModulesWithDispatchGroup:
  (dispatch_group_t)dispatchGroup
{
...

  BOOL initializeImmediately = NO;
  if (dispatchGroup == NULL) {
// ... condition not applied here
  }

// ... perf

  for (RCTModuleData *moduleData in _moduleDataByID) {
    if (moduleData.requiresMainQueueSetup) {
      dispatch_block_t block = ^{ // ----------------------> 2)
        if (self.valid &&
            ![moduleData.moduleClass
            isSubclassOfClass:[RCTCxxModule class]]
        ) {
// ...
          (void)[moduleData instance]; // ----------------> 1)
          [moduleData gatherConstants]; // ---------------> 1)
// ...
        }
      };

      if (initializeImmediately && RCTIsMainQueue()) {
// condition not applied here
      } else {
        if (dispatchGroup) {
          dispatch_group_async( // --------------------> 2)
          dispatchGroup, dispatch_get_main_queue(), block
```

```
        );
    }
  }
  _modulesInitializedOnMainQueue++;
  }
  }
...
}
```

1) Initialize and instantiate the native modules.

2) Apply the initialization on the main queue as indicated by requiresMainQueueSetup. As mentioned, this operation is part of the prepareBridge dispatch queue group.

At this point, the **native modules** are in the form of RCTModuleData stored in _moduleDataByID. Among those, the **native modules** that require the main queue setup are initialized and are instantiated up front. The rest of the **native modules** are instantiated on the run in the next phases. Before we move on to those phases, we look at requiresMainQueueSetup.

6.5.2.1 requiresMainQueueSetup

requiresMainQueueSetup is a class method defined in RCTBridgeModule that can be overridden by any **native modules**. When returning true, it indicates that the **native module** requires the main queue setup, meaning to be set up in the main queue. This is the explicit type of requiring the main queue setup. And as we just saw, modules that require the main queue setup are instantiated up front during bootstrap.

There are also **native modules** that require the main queue setup implicitly. More specifically, if a native module either has a custom init method or overrides the constantsToExport, it is determined as requiring the main queue setup. This implicitly is also highlighted during bootstrap with the following warning message:

Module HelloWorldManager requires main queue setup since it overrides `constantsToExport` but doesn't implement `requiresMainQueueSetup`. In a future release React Native will default to initializing all native modules on a background thread unless explicitly opted-out of.

The actual code that reflects this logic is inside the setUp method of RCTModuleData (Listing 6-17). Actually, the sole purpose of this method is to determine whether the **native module** requires a main queue.

Listing 6-17. Set up the RCTModuleData

```
- (void)setUp
{
// ... irrelevant logic
  _hasConstantsToExport =
  [_moduleClass instancesRespondToSelector:
    @selector(constantsToExport)
  ];

  const BOOL implementsRequireMainQueueSetup =
  [_moduleClass respondsToSelector:
  @selector(requiresMainQueueSetup)];

  if (implementsRequireMainQueueSetup) {
    _requiresMainQueueSetup =
    [_moduleClass requiresMainQueueSetup];
  } else {
```

```objc
    static IMP objectInitMethod;
    static dispatch_once_t onceToken;
    dispatch_once(&onceToken, ^{
      objectInitMethod =
      [NSObject instanceMethodForSelector:@selector(init)];
    });

    const BOOL hasCustomInit = !_instance &&
  [_moduleClass instanceMethodForSelector:@selector(init)]
  != objectInitMethod;

    _requiresMainQueueSetup =
    _hasConstantsToExport || hasCustomInit;
    if (_requiresMainQueueSetup) {
      const char *methodName = "";
      if (_hasConstantsToExport) {
        methodName = "constantsToExport";
      } else if (hasCustomInit) {
        methodName = "init";
      }

      RCTLogWarn(
      @"Module %@ requires main queue setup since it overrides
      `%s` but doesn't implement "
        "`requiresMainQueueSetup`. In a future release React
      Native will default to initializing all native modules "
          "on a background thread unless explicitly opted-
          out of.",
          _moduleClass,
          methodName);
    }
  }
}
```

We know that RCTModuleData is initialized and instantiated in two methods, _registerModulesForClasses and registerExtraModules in RCTCxxBridge. And the setUp method is eventually called from there.

6.5.2.2 Threads and Locks

One difficulty in understanding the flow (Figure 6-5) is the threading model and locks. Some locks are nested down to the call stack and are working on different phases, which obscure the actual mechanics.

The first lock we encounter is across phase 0 and phase 1, where a dispatch barrier is applied on a dispatch queue, RCTModuleClassesSyncQueue, when we add the native module classes to RCTModuleClasses in RCTRegisterModule (Listing 6-18).

Listing 6-18. Lock in phase 0

```
...
  dispatch_barrier_async(RCTModuleClassesSyncQueue, ^{
    [RCTModuleClasses addObject:moduleClass];
  });
...
```

This is to ensure that all the module classes have been stored successfully before we read from RCTModuleClasses in phase 1 (Listing 6-19).

Listing 6-19. Waiting for lock in phase 1

```
- (void)start
{
...
  (void)[self _initializeModules:RCTGetModuleClasses()
  withDispatchGroup:prepareBridge lazilyDiscovered:NO];
...
}
```

Inside `RCTGetModuleClasses()`, `dispatch_sync` is used to wait for all the dispatch barriers to complete (Listing 6-20).

Listing 6-20. RCTGetModuleClasses

```
NSArray<Class> *RCTGetModuleClasses(void)
{
  __block NSArray<Class> *result;
  dispatch_sync(RCTModuleClassesSyncQueue, ^{
    result = [RCTModuleClasses copy];
  });
  return result;
}
```

The second lock is in phase 1 which is applied around a dispatch group, `prepareBridge`. Firstly, this dispatch group is passed all the way down to `_prepareModulesWithDispatchGroup` where blocks are created for each native module and are shot to the main thread (Listing 6-21).

Listing 6-21. Passed down to _prepareModulesWithDispatchGroup

```
- (void)_prepareModulesWithDispatchGroup:(dispatch_group_t)
dispatchGroup
{
...
  for (RCTModuleData *moduleData in _moduleDataByID) {
    if (moduleData.requiresMainQueueSetup) {
      dispatch_block_t block = ^{
...
      };
...
      if (dispatchGroup) {
        dispatch_group_async(
```

```
        dispatchGroup, dispatch_get_main_queue(), block
      );
    }
    _modulesInitializedOnMainQueue++;
  }
 }
...
}
```

Next, the dispatch group is used (1) to initialize the bridge on the *JavaScript* thread as well as (2) to load the bundle (Listing 6-22).

Listing 6-22. Init bridge and load the bundle

```
- (void)start
{
...
  dispatch_group_enter(prepareBridge); // ----------------> 1)
  [self ensureOnJavaScriptThread:^{
    [weakSelf _initializeBridge:executorFactory];
    dispatch_group_leave(prepareBridge); // --------------> 1)
  }];

  dispatch_group_enter(prepareBridge); // ----------------> 2)
  __block NSData *sourceCode;
  [self loadSource:^(NSError *error, RCTSource *source) {
    if (error) {
      [weakSelf handleError:error];
    }

    sourceCode = source.data;
    dispatch_group_leave(prepareBridge); // --------------> 2)
  }
...
}
```

Lastly, the *JavaScript* execution can start after all the prerequisites are met (Listing 6-23).

Listing 6-23. Execute JavaScript after everything is done

```
- (void)start
{
...
  dispatch_group_notify(
    prepareBridge,
    dispatch_get_global_queue(QOS_CLASS_USER_INTERACTIVE, 0),
    ^{
      RCTCxxBridge *strongSelf = weakSelf;
      if (sourceCode && strongSelf.loading) {
        [strongSelf executeSourceCode:sourceCode sync:NO];
      }
    }
  );
...
}
```

6.5.3 Phase 2, Native Module on the JavaScript Layer

The last step of **native module** initialization occurs on the *JavaScript* layer.

Again, let's look at the big picture (Figure 6-6) to understand what happens after the *JavaScript* execution starts. This step involves direct native-to-JS communication through the global object. More specifically, *JavaScript* and native layers both inject functions and classes to global objects for other sides to call at a certain stage.

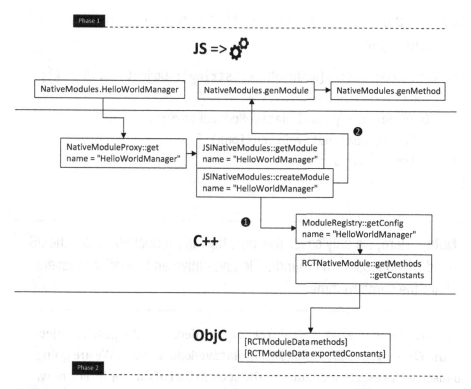

Figure 6-6. *React Native bootstrap (phase 2)*

We have seen that to import a **native module**, we do not use the ordinary ES6 require(). Instead, we use NativeModules.xxx which is the actual entry point of native module initialization on the *JavaScript* layer.

Let's see what happens inside (Listing 6-24).

Note   All the relevant source code files on the *JavaScript* layer are located in react-native/Libraries/BatchedBridge.

Listing 6-24. Phase 2-0, reference NativeModules on the JavaScript layer

```
let NativeModules: {[moduleName: string]: Object, ...} = {};
if (global.nativeModuleProxy) {
  NativeModules = global.nativeModuleProxy;
} else if (!global.nativeExtensions) {
// ... irrelevant logic
}
```

Note   Here, we only cover the logic flow in production where the JS bundle is loaded from a bundle file and native and JavaScript layers share the same runtime.

Here, the native `nativeModuleProxy` is injected to the `global` object on the *C++* layer, which is backed by `NativeModuleProxy`. We are going to discuss the exact mechanics in the second half of this topic. For now, we need to know that the `NativeModules.xxx` will invoke the getter of `NativeModuleProxy` (Listing 6-25).

Listing 6-25. Phase 2-1, invoke the get method of NativeModuleProxy@ JSIExecutor on the native layer

```
class JSIExecutor::NativeModuleProxy : public jsi::HostObject {
public:
  NativeModuleProxy(
    std::shared_ptr<JSINativeModules> nativeModules
  ) : weakNativeModules_(nativeModules) {}
```

```
Value get(Runtime &rt, const PropNameID &name) override //-> 1)
{
  if (name.utf8(rt) == "name") {
    return jsi::String::createFromAscii(rt, "NativeModules");
  }

  auto nativeModules = weakNativeModules_.lock();
  if (!nativeModules) {
    return nullptr;
  }

  return nativeModules->getModule(rt, name); // ---------> 2)
}

void set(Runtime &, const PropNameID &, const Value &) override
{
  throw std::runtime_error(
  "Unable to put on NativeModules: Operation unsupported");
}
private:
  std::weak_ptr<JSINativeModules> weakNativeModules_;
};
```

1) This is the getter method that gets called whenever we import a **native module**.

2) Move on to the next step (Listing 6-26).

Listing 6-26. Phase 2-2, getModule@JSINativeModules on the native layer

```cpp
Value JSINativeModules::getModule(Runtime &rt, const PropNameID
&name) {
  if (!m_moduleRegistry) {
    return nullptr;
  }

  std::string moduleName = name.utf8(rt);

  const auto it = m_objects.find(moduleName); // ----------> 1)
  if (it != m_objects.end()) {
    return Value(rt, it->second); // ---------------------> 1)
  }

  auto module = createModule(rt, moduleName); // ----------> 2)
  if (!module.hasValue()) {
  // Allow lookup to continue in the objects own properties,
    which allows for
  // overrides of NativeModules
    return nullptr;
  }

  auto result =
    m_objects.emplace(
      std::move(moduleName),std::move(*module)
    ).first; // --------------------------------------------> 3)
  return Value(rt, result->second); // -------------------> 4)
}
```

1) Check if the **native module** information has already been cached in m_objects. Return the cached value if that's the case.

2)   Move to the next step and create the **native module** information. This step will eventually call a *JavaScript* method to create the native module information (Listing 6-27).

3)   Add the newly created **native module** information to the cache.

4)   Return the newly created **native module** information to the *JavaScript* layer.

Listing 6-27. Phase 2-3, createModule@JSINativeModules on the native layer

```
folly::Optional<Object> JSINativeModules::createModule(
  Runtime &rt,
  const std::string &name
) {
...
  if (!m_genNativeModuleJS) { // -------------------------> 2)
    m_genNativeModuleJS =
    rt.global().getPropertyAsFunction(rt, "__fbGenNativeModule");
  }

  auto result = m_moduleRegistry->getConfig(name); // -----> 1)
  if (!result.hasValue()) {
    return folly::none;
  }

  Value moduleInfo = m_genNativeModuleJS->call( // --------> 2)
    rt,
    valueFromDynamic(rt, result->config),
    static_cast<double>(result->index)
  );
```

```
CHECK(!moduleInfo.isNull())
<< "Module returned from genNativeModule is null";

folly::Optional<Object> module(
moduleInfo.asObject(rt).getPropertyAsObject(rt, "module"));
```

...

```
return module; // ---------------------------------------> 3)
}
```

1) Fetch the native module metadata from
   m_moduleRegistry, which is the *C++* counterpart
   of the mentioned data structures that store
   RCTModuleData. In this step, all the methods and
   constants are extracted from the **native module**
   from the RCTModuleData generated in phase 1.

2) Invoke the __fbGenNativeModule with the relevant
   information (Listing 6-28).

3) Return the result of __fbGenNativeModule, the
   object of which is returned eventually to the
   JavaScript layer.

Listing 6-28. Phase 2-4, __fbGenNativeModule@NativeModules on
the JavaScript layer

```
function genModule(
  config: ?ModuleConfig,
  moduleID: number,
): ?{
  name: string,
  module?: Object,
  ...
```

```
} {
  if (!config) { return null; }

  const [
    moduleName,
    constants,
    methods,
    promiseMethods,
    syncMethods
  ] = config;
...

  if (!constants && !methods) {
    // Module contents will be filled in lazily later
    return {name: moduleName};
  }

  const module = {};
  methods && methods.forEach((methodName, methodID) => {
// -> 1)
    const isPromise =
    promiseMethods && arrayContains(promiseMethods, methodID);

    const isSync =
    syncMethods && arrayContains(syncMethods, methodID);
...

    const methodType =
    isPromise ? 'promise' : isSync ? 'sync' : 'async';

    module[methodName] = genMethod(
      moduleID, methodID, methodType
    ); // ----------------------------------------------> 2)
  });
```

```
  Object.assign(module, constants);
...
  return {name: moduleName, module};
}

...

global.__fbGenNativeModule = genModule; // ----------------> 3)
...
```

1) Iterate through all the methods for this
   native module.

2) Create the *JavaScript* layer counterparts for those
   methods.

3) Inject the genModule as __fbGenNativeModule so it
   can be invoked from the native layer.

6.5.3.1 The Nature of a Native Call

Lastly, let's look at the genMethod. At this point, the mechanic of a native
call should be crystal clear to us (Listing 6-29).

Listing 6-29. Phase 2-5, genMethod@NativeModules on the
JavaScript layer

```
function genMethod (
  moduleID: number, methodID: number, type: MethodType
) {
  let fn = null;
  if (type === 'promise') {
    fn = function promiseMethodWrapper(...args: Array<any>) {
      // In case we reject, capture a useful stack trace here.
      const enqueueingFrameError: ExtendedError = new Error();
```

```
  return new Promise((resolve, reject) => { // --------> 1)
    BatchedBridge.enqueueNativeCall( // ---------------> 2)
      moduleID,
      methodID,
      args,
      data => resolve(data), // ----------------------> 1)
      errorData => reject(updateErrorWithErrorData( // --> 1)
        errorData, enqueueingFrameError)
      ),
    );
  });
};
} else {
  fn = function nonPromiseMethodWrapper(...args:
  Array<any>) {
    const lastArg =
    args.length > 0 ? args[args.length - 1] : null;

    const secondLastArg =
    args.length > 1 ? args[args.length - 2] : null;

    const hasSuccessCallback = typeof lastArg === 'function';

    const hasErrorCallback =
    typeof secondLastArg === 'function';

    hasErrorCallback && invariant(hasSuccessCallback,
      'Cannot have a non-function arg after a function arg.',
    );

    const onSuccess = hasSuccessCallback ? lastArg : null;
    const onFail = hasErrorCallback ? secondLastArg : null;
    const callbackCount =
    hasSuccessCallback + hasErrorCallback;
```

```
    args = args.slice(0, args.length - callbackCount);
    if (type === 'sync') {
      return BatchedBridge.callNativeSyncHook( // -------> 3)
        moduleID,
        methodID,
        args,
        onFail,
        onSuccess,
      );
    } else {
      BatchedBridge.enqueueNativeCall( // ---------------> 2)
        moduleID,
        methodID,
        args,
        onFail,
        onSuccess,
      );
    }
  };
}
fn.type = type;
return fn;
}
```

1) Wrap the promise around the actual native call.

2) Carry out the asynchronous native call using
   enqueueNativeCall with the moduleID and
   methodID.

3) Carry out the synchronous native call using
   callNativeSyncHook with the moduleID and
   methodID.

We reached our last stop on the *JavaScript* layer, the native call. As you can see, all the native calls are essentially converged to two methods that are injected from the native layer (Listing 6-30).

Listing 6-30. enqueueNativeCall, @MessageQueue on the JavaScript layer

```
enqueueNativeCall(
  moduleID: number,
  methodID: number,
  params: any[],
  onFail: ?Function,
  onSucc: ?Function,
) {
  this.processCallbacks(
moduleID, methodID, params, onFail, onSucc
  );

...

  this._queue[MODULE_IDS].push(moduleID);
  this._queue[METHOD_IDS].push(methodID);

  this._queue[PARAMS].push(params);

  const now = Date.now();
  if (
    global.nativeFlushQueueImmediate &&
    now - this._lastFlush >= MIN_TIME_BETWEEN_FLUSHES_MS
// -> 3)
  ) {
    const queue = this._queue;
    this._queue = [[], [], [], this._callID];
```

```
    this._lastFlush = now;
    global.nativeFlushQueueImmediate(queue); // -----------> 1)
  }
}
...
callNativeSyncHook(
  moduleID: number,
  methodID: number,
  params: any[],
  onFail: ?Function,
  onSucc: ?Function,
): any {
  this.processCallbacks(
    moduleID, methodID, params, onFail, Succ
  );

  return global.nativeCallSyncHook(
moduleID, methodID, params
  ); // ------------------------------------------------------> 2)
}
```

1) nativeFlushQueueImmediate for asynchronous method calls.

2) nativeCallSyncHook for synchronous ones. Both of the preceding calls accept the module ID and method ID procured in the last few steps with the NativeModuleProxy, another entity injected from the native layer.

3) A queue that aggregates method calls within five milliseconds for asynchronous calls.

Next, we will examine the missing pieces in the bootstrap process discussed earlier, the *C++* layer that interacts directly with the **JavaScriptCore**. We will answer three specific unresolved questions: (1) how the bundle is executed through **JavaScriptCore**, (2) how the two-way communication is facilitated between **JavaScriptCore** and the *React Native* runtime, and (3) how the **native module** metadata are stored in the *C++* layer, which reveals the mechanism of method calls to the *Objective-C* layer.

6.5.4 Execute the Bundle

JSCRuntime is in the core of *JavaScript* and native communication, which is basically an encapsulation of **JavaScriptCore**. Let's firstly get familiar with some **JavaScriptCore** API and then get straight to its core.

JSEvaluateScript() runs a script in the form of a JSStringRef which can be created from an ordinary string using JSStringCreateWithUTF8CString(). And JSStringRelease() releases a JSStringRef. These functions are the building blocks of evaluateJavaScript, which is eventually called in the last step of *React Native* bootstrap (Section 4.3.2) to execute the bundle. Next, we look at the function of JSCRuntime to have a taste (Listing 6-31).

Listing 6-31. JSCRuntime::evaluateJavaScript

```
jsi::Value JSCRuntime::evaluateJavaScript(
    const std::shared_ptr<const jsi::Buffer> &buffer,
    const std::string &sourceURL) {
  std::string tmp(
    reinterpret_cast<const char *>(buffer->data()),
    buffer->size()
  );
```

```
JSStringRef sourceRef =
JSStringCreateWithUTF8CString(tmp.c_str());

JSStringRef sourceURLRef = nullptr;
if (!sourceURL.empty()) {
   sourceURLRef = JSStringCreateWithUTF8CString(
   sourceURL.c_str());
}
JSValueRef exc = nullptr;
JSValueRef res =
    JSEvaluateScript( // -------------------------------> 1)
    ctx_, sourceRef, nullptr, sourceURLRef, 0, &exc);
JSStringRelease(sourceRef);
if (sourceURLRef) {
  JSStringRelease(sourceURLRef);
}
checkException(res, exc);
return createValue(res);
}
```

1)   This is where the bundle got executed eventually.

6.5.5 The Two-Way Communication

Again, let's get to know some **JavaScriptCore** API first. We know that
the communication is pivoting around the global object. We use
JSContextGetGlobalObject() to get the *C++* representative of this object.
We can then inject native instances and functions to this object to be called
by the *JavaScript* layer.

The native instances are injected into the global object in *JavaScript*
in three steps:

1) Map **C++** classes to *JavaScript* using
   JSClassCreate() using a JSClassDefinition.

2) Instantiate such class using JSObjectMake().

3) Inject the instance to the global object using
   JSObjectSetProperty().

Next, we look at the code that injects the NativeModuleProxy to the global object, which facilitates the two-way communication that establishes the **native modules** on the *JavaScript* layer (Listing 6-32).

Listing 6-32. Inject nativeModuleProxy

```
void JSIExecutor::initializeRuntime() {
  SystraceSection s("JSIExecutor::initializeRuntime");
  runtime_->global().setProperty( // --------------------> 1,2)
    *runtime_,
    "nativeModuleProxy",
    Object::createFromHostObject( // ----------------------> 3)
      *runtime_, std::make_shared<NativeModuleProxy>(
        nativeModules_
      )
    )
  );
...
```

1) global() is a wrapper function that gets the global
   object using JSContextGetGlobalObject() and
   returns it wrapped with a jsi::Object.

2) jsi::Object::setProperty() is the wrapper for
   JSObjectSetProperty().

3) jsi::Object::createFromHostObject is the
   wrapper of JSClassCreate() and JSObjectMake().

This is how the object `nativeModuleProxy` is made available to the *JavaScript* layer. And other critical functions such as `nativeFlushQueueImmediate()` and `nativeCallSyncHook()` are injected to global objects in a similar way.

6.5.6 The Native Module Metadata

As discussed, the metadata is also stored in the *C++* layer. This is achieved by saving the reference of `RCTModuleData` in `RCTNativeModule` which is in turn stored in `Instance::moduleRegistry_`.

`RCTNativeModule` works as a simple *C++* wrapper of `RCTModuleData`. Let's take a look at how a method is invoked as an example (Listing 6-33).

Listing 6-33. Method invocation from C++

```
static MethodCallResult
invokeInner(RCTBridge *bridge, RCTModuleData *moduleData,
unsigned int methodId, const folly::dynamic &params)
{
  if (!bridge || !bridge.valid || !moduleData) {
    return folly::none;
  }

  id<RCTBridgeMethod> method = moduleData.methods
  [methodId];//>1)
...

  NSArray *objcParams = convertFollyDynamicToId(params);
  @try {
        id result =
        [method invokeWithBridge:bridge
        module:moduleData.instance arguments:objcParams]; // -> 2)
```

```
  return convertIdToFollyDynamic(result);
} @catch (NSException *exception) {
  // Pass on JS exceptions
  if ([exception.name hasPrefix:RCTFatalExceptionName]) {
    @throw exception;
  }
...
}

  return folly::none;
}
```

1) Get the method object from RCTModuleData.

2) Invoke the method. Internally, it uses NSInvocation to invoke the method dynamically.

6.5.7 Wrap Up

It's a pretty heavy section. It takes significant effort to write, and I suppose the reading effort would be equal if not more. With an eye for detail, you might have answered several practical questions that are not well documented already, for instance:

1) What is the app bootstrap process like? The start render time is one of the key factors to one of the key metrics to five-point apps. By answering this question, we know the initialization of our **native modules** could block the bootstrap process. So we shall consider making **native modules** that are not essential or need a long time to be loaded lazily.

2) What does it mean by `requiresMainQueueSetup`? This is an actual follow-up question of the previous one. More specifically, **native modules** that require the main queue setup are those that need to be initialized up front and could block the bootstrap. By answering this question, we also know that there are actually two types of `requiresMainQueueSetup`, explicit and implicit.

3) At which point native modules are instantiated? We know that only **native modules** that require the main queue setup are instantiated up front; the rest stay in the form of class metadata and will only be instantiated in an on-demand way. Answering this question could be beneficial to multibridge settings. This setting is common for apps that use *React Native* for parts of its features. Here, lazy loading can be used to improve memory footprint as it gives the option to each bridge to load only **native modules** that are needed.

4) What is lazy loading exactly? We haven't fully answered this question just yet. We know that native modules that do not require the main queue setup are lazily loaded. And you might have noticed that `RCTBridge` offers a `registerAdditionalModuleClasses` to enable lazy loading. We will leave it to you to explore in that multibridge is not a common scenario that most of our readers would confront.

5) What is exactly a native method call? We know that the nature of native method calls are two *C++* functions injected to the global

object, `nativeFlushQueueImmediate` and `nativeCallSyncHook`. By answering this question, we know what to look at when there is a bottleneck imposed by the bridge.

It's sometimes essential to understand the underlying logic for fixing hard bugs or deep squeezing the performance. Moreover, I found the insight of the internal mechanism is beneficial for everyday development activities such as decision making, filtering answers on Stack Overflow and issues on GitHub, as well as discussing pull requests. It's like understanding the soil properties before building a skyscraper or understanding the aerodynamics before making an aircraft. At the end of the day, a solid understanding leads to a solid product, a **05 app**.

Leaving aside all practical purposes, an inside-out understanding is always fun. Next, let's continue this journey by understanding the animation mechanism. It will be another intensive albeit fun one.

6.6 Animation Inside Out

In this section, we examine the underlying mechanisms of a *native event*, an *animated value*, and a *value interpolation/calculation*, which are the three major building blocks of the *native driver* that enables the native-level performant animation.

The secret behind the performance is direct native-to-native communication that is completely free of *JavaScript* thread intervention. The relationship between the event source (user gestures) and the receivers (**component**) is a directed graph connected with *animation nodes* (will be discussed very soon). After this graph is defined in the *JavaScript* layer, it is pushed down altogether to the animation subsystem of the **React Native** runtime to keep record. Then all animation can be performed purely in the native layer.

Before we move on, let's have a look at the big picture (Figure 6-7).
Technically, all the animation entities listed earlier are represented by
the data structure *animated node*. In Section 3.4.2, we used the *value
calculation* (Section 3.3.2.3) technique to derive the **component props** in
animation from the *native event*. What this technique creates is nothing
but an *animated node graph (ANG)*. Those *animated nodes* (1) are
connected with each other within the *ANG* and (2) are attached to both
the event source, the ScrollView in our case, and the event receiver, the
SpinningEnvelope **component**. We will revisit this relationship very soon
in Section 6.6.1.1, so don't worry if you cannot recall the implementation
details from the case study. Lastly, all the preceding relationships are
declared on the *JavaScript* layer and are passed down to the native layer.
ANG is the key information for the *native layer* to carry out animation
without the involvement of the *JavaScript* thread. More specifically, the
animation can be carried out by (1) relaying a *native event* from the source
all the way to the receivers through the *ANG* and (2) deriving the result of
the *value calculation/interpolation* along the way.

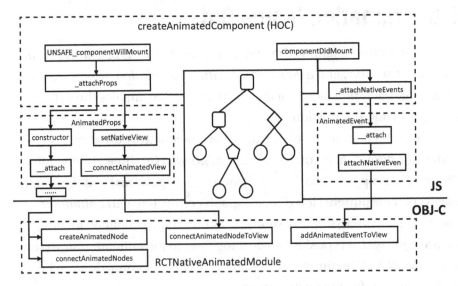

Figure 6-7. *Internal architecture of the native driver*

Let's track and trace from the entry point createAnimatedComponent() (Listing 6-34). This is where all animation elements are declared, that is, establish the *ANG* (Section 6.6.1), bind the event receiver (Section 6.6.2), and attach the event source (Section 6.6.3).

Note   Code for *JavaScript*-driven animation is removed on purpose for clarity. We also remove the logic of node detaching for simplicity.

Listing 6-34.   createAnimatedComponent

```
function createAnimatedComponent<Props: {+[string]: mixed,
...}, Instance>(
  Component: React.AbstractComponent<Props, Instance>,
): AnimatedComponentType<Props, Instance> {
  invariant(
    typeof Component !== 'function' || // ----------------> 1a)
      (Component.prototype && Component.prototype.
      isReactComponent),
    '`createAnimatedComponent` does not support stateless
    functional components; ' +
      'use a class component instead.',
  );

  class AnimatedComponent extends React.Component<Object> {//> 1)
    _component: any;
...

    _propsAnimated: AnimatedProps;
...

    _attachNativeEvents() {
      // Make sure to get the scrollable node for components
        that implement
```

```
      // `ScrollResponder.Mixin`.
      const scrollableNode = this._component?.getScrollableNode
        ? this._component.getScrollableNode()
        : this._component;

      for (const key in this.props) {
        const prop = this.props[key];
        if (prop instanceof AnimatedEvent && prop.__isNative) {
          prop.__attach(scrollableNode, key); // ----------> 5)
...
        }
      }
    }
...
    _attachProps(nextProps) { // ------------------------> 3)
    const oldPropsAnimated = this._propsAnimated;

    this._propsAnimated = new AnimatedProps(
    nextProps,
    this._animatedPropsCallback,
  );
...
}

    _setComponentRef = setAndForwardRef({
      getForwardedRef: () => this.props.forwardedRef,
      setLocalRef: ref => {
        this._prevComponent = this._component;
        this._component = ref; // ------------------------> 2)
...
    },
    });
```

```
    render() {
    const props = this._propsAnimated.__getValue();
    return (
      <Component
        {...props}
        ref={this._setComponentRef}
...
      />
    );
  }

    UNSAFE_componentWillMount() { // ---------------------> 3)
    this._attachProps(this.props);
    }

    componentDidMount() {
...

    this._propsAnimated.setNativeView(this._component); // > 4)
    this._attachNativeEvents(); // ----------------------> 5)
}
    }

    return React.forwardRef( // --------------------------> 1b)
function AnimatedComponentWrapper(props, ref
  ) {
    return (
      <AnimatedComponent
        {...props}
        {...(ref == null ? null : {forwardedRef: ref})}
      />
    );
  });
}

module.exports = createAnimatedComponent;
```

1) `createAnimatedComponent` is the entry point of all animation-related logic. It is a standard **HOC**. It wraps the **component** passed in with the `AnimatedComponent` which, in its *life cycle methods*, sets up the metadata (events, props, values) related to animation. Two points worth noting here are: (a) functional components are not supported, and (b) it uses the technique of *ref forwarding* which we introduced in Section 4.5.3.4.

2) Set the ref (Section 4.3.2.1) to `this._component`.

3) Set up the *ANG* with the starting point set to `_propsAnimated`. We will know very soon that `_propsAnimated: AnimatedProps` is also one type of *animated node*. This step will be discussed in detail in Section 6.6.1.

4) Bind the `_propsAnimated` with the current **component**, which connects the *ANG* to the event receiver. This step will be discussed in Section 6.6.2.

5) Attach the *native event* to the current **component**, which connects the *ANG* to the event source. Note that only `ScrollView` is supported by vanilla **React Native**, which is sufficient for most scenarios that involve a gesture. This step will be discussed in Section 6.6.3.

Next, we look at how the *ANG* is established from the entry point of `UNSAFE_componentWillMount` in step 3. Step 4 that connects *ANG* to the receiver end and step 5 that connects *ANG* to the sender end will be examined in detail in Sections 6.6.2 and 6.6.3, respectively. Then in Section 6.6.4, we will see how events are transmitted end to end.

6.6.1 Establish the Animated Node Graph

Let's recall the pull-to-refresh animation we implemented in Section 3.4.2. As a reminder, we use *value calculation* to define the animation behavior. Listing 6-35 shows the original code.

Listing 6-35. Value calculation for pull-to-refresh

```
...
<LoomingSpinningEnvelope
  color={'#6291f0'}
  size={45}
  style={{
    opacity:
      Animated.add(
        Animated.multiply(
          this.userPulling,
          this.pullDownPos.interpolate({
            inputRange: [-loadingIndicatorOffset, 0],
            outputRange: [0.5, 0]
          })
        ),
        Animated.multiply(
          this.autoScrolling,
          this.pullDownPos.interpolate({
            inputRange: [-loadingIndicatorOffset, 0],
            outputRange: [1, 0]
          })
        ),
      )
  }}
/>
...
```

Data structure wise, all the individual *animated values*, the *value calculation* (e.g., `Animated.multiply()`), and *value interpolation* are different forms of *animated nodes*. The invocation of animation-related functions essentially instantiates the corresponding subclasses of *animated nodes*. The cascading invocation of such functions incorporates those *animated nodes* together to form the mentioned *ANG*. The calculated result of such *value calculation* is represented by the root of the tree and is eventually attached to **props** of a **component**, the process of which will be examined in Section 6.6.3.

A copy of the *ANG* is maintained in the native layer as well. This is achieved majorly with two methods `createAnimatedNode:` and `connectAnimatedNode:` residing in `RCTNativeAnimatedModule`. These two methods are invoked as side effects when the *ANG* is established, which we will examine later in this section.

Programmatically, the *ANG* is established using two key *animated node* methods: `__attach()` and `__makeNative()`. `__attach()` is used for establishing the *ANG* on the ***JavaScript*** layer, while `__makeNative()` is for establishing the native layer representative.

Note   The following logic is a bit hard to be interpreted as the key methods reside in different classes within the `AnimatedNode` inheritance hierarchy. And those methods are to establish *ANG* with another kind of hierarchy.

6.6.1.1 JavaScript Pass

The ***JavaScript*** pass starts from step 3 of `createAnimatedComponent`, from where an `AnimatedProps` is instantiated, and all the *animated nodes* are attached. Let's get started from that point by looking at the implementation of _attachProps in createAnimatedComponent. Basically, this method instantiates an AnimatedProps and invokes the __attach() method of it (Listing 6-36).

Listing 6-36. __attachProps

```
...
_attachProps(nextProps) {
...

  this._propsAnimated = new AnimatedProps( // -------------> 1)
    nextProps,
    this._animatedPropsCallback,
  );
...
}
...

class AnimatedProps extends AnimatedNode {
  _props: Object;
...

  constructor(props: Object, callback: () => void) {
    super();
...

    this.__attach(); // ------------------------------------> 2)
  }

  __attach(): void {
    for (const key in this._props) {
      const value = this._props[key];
      if (value instanceof AnimatedNode) {
        value.__addChild(this); // -----------------------> 3)
      }
```

```
    }
  }
...
}
```

1) Continued from step 3 in
   createAnimatedComponent.

2) Call __attach() of AnimatedProps and move on.

3) Call __addChild() of all the _props that are
   animated.

Here, __attach() and addChild() are the paired methods calling each
recursively. In particular, __attach() calls all the parent's addChild()
which in turn calls the __attach() of the respective parent and traverses
the complete *ANG*.

The preceding recursion resides in AnimatedWithChildren from which
all nodes except for the starting node inherit (Listing 6-37).

Listing 6-37. AnimatedWithChildren

```
class AnimatedWithChildren extends AnimatedNode {
  _children: Array<AnimatedNode>;

  constructor() {
    super();
    this._children = [];
  }

  __makeNative() { // ------------------------------------> 3)
    if (!this.__isNative) {
      this.__isNative = true;
      for (const child of this._children) {
        child.__makeNative();
        NativeAnimatedHelper.API.connectAnimatedNodes(
```

```
        this.__getNativeTag(),
        child.__getNativeTag(),
      );
    }
  }
  super.__makeNative();
}

__addChild(child: AnimatedNode): void { // -------------> 1)
  if (this._children.length === 0) {
    this.__attach(); // -------------------------------> 2)
  }
  this._children.push(child); // ----------------------> 1)
  if (this.__isNative) {
... // -----------------------------------------------> 3)
  }
}
...
}
```

1) __addChild is called from __attach of the
   children node.

2) Call __attach of the current node to recursively
   attach all the nodes downward the tree hierarchy.

3) Native pass (Section 6.6.1.2).

Figure 6-8 shows the animated node graph generated.

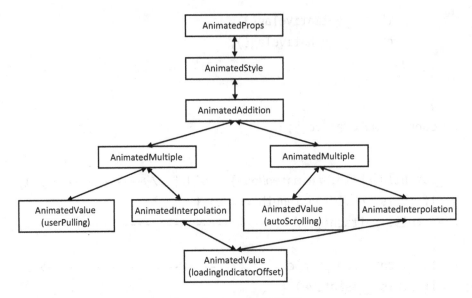

Figure 6-8. An animated node graph (ANG)

6.6.1.2 Native Pass

Like **components**, *animated nodes* all have their native layer representatives of the same type. The native layer counterpart is created using __makeNative which in turn calls two native methods from RCTNativeAnimatedModule, createAnimatedNode() and connectAnimatedNode().

Let's start by revisiting the __makeNative() (Listing 6-38).

Note   We haven't seen the entry point of the native pass yet, which will be covered in Section 6.6.3.

Listing 6-38. __makeNative

```
...
__makeNative() {
  if (!this.__isNative) {
    this.__isNative = true; // ---------------------------> 1)
    for (const child of this._children) {
      child.__makeNative(); // ---------------------------> 2)
      NativeAnimatedHelper.API.connectAnimatedNodes( // ---> 4)
        this.__getNativeTag(), // --------------------------> 3)
        child.__getNativeTag(),
      );
    }
  }
  super.__makeNative();
}
...
```

1) Set the __isNative to true to flag that this node is native for the following logic.

2) Recursively make all the children nodes native. Note that in the respective animated node classes, the parent's makeNative() is also called to traverse the whole graph.

3) Call __getNativeTag() to generate a tag for the current *animated node* and to call one of the key native methods, createAnimatedNode(), to register the current node.

4) Call the other key native method, connectAnimatedNode(), to make connection between the current node and its child.

Next, we look at the __getNativeTag(). This method resides in the AnimatedNode, the superclass of all nodes (Listing 6-39).

Listing 6-39. __getNativeTag

```
__getNativeTag(): number {

...

  const nativeTag =
    this.__nativeTag ?? NativeAnimatedHelper.generateNewNode
    Tag();

  if (this.__nativeTag == null) {
    this.__nativeTag = nativeTag;
    NativeAnimatedHelper.API.createAnimatedNode( // -------> 1)
      nativeTag,
      this.__getNativeConfig(),
    );
    this.__shouldUpdateListenersForNewNativeTag = true;
  }

  return nativeTag;
}
```

　　1)　Call createAnimatedNode() from step 3 in
　　　　__makeNative().

Lastly, we look at the two key native methods in RCTNativeAnimated Module. In fact, those two methods are thin wrappers of their counterparts in RCTNativeAnimatedNodesManager.

The AnimatedNode is created in the native layer using createAnimated Node:config: (Listing 6-40).

Listing 6-40. createAnimatedNode:config:

```
RCT_EXPORT_METHOD(createAnimatedNode:(double)tag
                config:(NSDictionary<NSString *, id> *)
                config)
{
  [self addOperationBlock:^(RCTNativeAnimatedNodesManager
  *nodesManager) {
    [nodesManager createAnimatedNode:[NSNumber numberWith
    Double:tag] config:config];
  }];
}
```

The heavy lifting is carried out by RCTNativeAnimatedNodesManager which encapsulates all the *animated node* records and operations (Listing 6-41).

Listing 6-41. createAnimatedNode:config: (internal call)

```
- (void)createAnimatedNode:(nonnull NSNumber *)tag
                config:(NSDictionary<NSString *, id> *)
                config
{
  static NSDictionary *map;
  static dispatch_once_t mapToken;
  dispatch_once(&mapToken, ^{ // --------------------------> 1)
    map = @{@"style" : [RCTStyleAnimatedNode class],
            @"value" : [RCTValueAnimatedNode class],
            @"props" : [RCTPropsAnimatedNode class],
            @"interpolation" : [RCTInterpolationAnimated
            Node class],
            @"addition" : [RCTAdditionAnimatedNode class],
            @"diffclamp": [RCTDiffClampAnimatedNode class],
```

```
        @"division" : [RCTDivisionAnimatedNode class],
        @"multiplication" : [RCTMultiplicationAnimated
        Node class],
        @"modulus" : [RCTModuloAnimatedNode class],
        @"subtraction" : [RCTSubtractionAnimated
        Node class],
        @"transform" : [RCTTransformAnimatedNode class],
        @"tracking" : [RCTTrackingAnimatedNode class]};
});

NSString *nodeType = [RCTConvert NSString:config[@"type"]];
Class nodeClass = map[nodeType]; // --------------------> 1)
if (!nodeClass) {
  RCTLogError(@"Animated node type %@ not supported
  natively", nodeType);
  return;
}

RCTAnimatedNode *node = [[nodeClass alloc] initWithTag:tag
config:config]; // ------------------------------------> 1)
  node.manager = self;
  _animationNodes[tag] = node; // ------------------------> 2)
  [node setNeedsUpdate]; // ------------------------------> 3)
}
```

1) Take the factory pattern to create the corresponding *animated node* class according to the config string passed in from the **JavaScript** layer. Note that the relationship between native classes and **JavaScript** ones is 1:1.

2) Store the created *animated node* instance in a map.

3) Set "needs update" for the newly created node. This flag will be used in Section 6.6.4.

The relationship among them has been recorded in the native layer by connectAnimatedNode:childTag (Listing 6-42).

Listing 6-42. connectAnimatedNode:childTag:

```
RCT_EXPORT_METHOD(connectAnimatedNodes:(double)parentTag
                   childTag:(double)childTag)
{
  [self addOperationBlock:^(RCTNativeAnimatedNodesManager
  *nodesManager) {
    [nodesManager connectAnimatedNodes:[NSNumber number
    WithDouble:parentTag] childTag:[NSNumber number
    WithDouble:childTag]];
  }];
}
```

Again, the actual work is carried out by RCTNativeAnimatedNodesManager which establishes the same *ANG* as in the ***JavaScript*** layer (Listing 6-43).

Listing 6-43. connectAnimatedNode:childTag: (internal call)

```
- (void)connectAnimatedNodes:(nonnull NSNumber *)parentTag
                   childTag:(nonnull NSNumber *)childTag
{
  RCTAssertParam(parentTag);
  RCTAssertParam(childTag);

  RCTAnimatedNode *parentNode = _animationNodes[parentTag];
  RCTAnimatedNode *childNode = _animationNodes[childTag];

  RCTAssertParam(parentNode);
  RCTAssertParam(childNode);
```

```
[parentNode addChild:childNode]; // --------------------> 1)
[childNode setNeedsUpdate]; // --------------------------> 2)
}
```

1) Establish the same parent-to-children relationship as in the *JavaScript* layer.

2) Set "needs update" for the child node. This flag will be used in Section 6.6.4.

6.6.2 Bind the Event Receiver

We know that the starting point of the graph is attached to the **component** in animation, which is the AnimatedProps (Listing 6-44).

Listing 6-44. AnimatedProps

```
class AnimatedProps extends AnimatedNode {
...
  __makeNative(): void {
    if (!this.__isNative) {
      this.__isNative = true;
      for (const key in this._props) {
        const value = this._props[key];
        if (value instanceof AnimatedNode) {
          value.__makeNative();
        }
      }
      if (this._animatedView) {
        this.__connectAnimatedView(); // ------------------> 2)
      }
    }
  }
}
```

```
setNativeView(animatedView: any): void { // -------------> 1)
  if (this._animatedView === animatedView) {
    return;
  }
  this._animatedView = animatedView;
  if (this.__isNative) {
    this.__connectAnimatedView();
  }
}

__connectAnimatedView(): void {
  invariant(this.__isNative, 'Expected node to be marked as
  "native"');
  const nativeViewTag: ?number = ReactNative.findNodeHandle(
    this._animatedView,
  );
...
  NativeAnimatedHelper.API.connectAnimatedNodeToView(
// --> 3)
    this.__getNativeTag(),
    nativeViewTag,
  );
}
...
}
```

1) The _animatedView is set by step 2 of
   createAnimatedComponent.

2) This is the critical line within __makeNative().
   Though we haven't encountered the entry point of
   this method yet, we know that it is recursively called
   for all nodes within the *ANG*.

3) Call the native method
   `connectAnimatedNodeToView()` to make the
   connection.

Next, we look at the native layer implementation. Similarly, here the **native module** `RCTNativeAnimatedModule` provides merely a thin wrapper to `RCTNativeAnimatedNodesManager` (Listing 6-45).

Listing 6-45. connectAnimatedNodeToView:viewTag:

```
RCT_EXPORT_METHOD(connectAnimatedNodeToView:(double)nodeTag
                  viewTag:(double)viewTag)
{
  NSString *viewName = [self.bridge.uiManager
viewNameForReactTag:[NSNumber numberWithDouble:viewTag]];
  [self addOperationBlock:^(RCTNativeAnimatedNodesManager
*nodesManager) {
    [nodesManager connectAnimatedNodeToView:[NSNu
mber numberWithDouble:nodeTag] viewTag:[NSNumber
numberWithDouble:viewTag] viewName:viewName];
  }];
}
```

Lastly, we look at the actual native implementation of the `connectAnim atedNodeToView:viewTag:viewName:` (Listing 6-46).

Listing 6-46. connectAnimatedNodeToView:viewTag:viewName: (internal call)

```
- (void)connectAnimatedNodeToView:(nonnull NSNumber *)nodeTag
                    viewTag:(nonnull NSNumber *)viewTag
                   viewName:(nonnull NSString *)viewName
```

```
{
  RCTAnimatedNode *node = _animationNodes[nodeTag];
  if ([node isKindOfClass:[RCTPropsAnimatedNode class]]) {
    [(RCTPropsAnimatedNode *)node connectToView:viewTag
    viewName:viewName bridge:_bridge]; // -----------------> 1)
  }
  [node setNeedsUpdate]; // -------------------------------> 2)
}
```

1) Register the native view in animation with the RCTPropsAnimatedNode.

2) Set "needs update" for the RCTPropsAnimatedNode. This flag will be used in Section 6.6.4.

6.6.3 Attach the Event Source

As usual, let's look back at the implementation layer where the event source is bound to ScrollView (Listing 6-47).

Listing 6-47. Revisit the Moment based on FlatList

```
...
<Animated.FlatList
  data={this.state.data}
  renderItem={this.renderItem}
  onViewableItemsChanged={this.onViewableItemsChanged}
  contentInset={{
    top: this.state.loading ?
        5: 0
  }}
```

```
scrollEventThrottle={1}
onScroll={
  Animated.event([{ // -----------------------------------> 1)
    nativeEvent: { contentOffset: { y: this.pullDownPos } }
  }], { useNativeDriver: true }) // --------------------> 2)
}
onScrollBeginDrag={this.beginDrag}
onScrollEndDrag={this.endDrag}
ref={this.getScrollViewRef}
onMomentumScrollEnd={this.onReset}
/>
...
```

1) Like *animated nodes*, the `Animated.event()` basically instantiates an `AnimatedEvent` which we will examine very soon.

2) By saying `nativeEvent` and `useNativeDriver: true`, we indicate that the event should be sent to the native layer. The *JavaScript* layer will receive the same event, so we can bind an additional callback to it if we want. This callback will still be subject to the performance penalty of the *JavaScript* layer.

Next, we examine the respective logic in `createAnimatedComponent`. More specifically, we look at how the `nativeEvent` object combined with the `onScroll` props is translated into metadata that is understandable by the native layer. Moreover, we will encounter the entry point of the *ANG* native pass (Section 6.6.1.2) in this process. Continue from step 5 in `_attachNativeEvents` (Listing 6-48).

Listing 6-48. _attachNativeEvents

```
_attachNativeEvents() {
...
  const scrollableNode = this._component?.getScrollableNode
    ? this._component.getScrollableNode()
    : this._component;

  for (const key in this.props) {
    const prop = this.props[key];
    if (prop instanceof AnimatedEvent && prop.__isNative) {
      prop.__attach(scrollableNode, key); // ----------------> 1)
      this._eventDetachers.push(() =>
        prop.__detach(scrollableNode, key)
      );
    }
  }
}
```

    1)   Call __attach() if we encounter an AnimatedEvent.
            __attach() is a wrapper of the method
            attachNativeEvent(). Let's get to those two
            methods directly (Listing 6-49).

Listing 6-49. _attach

```
__attach(viewRef: any, eventName: string) {
...
  this._attachedEvent = attachNativeEvent( // -------------> 1)
    viewRef,
    eventName,
    this._argMapping,
  );
}
```

```
...
function attachNativeEvent( // --------------------------> 1)
  viewRef: any,
  eventName: string,
  argMapping: $ReadOnlyArray<?Mapping>,
): {detach: () => void} {
...
  const traverse = (value, path) => { // -----------------> 2)
    if (value instanceof AnimatedValue) {
      value.__makeNative(); // ----------------------------> 3)

      eventMappings.push({
        nativeEventPath: path,
        animatedValueTag: value.__getNativeTag(),
      });
    } else if (typeof value === 'object') {
      for (const key in value) {
        traverse(value[key], path.concat(key));
      }
    }
  };
...

  traverse(argMapping[0].nativeEvent, []); // -------------> 4)

  const viewTag = ReactNative.findNodeHandle(viewRef);
  if (viewTag != null) {
    eventMappings.forEach(mapping => { // ----------------> 5)
      NativeAnimatedHelper.API.addAnimatedEventToView(
        viewTag,
        eventName,
        mapping,
```

```
    );
  });
}

return {
...
};
}
```

1) Here, we need to pay attention to the parameters passed through. viewRef is the **react ref** of the ScrollView; eventName is the prop name which is onScroll; this._argMapping is the first parameter passed to the Animated.event(), which is [{nativeEvent: {contentOffset:{ y: this. pullDownPos }}}].

2) Define a traverse() in a way that it can extract the path and associate it with the *animated value*. Here, the key path extracted is 'contentOffSet'.

3) Call the first __makeNative() of the *animated value* bound to the event. This leads to the cascading invocation of the same methods throughout the *ANG* (Section 6.6.1.2).

4) Invoke the traverse(). 💣 One caveat is that the nativeEvent should be the first element in the array.

5) Pass the mapping of the event path to the *animated value* down to the native layer.

For event attaching, we look at the native layer implementation. Here, we can find the same pattern that the **native module** RCTNativeAnimatedModule works as a thin layer that offloads the work to RCTNativeAnimatedNodesManager (Listing 6-50).

Listing 6-50. addAnimatedEventToView:eventName

```
RCT_EXPORT_METHOD(addAnimatedEventToView:(double)viewTag
                  eventName:(nonnull NSString *)eventName
                  eventMapping:(JS::NativeAnimatedModule::Event
                  Mapping &)eventMapping)
{
  NSMutableDictionary *eventMappingDict =
  [NSMutableDictionary new];
  eventMappingDict[@"nativeEventPath"] = RCTConvertVecToArray(
  eventMapping.nativeEventPath()); // --------------------> 1)

  if (eventMapping.animatedValueTag()) {
    eventMappingDict[@"animatedValueTag"] = // ------------> 1)
    @(*eventMapping.animatedValueTag());
  }

  [self addOperationBlock:^(RCTNativeAnimatedNodesManager
  *nodesManager) {
    [nodesManager addAnimatedEventToView:[NSNumber
    numberWithDouble:viewTag] eventName:eventName
    eventMapping:eventMappingDict]; // --------------------> 2)
  }];
}
```

1) Reorganize the parameters passed in from the *JavaScript* layer.

2) Pass it down to RCTNativeAnimatedNodesManager (Listing 6-51).

Listing 6-51. addAnimatedEventToView:eventName:eventMapping (internal call)

```
- (void)addAnimatedEventToView:(nonnull NSNumber *)viewTag
                eventName:(nonnull NSString *)eventName
      eventMapping:(NSDictionary<NSString*, id> *)eventMapping
{
  NSNumber *nodeTag = [RCTConvert NSNumber:eventMapping[
  @"animatedValueTag"]];
  RCTAnimatedNode *node = _animationNodes[nodeTag];

... // error check

  NSArray<NSString *> *eventPath =
    [RCTConvert NSStringArray:eventMapping[@"nativeEventPath"]];

  RCTEventAnimation *driver =
    [[RCTEventAnimation alloc] initWithEventPath:eventPath
    valueNode:(RCTValueAnimatedNode *)node]; // -----------> 1)

  NSString *key = [NSString stringWithFormat:@"%@%@", viewTag,
  RCTNormalizeAnimatedEventName(eventName)];
  if (_eventDrivers[key] != nil) {
    [_eventDrivers[key] addObject:driver]; // -------------> 2)
  } else {
    NSMutableArray<RCTEventAnimation *> *drivers =
    [NSMutableArray new];
    [drivers addObject:driver]; // ----------------------> 2)
    _eventDrivers[key] = drivers;
  }
}
```

1) Create the RCTEventAnimation using the eventPath
   passed down. We will come back to this class when
   we examine the event transmission pass. For now,
   we only need to know that this class keeps a record
   of the eventPath and the associated *animated
   value (node)*.

2) Record the event key which is basically the
   eventPath concatenated with the **react tag**.

6.6.4 Native Event Transmission

Now it's time to connect everything up. We know that gesture-driven
animation starts from the gesture on the RCTScrollView; let's start from
there (Listing 6-52).

Listing 6-52. Event source of RCTScrollView

```
- (void)scrollViewDidScroll:(UIScrollView *)scrollView
{
  NSTimeInterval now = CACurrentMediaTime();
  [self updateClippedSubviews];

  if (_allowNextScrollNoMatterWhat ||
      (_scrollEventThrottle > 0 && _scrollEventThrottle < MAX
      (0.017, now - _lastScrollDispatchTime))) { // -------> 2)
...
      RCT_SEND_SCROLL_EVENT(onScroll, nil); // ------------> 1)
...

    // Update dispatch time
    _lastScrollDispatchTime = now;
    _allowNextScrollNoMatterWhat = NO;
  }
```

```objc
  RCT_FORWARD_SCROLL_EVENT(scrollViewDidScroll : scrollView);
}

...

#define RCT_SEND_SCROLL_EVENT(_eventName, _userData)      \
  {                                                       \
    NSString *eventName = NSStringFromSelector(@selector
    (_eventName));                                        \
    [self sendScrollEventWithName:eventName scrollView:_
    scrollView userData:_userData];                       \
  }

...

- (void)sendScrollEventWithName:(NSString *)eventName
                     scrollView:(UIScrollView *)scrollView
                       userData:(NSDictionary *)userData
{
  if (![_lastEmittedEventName isEqualToString:eventName]) {
    _coalescingKey++;
    _lastEmittedEventName = [eventName copy];
  }
  RCTScrollEvent *scrollEvent = [[RCTScrollEvent alloc]
                initWithEventName:eventName
                         reactTag:self.reactTag
            scrollViewContentOffset:scrollView.contentOffset
            scrollViewContentInset:scrollView.contentInset
             scrollViewContentSize:scrollView.contentSize
                  scrollViewFrame:scrollView.frame
              scrollViewZoomScale:scrollView.zoomScale
                         userData:userData
```

```
                        coalescingKey:_coalescingKey];
  [_eventDispatcher sendEvent:scrollEvent]; // ------------> 1)
}
```

1) Send an event with all the information included.

2) Set a throttle to 17 milliseconds. For *JavaScript*-powered animation, this throttle is reasonable. This throttle could be removed for native-powered animation.

The event is eventually sent to RCTNativeAnimatedModule which, again, passes it down to RCTNativeAnimatedNodesManager for the hard work (Listing 6-53). With all the relevant information for event transmission registered (Sections 6.6.2 and 6.6.3), RCTNativeAnimatedNodesManager is able to dispatch the event to the destined *animated node* through the *ANG*.

Listing 6-53. Event dispatcher

```
// # RCTNativeAnimatedModule
- (void)eventDispatcherWillDispatchEvent:(id<RCTEvent>)event
{
...
  RCTExecuteOnMainQueue(^{
    [self->_nodesManager handleAnimatedEvent:event];
  });
}

// # RCTNativeAnimatedNodesManager
- (void)handleAnimatedEvent:(id<RCTEvent>)event
{
  if (_eventDrivers.count == 0) {
    return;
  }
```

```
NSString *key = [NSString stringWithFormat:@"%@%@",
  event.viewTag, RCTNormalizeAnimatedEventName(event.eventName)];

NSMutableArray<RCTEventAnimation *> *driversForKey =
                                  _eventDrivers
                                  [key]; // > 1)
if (driversForKey) {
  for (RCTEventAnimation *driver in driversForKey) {
// ---> 1)
    [self stopAnimationsForNode:driver.valueNode];
    [driver updateWithEvent:event]; // -----------------> 2)
  }

  [self updateAnimations]; // --------------------------> 3)
  }
}
```

1) Find the animation drivers related to the event and
    iterate through them. This information is populated
    in Section 6.6.3.

2) The updateWithEvent depth first searches the *ANG*
    to identify all the event receivers (Section 6.6.4.1).

3) The updateAnimations breadth first searches
    the *ANG* to update all the associated *animated*
    nodes and eventually updates the event receiver, a
    component (Section 6.6.4.2).

Next, we see how the **component** got updated in this process by
examining steps 2 and 3 closer in the following two sections.

6.6.4.1 Identify Receivers

The depth-first search is carried out by searching through the children of the *animated node*. As mentioned, this search is used to identify all the receivers (Listings 6-54 and 6-55).

Listing 6-54. Depth-first search to mark the receivers (updateWithEvent)

```
- (void)updateWithEvent:(id<RCTEvent>)event
{
  NSArray *args = event.arguments;
  id currentValue = args[2];
  for (NSString *key in _eventPath) { // ------------------> 1)
    currentValue = [currentValue valueForKey:key];
  }

  _valueNode.value = ((NSNumber *)currentValue).doubleValue;//>2)
  [_valueNode setNeedsUpdate]; // ------------------------> 3)
}
```

1) Extract the value from the event using the _eventPath populated in Section 6.6.3.

2) Update the *animated node* with the value extracted.

3) setNeedsUpdate cascading calls the same method of all the children of the animated node. See the logic in the next snippet.

Listing 6-55. Depth-first search to mark the receivers (setNeedsUpdate)

```
- (void)setNeedsUpdate
{
  _needsUpdate = YES; // ------------------------------------> 1)
  for (RCTAnimatedNode *child in _childNodes.
objectEnumerator) {
    [child setNeedsUpdate]; // ---------------------------> 2)
  }
}
```

1) Mark self as "needs update."

2) Cascading marks all children as "needs update."
   Take the example *ANG* we used in Section 6.6.1.1;
   the resulting state of the data structure is given in
   Figure 6-9.

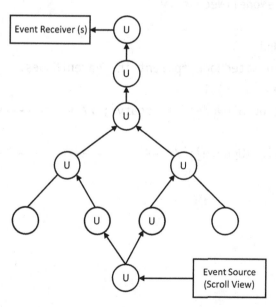

Figure 6-9. *Update pass within an animated node graph (ANG)*

417

6.6.4.2 Update

Let's continue from step 3 in handleAnimatedEvent (Listing 6-56).

Listing 6-56. Breadth-first search to update (updateAnimations)

```
// # RCTNativeAnimatedNodesManager
- (void)updateAnimations
{
  [_animationNodes enumerateKeysAndObjectsUsingBlock:
  ^(NSNumber *key, RCTAnimatedNode *node, BOOL *stop) {
    if (node.needsUpdate) {
      [node updateNodeIfNecessary]; // --------------------> 1)
    }
  }];
}

// # RCTAnimatedNode
- (void)updateNodeIfNecessary
{
  if (_needsUpdate) {
    for (RCTAnimatedNode *parent in _parentNodes.
    objectEnumerator) {
      [parent updateNodeIfNecessary]; // ------------------> 2)
    }
    [self performUpdate]; // ----------------------------> 3)
  }
}
```

1) Iterate through the registered *animated nodes* and carry out the updateNodeIfNecessary() of all nodes.

2) The update of *ANG* is carried out as a breadth-first search (BFS). Here, all parent nodes need to be updated first before the current node is updated. The stop condition of the BFS is false in needsUpdate, so the values can be directly used for nodes that have been updated.

3) Perform the actual update of the *animated node.*

Let's take a look at the performUpdate of RCTAdditionAnimatedNode continued from step 3 (Listing 6-57).

Listing 6-57. Breadth-first search to update (performUpdate)

```
// # RCTAdditionAnimatedNode
- (void)performUpdate
{
  [super performUpdate]; // -------------------------------> 1)
  NSArray<NSNumber *> *inputNodes = self.config[@"input"];
  if (inputNodes.count > 1) {
    RCTValueAnimatedNode *parent1 = (RCTValueAnimatedNode *)
    [self.parentNodes objectForKey:inputNodes[0]];
    RCTValueAnimatedNode *parent2 = (RCTValueAnimatedNode *)
    [self.parentNodes objectForKey:inputNodes[1]];
    if ([parent1 isKindOfClass:[RCTValueAnimatedNode class]] &&
        [parent2 isKindOfClass:[RCTValueAnimatedNode class]]) {
      self.value = parent1.value + parent2.value;
    }
  }
}
```

1) Before the calculation of the current node, perform the search on related nodes through RCTPropsAnimatedNode (Listing 6-58).

Listing 6-58. Breadth-first search to update (RCTPropsAnimated Node::performUpdate)

```
- (void)performUpdate
{
  [super performUpdate];

  if (!_connectedViewTag) {
    return;
  }

  for (NSNumber *parentTag in self.parentNodes.keyEnumerator) {
    RCTAnimatedNode *parentNode =
    [self.parentNodes objectForKey:parentTag];

    if (
      [parentNode isKindOfClass:[RCTStyleAnimatedNode class]]
    ) {
      [self->_propsDictionary addEntriesFromDictionary:
      [(RCTStyleAnimatedNode *)parentNode
      propsDictionary]];// 1)
    } else if (
      [parentNode isKindOfClass:[RCTValueAnimatedNode class]]
    ) {
      NSString *property =
      [self propertyNameForParentTag:parentTag];

      id animatedObject =
      [(RCTValueAnimatedNode *)parentNode animatedObject];
```

```
    if (animatedObject) {
      self->_propsDictionary[property] =
      animatedObject;// > 1)
    } else {
      CGFloat value =
      [(RCTValueAnimatedNode *)parentNode value];
      self->_propsDictionary[property] = @(value); // ---> 1)
    }
  }
}

if (_propsDictionary.count) {
  [self updateView]; // --------------------------------> 2)
}
}
```

1) Populate the _propsDictionary with the properties in change.

2) Update the views using the _propsDictionary. See in Listing 6-59 the implementation of updateView.

Listing 6-59. updateView

```
- (void)updateView
{
  if (_managedByFabric) {
    ...
  } else {
    [_bridge.uiManager
    synchronouslyUpdateViewOnUIThread:_connectedViewTag
                          viewName:_connectedViewName
                             props:_propsDictionary];
  }
}
```

6.7 Adaptive to All Screens, Layout Design

In the experience of the author, the various widths of phones rarely cause issues. The heights do. Unscrollable vertical layout could easily mess up the UI, especially on small screens. Here are some hints from the battle-ironed methods to do a vertical layout that is adaptable to any screens:

1) 🚀 Do not use an absolute value for height.

2) 🚀 Make all **components** layoutable, that is, the layout of a **component** should be able to be extrapolated from its **flex** attributes with no surprise. To achieve this, all customized **components** should be designed to behave the same as stock **components** – they can maintain their inheritance layouts while respecting **flex** attributes passed down from the consumer. Practically, *the spread operator* on the **style props** is your friend.

3) 🚀 Do not overabstract. Try to make the **component** hierarchy flatten and to put in one place all **components** involved in one screen. So they can be programmed, reasoned, and debugged in one place. Combined with the second hint, you will find coding layout a breeze. Moreover, the animation code can benefit from this practice too.

4) 🚀 Make the best of available space by using *intrinsic sizes* combined with flexGrow. More specifically, (a) let the **components** with solid intrinsic size occupy the space they need (nonnegotiable space) and (b) leverage flexGrow to distribute the gaps left among those **components**. In some cases, the

size of some **components** (such as text size) is also
negotiable. Discuss with your designer if that's
the case.

5) 🚀 Use raw calculation based on screen height as the
last resort. It is not very scalable (in terms of adding
new **components**) and hard to maintain.

6.8 Time to Say Goodbye

We have completed the journey of ***React Native***. From programming
techniques to internal mechanisms, I hope this journey is exciting and
fruitful to you too. Nonetheless, the topics discussed in this book are
far from enough to cover the complete enormous ecosystem of ***React
Native*** which arises based on a whole lot of ***JavaScript*** projects that
are equally significant, sophisticated, and complex. They are, namely,
Yoga that makes flexbox possible on mobile development; **Metro** that
enables hot reload and debugging of ***JavaScript***; NodeJS and Webpack
that establish the foundation to most ***React Native*** projects; **Babel** that
enables ***JSX***; **JavaScriptCore** and **Hermes** that provide the ***JavaScript***
runtime; **TypeScript** that makes ***JavaScript*** a safer language; **Jest** that
is a framework to write unit tests in ***JavaScript***; and lastly but most
importantly, ***React*** that defines the modernized program paradigm
accompanied with the reconciliation/rendering mechanism.

There are also a plethora of awesome third-party libraries that haven't
been examined. There are *react-native-fast-image, react-native-vector-
icons,* and *react-native-svg* for image rendering and caching; *react-native-
reanimated, react-native-gesture, react-native-gesture-handler,* and
react-native-lottie that extend the ***React Native*** animation capacity; *react-
navigation* that offers a declarative way for page routing; *react-native-video*
that enables multimedia; and *recyclerlistview* that enhances the long list
performance in ***React Native***, just to name a few.

React Native and its ecosystem is ever iterating. **Turbo modules** and **Fabric** are on the horizon; the practice of great front end (share code across all platforms including desktop and the Web) is still behind the walls of big corporations; and excellent developers and teams are continuously creating new awesome projects filling almost every capillary requirement and pain point. Hopefully when you are reading this book, these new architectural optimizations and methodologies are available to the community.

From first-party to third-party projects, from coding guides to n-times efficiency methodologies, it's simply not possible to cover the complete ecosystem that is moving forward, regardless of how much I would like to. All the preceding unexplored territories could be side tasks in the future. You may also choose your next adventure in accordance with your project goal to make the greatest impact.

It is worth noting that the principles in this book are subjective from my point of view and are also subjective to be challenged. Having been working on projects of various scales, from startup apps with thousands of users to full-fledged Internet systems that are used by hundreds of millions, I believe there is a "best practice" suitable for each team under each particular circumstances. It is the development team to define what it is. So please use the guides in this book as scale weights, instead of rules, when making your own decisions. Please bear in mind that these are just opinions derived from years of working on the technology by a developer just like yourself. Feel free to revise, enhance, or undermine some of the opinions based on your specific circumstance. Feel free to contact me (holmeshe@hotmail.com) if you want to discuss it with me.

We have accomplished our adventure of *Manyface*. After having thoroughly explored it, the adventurous region has now turned into a playground with maps and guidance. A good idea is to use *Manyface* as a reference app to experiment on when you are tackling technical difficulties, making design decisions, or trying to understand platform/ network particularities. With the understanding of both the regime of application and the regime of framework, you are now more than capable of doing it.

Let's conclude it here. Happy hacking, and Valar Morghulis (ˆ°ʃˆ°).

Index

A, B

Android version
project setup, 159
asynchronous, 163, 164
hello() method, 162
HelloWorldManager, 160
implementation, 161, 162
Kotlin class, 160
ManyfacePackage, 161–163
subdirectory, 159
Animated node graph (ANG), 386,
391, 395, 396, 417
Animation
AnimatedProps, 402
createAnimatedComponent()
method, 387–390
event source, 385
internal architecture, 386
interpolation/calculation, 385
node graph
AnimatedWithChildren, 394
createAnimatedNode,
399–402
getNativeTag(), 398
JavaScript pass, 392–396
makeNative(), 396, 397
native pass, 396
pull-to-refresh, 391, 392

value calculation, 391, 392
nodes, 386
receiver option, 402–405
source process
addAnimatedEventToView,
410, 411
attach() method, 407
attachNativeEvents, 407
FlatList, 405–412
transmission
depth-first search, 417
dispatcher, 414, 415
handleAnimatedEvent, 418
performUpdate, 419
RCTPropsAnimated
Node, 420
RCTScrollView, 412, 414
receiver identification,
416, 417
update, 418–421
updateView, 421
Animation technique
gesture-driven, 134–145
glimmering skeleton view, 89
layout (see Layout animation)
setState() method, 90
user experience, 90
value (see Value animation)

R

Printed in the United States
by Baker & Taylor Publisher Services

Printed in the United States
by Baker & Taylor Publisher Services